FORTUNE ADVISER
1999

FORTUNE ADVISER 1999

By the Editors of FORTUNE

FORTUNE BOOKS
TIME INC. HOME ENTERTAINMENT
1271 AVENUE OF THE AMERICAS
NEW YORK, N.Y. 10020

FORTUNE ADVISER 1999
FIRST PRINTING 1998
ISSN 1096-1070
ISBN 1-883013-40-2

FORTUNE ADVISER STAFF:
EDITORIAL DIRECTOR: JOE McGOWAN
EDITOR: VALERIE J. MARCHANT
DESIGNER: LAURA IERARDI, LCI DESIGN
COPY EDITORS: EDITH FIROOZI FRIED, CHARLES J. ATTARDI
EDITORIAL OPERATIONS: DAVID V. RILE

SPECIAL THANKS TO: GEOFFREY COLVIN, CAROL GWINN, ILENE HOFFMAN, JOAN HOFFMAN,
EILEEN NAUGHTON, RIK KIRKLAND, CAROLYN SAMPSON, DAVID SLOAN, THOMAS STEWART, AND ANNA YELENSKAYA

TIME INC. HOME ENTERTAINMENT
PRESIDENT: DAVID GITOW
DIRECTOR, CONTINUITIES AND SINGLE SALES: DAVID ARFINE
DIRECTOR, CONTINUITIES & RETENTION: MICHAEL BARRETT
DIRECTOR, NEW PRODUCTS: ALICIA LONGOBARDO
GROUP PRODUCT MANAGERS: ROBERT FOX, MICHAEL HOLAHAN
PRODUCT MANAGERS: CHRISTOPHER BERZOLLA, ALISON EHRMANN, ROBERTA HARRIS, STACY HIRSCHBERG,
KENNETH MAEHLUM, JENNIFER McLYMAN, DAN MELORE
MANAGER, RETAIL AND NEW MARKETS: TOM MIFSUD
ASSOCIATE PRODUCT MANAGERS: CARLOS JIMENEZ, DARIA RAEHSE, BETTY SU, CHERYL ZUKOWSKI
ASSISTANT PRODUCT MANAGERS: JENNIFER DOWELL, MEREDITH SHELLEY, LAUREN ZASLANSKY
EDITORIAL OPERATIONS DIRECTOR: JOHN CALVANO
BOOK PRODUCTION MANAGER: JESSICA McGRATH
BOOK PRODUCTION COORDINATOR: JOSEPH NAPOLITANO
FULFILLMENT DIRECTOR: MICHELLE GUDEMA
ASSISTANT FULFILLMENT MANAGER: RICHARD PEREZ
FINANCIAL DIRECTOR: TRICIA GRIFFIN
ASSOCIATE FINANCIAL MANAGER: AMY MASELLI
ASSISTANT FINANCIAL MANAGER: STEVEN SANDONATO
MARKETING ASSISTANT: SARAH HOLMES

WE WELCOME YOUR COMMENTS AND SUGGESTIONS ABOUT FORTUNE BOOKS. PLEASE WRITE US AT:

FORTUNE BOOKS
ATTENTION: BOOK EDITORS
P.O. BOX 11016
DES MOINES, IA 50336-1016

IF YOU WOULD LIKE TO ORDER ADDITIONAL COPIES OF ANY OF OUR BOOKS, PLEASE CALL US AT 1-800-327-6388
(MONDAY THROUGH FRIDAY, 7:00 AM–8:00 PM, OR SATURDAY, 7:00 AM–6:00 PM).

TO ORDER FORTUNE MAGAZINE, PLEASE CALL (800) 621-8000.

CONTENTS

▲▼▲

CHAPTER FOUR
INVESTMENT STRATEGIES FOR A SECURE FUTURE

▼

CHAPTER FIVE
RETIRING WELL: A GUIDE TO PROSPERITY

▼

CHAPTER SIX
HOT STUFF IN THE DIGITAL WORLD

▼

APPENDIX: FORTUNE LISTS

▼

CHAPTER ONE

▲▼▲

THE FUTURE IS NOW

ECONOMIC WARFARE: AND THE WINNER IS ...

BY JUSTIN FOX

▲▼▲

*Capitalism conquered communism
in the Cold War. No contest.
Figuring out which model of
capitalism—from the Anglo-
American to the German and
Japanese brands—isn't as easy.*

▲▼▲

Back when the Berlin Wall fell in 1989, it at first seemed so simple. Capitalism had won. Communism had lost. Game over.

That's when things got interesting. Sure, capitalism had won. But which capitalism? The Anglo-American kind, with democracy, a common-law legal system, a relatively modest role for government, and a tradable security for every occasion? Or maybe the German kind, with a heavy-handed government, exhaustive worker training, and a financial system ruled by a few big banks? Or how about Chilean capitalism, which featured mostly free markets, controls on capital flows, and (until a few years ago) a scary general running the show?

In the late 1980s and early 1990s, a lot of people thought they had the answer: Japanese capitalism. "The Cold War is over, and Japan won," Japan expert Chalmers Johnson famously said. It sure looked that way. Japan had humbled the U.S. auto and consumer electronics industries, and had taken much of the world's semiconductor business away from the U.S. companies that had created it. Even as the Tokyo stock market began to slide after 1989, Japanese banks were still seemingly capable of buying up all their competition if they so chose. And Japanese real estate investors owned most of Hawaii, much of California, and Rockefeller Center.

In Japanese capitalism, most big corporations followed an industrial strategy plotted by the government. Their goal, for the most part, was economic growth and an ever larger worldwide market share, not profitability. They could rely on virtually unlimited credit from their banks, which were also following the government's advice, and virtually unlimited hours from their employees, who in turn were assured that they had jobs for life.

By 1995, Japan's bear market was so entrenched and its economy so anemic that it was clear the country had some problems, but other East Asian countries that had followed a similar economic model were still thriving. It was the "East Asian Miracle," as the World Bank put it in a famous report in 1993, and it looked as if there was something to be said for following a deliberate industrial strategy, rather than just leaving economic decisions to individual consumers and investors.

We all know what happened after that: Financial crises in Thailand and South Korea in 1997 started regionwide free fall that exposed the weaknesses of the East Asian way. Basically, all that collaboration between government and corporations and banks precluded independent, skeptical judgments of which investments made sense and which did not. So lots of money and resources was poured into projects (car plants, housing developments, dams) that had no hope of paying off. And since investors do in the end need to get their money back, this could not go on forever. Hence the crash.

Asia's fall was interpreted in the U.S. as a resounding endorsement of the American Way. Here, where the government's main role in business and finance is that of a referee, investment decisions are based on hard-nosed assessments of what will make money and what won't. When these decisions nonetheless go wrong, the American system is also much better equipped to deal with failure, via bankruptcy, lawsuits, and the like. Perhaps most important of all, American-style capitalism allows for suprises, for wondrous technological and financial innovations that no government planners could dream up.

So now the war of capitalisms is really over, and the Anglo-American brand has won, right? It's easy to find people who believe this. "The American economy is in the eighth year of sustained growth that transcends the "German miracle" and the "Japanese miracle" of earlier decades," publisher and real estate developer Mortimer Zuckerman wrote in *Foreign Affairs* last year

[1998]. "This is no fluke. The unique American brand of entre-preneurial bottom-up capitalism is made up of structural elements that have wrought the stunning economic success of the 1990s and are likely to provide the basis for extending America's com-parative advantage over time."

The problem with this sort of American triumphalism is that, contrary to what you might have heard, history's not over yet. A few years ago all the hard economic data pointed to the over-whelming superiority of the Japanese way of doing things—and look what happened to Japan. In the 1990s the U.S. economy has been the most consistent performer around, but it has not been spectacularly outperforming its industrialized-nation peers as Japan did in the 1960s, 1970s, and 1980s.

There are also some clear dangers to assuming that what works for the U.S., with its vast wealth, ample natural resources, and huge domestic market, makes sense for every other nation on earth. In fact, while the outbreak of the Asian financial crisis pointed up the weaknesses of government-guided capitalism, the crisis could also be interpreted as proof that allowing capital to flow freely across borders and exchange rates to be set by mar-kets isn't such a great idea for developing countries. In the latter half of 1998, even investors in U.S. stocks and bonds were get-ting jitters about the ever more chaotic nature of global finance.

This is not to say that the 1990s hasn't been a pretty great decade for the U.S., or that the American economy hasn't shown a remarkable resilience over the years. It's just that there's a bet-ter way to go about looking at the economic events of the last century or so than as a competition between the American way, the German way, the Japanese way, or whatever other way suits your fancy. This better way comes to us from, of all people, the nation's academic economists. In the past decade some of them have begun looking closely at just what causes long-term eco-nomic growth—which in the end is the only way to judge the success of any economic system. The inquiry is far from com-plete, and what the economists have come up with so far isn't shocking. But it is enlightening.

One method of studying the phenomenon is to line up GDP growth data on a group of countries, against their political and economic characteristics, and see what statistical patterns emerge. The best known of these studies is by Harvard professor Robert Barro, who examined data from more than 100 countries and concluded that "the growth rate of real per capita GDP is enhanced by better maintenance of the rule of law, smaller government consumption, and lower inflation. Increases in political rights initially increase growth but tend to retard growth once a moderate level of democracy has been attained. Growth is also stimulated by greater starting levels of life expectancy and of male secondary- and higher-level schooling, lower fertility rates, and improvements in the terms of trade."

Another recent statistical study has shown a positive link between well-developed banking systems and stock markets and long-term growth, and yet another has shown that countries with legal systems based on English common law tend to have the best-developed financial markets.

Meanwhile, the leading theorist of growth, Stanford's Paul Romer, has argued that encouraging the discovery of new technologies is the one reliable way to boost long-term growth. Romer figures this means the U.S. should encourage more smart young people to do graduate work in engineering and applied sciences. Historical research into the chemical industry, the first real high-tech industry, bears him out: Britain lost its early lead in chemicals to Germany in the latter half of the 19th century largely because top German universities churned out practically trained chemists while top British universities stuck to graduating Latin scholars.

Now, all this isn't quite as satisfying as concluding that the U.S. has kicked Japan's (or Germany's, or Korea's, or the Soviet Union's) butt. It is, however, useful information for any nation that prefers to remain unkicked.

WILL THE REAL INTERNET PLEASE STAND UP?

BY MELANIE WARNER

▲▼▲

*Consumer Internet companies get
all the attention, but companies
that sell software and services to
other companies are going to
make the big bucks from
the Web revolution.*

▲▼▲

The Internet has a dirty little secret. Don't get your hopes up—it's got nothing to do with all those cheesy cyberporn sites that keep spamming you. No, the secret is about how people are going to make ridiculous amounts of money from the Internet. Forget selling books, CDs, Caribbean travel packages, or banner ads on the Web. The real Internet gold will be mined by those selling software and services not to fickle Web consumers but to companies with huge information-technology budgets. As more and more large corporations enter the Internet Age and build sophisticated corporate Internets, or intranets (80% of all FORTUNE 500 companies now have them), both internal operations like travel and expense reporting and payroll accounting and external dealings with suppliers, distributors, and customers are shifting to Web-based applications.

What's happening here is nothing short of a paradigm shift. Companies are migrating many of their corporate functions from a client/server model where large network servers interact with a big hairball of software on each employee's desktop PC to a world where every employee uses just one piece of software, a Web browser, to access information and perform a whole range of tasks. This emerging market of Web-based enterprise software, as it's called, consists of techie-sounding subdivisions like ORM (operations resource management) and EAM (enterprise asset management) and is completely arcane. It's also big business. Technology research firm International Data Group estimates that business-to-business transactions on the Internet will reach $300 billion by the year 2002. Look for Web-based enterprise software companies to be the next big wave of wealth-generating Internet stocks.

Which is why entrepreneurs all over Silicon Valley are devoting tons of brain hours to starting up enterprise software and E-commerce companies. Nothing fires up the entrepreneurial spirit quite like the words "paradigm shift." One of the hottest of these companies is Marimba, based in Mountain View, Calif. Want to know what Marimba does? It builds software that will help large companies use their intranets to distribute more software. Or as they might put it, "drive down the cost of distributing, managing, and maintaining mission-critical applications throughout the extended enterprise." Yikes. But if you're a chief information officer at a FORTUNE 500 company, Marimba's product can be really thrilling stuff, because it makes a company's information technology network more efficient. Instead of having a techie physically invade employees' offices each time new software needs to be installed on each and every desktop computer, Marimba's product enables companies to automatically send the software over its intranet.

Other companies are tackling similar kinds of automation. Ariba, a two-year-old startup based in Sunnyvale, Calif., is selling software that allows customers to purchase all forms of mundane but essential office supplies with their Web browser, from furniture and telephones right down to paper clips. Orders are instantly routed to the department honcho who needs to approve them and then sent electronically to the vendor filling the order. Or take Kana Communications, whose software automatically sorts customer E-mails, routes them to the appropriate department, and chooses among boilerplate responses to shoot back a reply to the customer. It also gleans information about a company's customers from the E-mails and compiles data on the company's intranet where it can be accessed throughout the organization. So if you happen to be driving through Silicon Valley in the dark hours and see dim lights glowing from inside one of the low-slung, architecturally challenged office buildings that house high-tech startups, don't think there's some cool new Website being designed in there. Think instead *non-mission-critical enterprise application solution.*

Unlike their sexier consumer Internet counterparts, enterprise software companies actually have believable earnings models, i.e. ones that don't start in the year 2010. This is largely because selling a product to perhaps half a dozen corporate IT people demands much lower marketing costs than trying to entice a large chunk of the entire Web audience of 60 million people to come to your site. The revenue model of enterprise software companies is also sweeter because product prices are higher (Ariba's average sale is more than $500,000) and because many companies also generate service revenue from installing and integrating their product in the digital jungle that is corporate IT networks.

Many of these companies building products to automate new areas of the enterprise may or may not survive on their own. Analysts like Don Keller at Price Waterhouse believe today's most promising enterprise software startups will eventually be gobbled up by the four giants—Baan, Oracle, PeopleSoft, and SAP—that do the heavy IT lifting for large companies and are eager to expand product offerings. But then again, paradigm shifts have a way of leaving corpses in their wake. When the business shifted in the '80s from mainframe computing to a client/server model, all the market leaders but one survived—IBM. Seismic technology transitions often prove too difficult for large companies to navigate skillfully, opening up wide holes for smaller, nimbler competitors. Indeed, many of today's nimble entrepreneurs believe not that they will be acquired by SAP or PeopleSoft but that they will *be* the next SAP or PeopleSoft.

Either way, a new market is coming, and whether it's the little guys or the big guys that dominate it, lots of new wealth will be created. And one day you might find yourself marveling at the lofty valuations of those crazy Java tools companies. And that, in essence is the beauty of money—it makes everything that generates it a whole lot more interesting.

WHERE'S THE LOOT COMING FROM?

BY BETHANY McLEAN

▲▼▲

High demand, a soaring stock market, and status-conscious top hogs have put a lot of pork into executive comp. Will a volatile market trim the fat?

▲▼▲

Not so long ago, a million dollars a year seemed like an absurdly extravagant income, and for nearly all the world's inhabitants, it is still the stuff of fairy tales. But in certain places in American business and finance—notably executive suites, Wall Street, and Silicon Valley—a million dollars a year today seems like ... chump change.

An overstatement? Not really. Consider that in 1997 the median CEO got total compensation of more than $3 million, according to a William M. Mercer survey. Travelers CEO Sandy Weill, who topped Mercer's charts, got an options-fueled $230.5 million. On Wall Street more than 400 Goldman Sachs bankers collected over $1 million. Only a few years ago it was unlikely that a research analyst could earn a million bucks. Yet last August, Jack Grubman, Salomon Smith Barney's top telecommunications analyst, made headlines with his new $25 million pay package.

Never have the numbers been so big, the rate of increase so dramatic, or the difference between the top and the bottom so extreme. In 1997, CEOs' total pay increased almost 30% above its 1996 level, according to the Mercer study. The New York controller's office says that Wall Streeters collected around $12 billion in bonuses, up 25% from 1996. (For a little perspective, consider that the average white-collar worker got a 4.2% raise last year.) Back in the 1960s the ratio of CEO pay to factory-worker pay was about 44 to one, according to the AFL-CIO; today it's over 300 to one. America's highest paid have reached the point where they think about money in a whole different way. "We're no longer talking salaries," says Lawrence Lieberman, managing director of the executive recruiter Orion Group. "We're talking wealth creation."

Why the soaring salaries? That old cliche about "bull market genius" explains a lot of what's going on—Wall Streeters who are collecting millions by being in the right place at the right time, corporate executives who are pocketing above-average salaries while their companies underperform their peers. "The rising market alone has moved lots of compensation to the point where it's completely unrealistic," says Peter Gonye, an executive recruiter at Egon Zehnder.

But there are a couple of more basic factors layered on top of the bull market that are pushing salaries skyward. One is simple supply and demand. Stressed-out financial-services headhunters say that even 30% to 50% pay increases are no longer enough to lure someone to a new job. Last year, Peter Crist, a Chicago-based recruiter, hired a 35-year-old mid-cap value manager with a good performance record away from a Boston firm. The manager got a "two, three, five" deal: a minimum of $2 million the first year, $3 million the second, and $5 million the third. Crist also said that big firms like General Electric, which historically have had lots of bench strength and little use for recruiters, were being forced to turn to search firms.

The other factor behind the monstrous sums—oddly enough—is the concept of pay for performance. That's always been the culture on Wall Street; even today, base salaries on the Street are usually under $200,000. It's the performance-based bonuses that can be ten times that amount. Obviously, performing in this market is none too challenging. In mid-1998, the market became far less forgiving—and corporate America's chieftains have yet to prove that they can perform in a less bullish arena.

In corporate America, pay for performance began to gain widespread popularity in the late 1980s. The common currency: stock options. Not only did options seem a clear way to link shareholders' interests with executives', but in accounting terms they are free money (companies needn't deduct the cost of options from their income statements, yet they can deduct it for tax purposes). No one foresaw that the bull market would turn reasonable-sounding grants into gazillions. Just under half the median CEO's compensation last year came from realized option gains; Mercer estimates that the median CEO is sitting on another $9 million or so in unrealized gains.

At this point, high compensation is a self-fulfilling prophecy. Boards of directors determine appropriate pay scales by—how else?—evaluating what everyone else is paying. "It's very much based on the concept of the Joneses next door," says Judy Fischer, director of Executive Compensation Advisory Services. This inflationary spiral spirals yet higher when it comes to recruiting rainmakers. You have to "make them whole"—pay them for any stock they are leaving behind—tack a substantial incentive onto that, and take into account what a competitor might pay to nab them. And when the person departs for the next job, his asking price is that much higher.

You might notice a certain irony in all this. The management mantra of the 1990s has been "teamwork." Yet we've created a star system in which those at the top collect the major share of the rewards. You also might think that it makes sense to ask, "Are these people really worth those sums?" The simple truth is that in many cases, we're all too fat, dumb, and happy to care. Last year Travelers' market capitalization increased by over $22 billion. Anyone want to quibble with Sandy Weill's $230 million? "It's ego pay, not economic pay," says Mercer consultant Yale Tauber. Whether Sandy Weill's services are worth $230 million is irrelevant. The money simply provides a means of measuring one's standing relative to one's peers.

What is irritating is that there's one element that's increasingly getting left out of both Wall Street and corporate compensation schemes: risk. If someone is putting a lot on the line, the potential for a huge payout doesn't seem so absurd. But that's not the way it works anymore. "For all the bravado, the Wall Street crowd is incredibly risk averse when it comes to their own money," says Egon Zehnder consultant Alan Hilliker. That risk aversion crops up in the form of guarantees—even if I sit on my butt for the next two years, you agree to pay me some exorbitant sum. In executive suites, that unwillingness to accept risk flows through every part of the compensation agreement—from what Mercer's Tauber calls "golden hellos" (we'll pay you to come) to retention bonuses (we'll pay you just to stick around) to golden parachutes (we'll pay you to leave). Those little perks come on top of the minimum requirement: replacing what the new recruit is leaving on the old company's buffet.

Some obvious suspects are squawking about all this. The AFL-CIO devotes a Website to executive overpayment. Rep. Martin Sabo (D-Minn.) is sponsoring a bill that would limit the tax deductibility for executive compensation to 25 times the salary of the company's lowest-paid full-time worker. And there are moves to link pay more closely to performance—for example, by setting the option's exercise price above the stock's current level or by indexing options to peer-group performance.

Still, people have been talking reform for years, and it's unwise to underestimate the ingenuity of those grown accustomed to deluxe salaries. Wall Streeters, nervous about a bear market, are becoming more appreciative of cash. Executives, too, will probably find clever ways to take the bite out of performance requirements or to get around a sliding stock market. Mercer notes that so-called megagrants—ones that have a face value of at least three times an executive's salary and bonus—are gaining popularity. And there are cases already in which companies have "repriced" options—lowered the exercise price to make up for a sagging stock. "If the market slides below 8000, a lot of options will be underwater. If it keeps slipping, expect to start hearing that the market isn't a good judge of performance," says Tauber. The sideways market that we entered into in the summer of 1998 will test not only individual investor's fortitude, but CEOs' true willingness to be paid for performance.

THE FUTURE OF THE NETWORKS IS BLURRED

BY MARC GUNTHER

▲▼▲

*Audiences are fleeing. Production
costs are rising. Advertisers are
grumbling. Something's wrong with
the picture at ABC, CBS, NBC,
and Fox.*

▲▼▲

Every summer, the big TV networks preview their fall season for critics who gather in a luxury hotel for a two-week marathon of screenings, parties, and celebrity chatter. Usually the mood is upbeat—this is the show biz equivalent of baseball's spring training, when every network dreams of high ratings and every new sitcom looks like the next *Seinfeld.*

But in the midst of the festivities in July 1998, the president of NBC Entertainment, Warren Littlefield, injected a sobering note. He took the stage to confirm speculation that General Electric, NBC's owner, was looking to spin off or sell NBC, perhaps by joining with a Hollywood production studio, a group of cable networks, or both. Without an alliance, he explained, NBC would struggle to compete with vertically integrated media giants like Disney and News Corp. that own broadcast, cable, and production assets. "Size does matter," said Littlefield. "We need partners. We need multiple revenue streams. We need more sandboxes in which to play."

The fact that NBC, the dominant TV network of the 1990s, felt ill equipped for the future reflected just how tough business has become for the over-the-air networks. Gradually, the idea has taken hold that the Big Four networks—ABC, CBS, NBC, and Fox—might never again make big money. "They're looking at a low-margin, breakeven business or worse going forward," said media analyst Tom Wolzien of Sanford C. Bernstein & Co. One striking sign of the times: Of the ten most profitable TV networks last year, nine were cablers like ESPN, Nickelodeon, USA, and

TNT, while only one, NBC, earned its keep as a broadcaster. In a speech to an industry convention, ABC Inc. President Bob Iger declared, "We're bound by an economic model of yesterday that no longer works today."

The root causes of the networks' woes were well known. Audience erosion looked to be unstoppable; for the first time ever, Nielsen reported that cable networks as a group attracted more viewers than the Big Four, albeit during some summer-rerun weeks. Programming costs were escalating, sometimes dramatically—desperate for hits, the networks agreed to new multi-million-dollar contracts with the NFL, the NBA, and the top-rated drama *ER* that more than doubled their costs. (Actually, $16 *billion* for the NFL, albeit over eight years.) Advertisers, meanwhile, warned that they would not pay higher and higher commercial rates for smaller audiences, although, with no real alternative, they continue to pay premium rates for popular network shows.

What remained unclear was how the networks would find a way out of their quandary. CBS, the network in the deepest trouble, has few hits and an older audience (average age: 52) that is shunned by Madison Avenue; its executives have all but given up on the idea of making money at the network, and they refuse even to say how much their network is losing. They argue that the CBS network should be assessed not as a stand-alone entity but as a way to spur profits at the company-owned TV stations, whose growth potential is greater. Programming at the network, as a result, is driven by the stations' needs for urban-oriented shows skewed to younger viewers. This is why CBS cast aside old favorite *Dr. Quinn, Medicine Woman* and welcomed late-night shock-jock Howard Stern.

NBC was in far better shape, with close to $500 million in profits in 1998, a slew of popular shows, a younger and more upscale audience, and most important, a forward-looking strategy. NBC had over the past decade assembled a cable portfolio that includes 100% of financial-news network CNBC, 50% of all-news MSNBC, and major stakes in A&E and the History Channel, all of which are growing in value. Using its broadcast network as leverage, NBC accumulated news and entertainment sites on the Internet at little cost, as well as a fledgling portal called Snap! The goal was to pursue eyeballs wherever they can be found. Even so, there was a sense in the industry, as well as within the company, that NBC remained too dependent on broadcasting and was headed for a fall—or a studio merger. For both CBS and NBC, possible partners include Viacom, which owns Paramount and the money-losing startup network UPN, and USA Networks, run by the acquisitive Barry Diller. Or Sony, a studio without a network, if a way could be found around foreign-ownership restrictions.

The models for networks of tomorrow are News Corp.'s Fox, Disney's ABC, and even Time Warner and Tribune Co.'s fledgling WB. These networks face the same profit pressures as CBS and NBC, but their value goes well beyond their direct contributions to their parent companies' earnings; they can be used to deliver programming to owned TV stations, to introduce hit shows that are owned by the company's production studios, and to promote other, more lucrative businesses. The Fox network, for example, creates the enormous syndication value in popular shows like *The Simpsons* and *The X-Files* owned by the Fox TV studio, and serves as a platform that Rupert Murdoch has used to launch news, sports, entertainment, and children's cable networks. ABC, meanwhile, is a powerful megaphone that Michael Eisner can deploy to promote Disney movies, theme parks, and cruise ships and to get the Disney brand name before millions of kids every Saturday morning. Yes, it's that much maligned idea called synergy, back in vogue again. "We're headed toward a vertically integrated global entertainment world," says Jamie Kellner, who runs the WB, the fast-growing network targeted at young viewers. "It is going to be a handful of very powerful large companies that are going to try to own shelf space and fill the shelf space and exploit the programing they own or create in many different arenas."

But if the broadcast networks are to retain their strategic value to these global giants, they must remain mass media; they need a steady supply of hits, which have been hard to come by in recent years. Nor can they afford to fall into the habit of losing money, year after year, particularly so long as they are owned by earnings-driven companies like GE and Disney. Their problem is that in 1998, the networks still do business much as they did in 1988 or 1978, before the growth of cable. They develop programs in a wasteful and frenetic manner, spending millions of dollars on pilots that never make it to the air. They rely on the same old studios and talent pool for ideas. They settle for look-alike sitcoms and dramas when bold, risky ideas are needed. They bombard viewers with a cacophony of promotion during the fall premiere weeks. And they glut the airwaves with reruns during the summer, all but inviting their audience to look elsewhere.

Some things are changing, albeit slowly and not necessarily for the better. To combat the rising costs of entertainment shows, the networks are programming more news—five nights a week of *Dateline* on NBC, three or four editions of *20/20* on ABC, a second *60 Minutes* on CBS. They are also trying to produce more of their own shows or share ownership with the studios; the danger there is that they will favor shows they own over better ideas from outsiders. To save money, ABC last summer tried out an improvisational comedy show (no expensive writers needed) and NBC imported an animated show from Great Britain.

But they need bigger ideas than those—new kinds of shows, new relationships with the studios and stations, perhaps even a willingness to program fewer prime-time hours. "If we continue to conduct business as usual, we won't be conducting much business at all," ABC's Iger said. The trouble is, most network executives are steeped in the old ways. Chris Carter, the brilliant creator of *The X-Files*, said recently that the next successful network executive "will be the person who reinvents network television." The truth is out there, as they say on his show; the networks' collective struggle to find, and define, their future should prove as fascinating as anything they put on their air.

CHAPTER TWO

▲▼▲

TITANS OF COMMERCE

CITIGROUP:
"ONE HELLUVA CANDY STORE!"

BY CAROL J. LOOMIS AND JAMES ALEY

▲▼▲

*That's what Sandy Weill calls the
megameld of his Travelers Group
and John Reed's Citicorp. Can
Citigroup's odd couple make it pay?*

▲▼▲

At the end of the most electric week in his life, Sanford I. Weill,
the chairman of Travelers Group, was in Augusta, Ga., for the
Masters golf tournament, switching frequently between green and
navy blue jackets. During the day, walking the glorious, story-
book grounds of the Augusta National course and lunching on its
clubhouse veranda, he wore the famous green jacket available to
only two slices of society: those golfers who have won the
Masters and the club's 300-odd members, whose ranks Weill
joined in 1995. Wherever he walked, Weill was stopped by people who wanted to congratulate him on the deal that had made
the week so remarkable: the stunning, crazy, could-you-ever-
have-imagined merger between Travelers and Citicorp.

On Thursday, Saturday, and Sunday evening of that early
April week in 1998 (but not on Friday, when he flew back to his
Connecticut home to celebrate Passover), Weill changed to navy
blue and served as host at dinners Travelers gave for customers.
A different set of 130 guests arrived each night, and they dined
in a billowy white tent put up alongside the Augusta house that
Travelers, for 40 years a television sponsor of the Masters, rents
each year. Then, toward the end of each dinner, Weill stepped
near the buffet table and launched into the tale of how he and
John S. Reed, chairman of Citicorp, had brought their companies
to this juncture.

In the air at those dinners, exerting a kind of counterforce,
was a sense of business history. This is not two large coastal
banks merging and spread-eagling the U.S. It is two very different financial services companies joining together in a way that

promises—and threatens—to transform the notion, long written into law, of what business activities are permissible for companies that own banks. It is also a merger that rides on, and preaches, the idea of revenue gains. These are to be gleaned, so the story goes, from Travelers' and Citi's "cross-selling" each other's products, from their reaching into geographies that are not now their strength, and from the proposition that one plus one might actually be made to equal more than two.

It is simultaneously a merger that raises enormous questions. The granddaddy of these is the matter of co-CEOs, which is the management architecture that Reed and Weill have adopted. The merger could not have happened had either insisted on being boss. Nor can the new company possibly thrive unless the arrangement endures for years and securely welds the two parts. And yet it is well known that co-CEOs are a management abomination, miserable to deal with on a church committee, much less at the top of a huge, deeply complex company. Weill and Reed have, of course, said it can work and have vowed that it will. In the job of making Citigroup fat and felicitous, it should help that its two monarchs have long known each other, though mostly as business friends rather than as buddies.

In fact, though both are highly intelligent, they are otherwise the Odd Couple. Reed, fit and Ivy League in looks—though his principal school was MIT and his degree is in metallurgy—is an analytical loner who dislikes talking to the press and sometimes seems to shun socialization entirely. In contrast, Weill has so many friends that his wife, Joan, was tortured when trying to cull the guest list to a number (173) when she threw him a surprise 65th birthday party in March.

A DEALER'S DEAL

When Weill tells the story of how the merger happened, he tends to leave out some details that FORTUNE learned from others: Fact is, Travelers held serious merger negotiations with J.P. Morgan in the summer of 1997, and had these borne fruit, they would surely have preempted a deal with Citi. But the Morgan talks foundered on disagreements about terms and management structure. Weill, throughout his history a nonstop dealmaker, then moved unfazed to the next project: his $9 billion acquisition of Salomon Inc. that fall.

You might think that would have sufficed for a while. But at a Travelers planning meeting that began in January 1998 and leaped to a day in early February, Weill asked for some musings about financial services companies that might make attractive merger partners. The name Citicorp surfaced promptly and drew snickering yeas of approval.

Weill called Reed next morning and made a date to talk with him the night of Wednesday, Feb. 25, when both were to be in Washington for a Business Council meeting. Weill gave no hint of his mission, and Reed came up with his own guess as to why he'd been called to this meeting: Weill, he thought, wanted to put the arm on him for a charitable contribution. When Reed learned that the contribution Weill had in mind was the totality of Citicorp, he was floored. The idea, he says, had never entered his thinking.

But the more Reed listened to Weill, the more sense it made. The two companies are amazingly complementary, displaying little overlap in what they do. Weill has spent his business life collecting distribution systems, which go by the names of Salomon Smith Barney, Travelers, Commercial Credit, and Primerica Financial Services (PFS). But Weill has just a minor presence overseas. With this merger, Weill will pick up one of the great international distribution systems in existence—it's called Citibank—and instantly become an overseas power.

Reed, meanwhile, is so committedly an internationalist that he is sometimes criticized for slighting domestic expansion. Via Weill, he is set to grab one of the strongest distribution operations in the U.S. Moreover, Travelers is an asset manager of size—running more than $200 billion in mutual funds and the like at the time of the merger—and this is a business area in which Citi has been weak and floundering around in search of a fix. Citi has also given short shrift to investment banking, choosing to spend elsewhere. But now Citi will have the ready-made help of Salomon Smith Barney, which along the way yearns for a road into Citi's huge roster of corporate banking clients.

You don't have to be as smart as John Reed to grasp that these two companies fit better than most, and on that night of the 25th, Reed listened to Weill with growing interest. But Reed knew relatively little about Travelers and could not immediately bone up, because he was set to leave on a long trip around the world. So he put vice chairman Paul Collins to studying Travelers and filling him in long distance. Reacting, Reed fell back on his habit of writing down the logic of a case to see whether it develops holes on paper, and from Singapore sent Weill a long fax detailing his thinking. By Thursday, March 19—not even a month having passed since Weill and Reed had met in Washington—Reed was back and the men were deep in serious conversation. At the end of two days of talks, Reed put his arm around Weill's shoulder and said, "Let's do it, partner." You don't flummox Weill often, but even he was stunned by how fast things were moving.

In the two weeks of behind-the-scenes tumult that followed before the deal was announced on April 6, Weill made three heads-up calls to Washington. One, in which Reed joined, was a largely ceremonial call to Weill's friend President Clinton. Another was to Secretary of the Treasury Robert Rubin. The third call, portentous, was to Federal Reserve Chairman Alan Greenspan. Weill asked, "You remember that thing I talked to you about last summer? Well, I've made a deal to merge with a bank, and I'd like to bring the other guy down to talk to you." Greenspan asked who the banker was. "It's John Reed," said Weill. Greenspan decided then he might just call the Fed's lawyer—and told Weill he'd get back to him with a date.

The heavy freight in this exchange is the Bank Holding Company Act, which has barred banking companies from engaging in most forms of insurance underwriting, a big business for Travelers. Consequently, it was never in the cards in this deal that Citi could buy Travelers. On the other hand, the absurdities of bank regulation make it possible for a nonbank—that's Travelers—to agree to buy a bank, apply to become a bank holding company, and commit to bring itself into compliance with the law within a prescribed period. The law specifically allows two years for this to happen and holds out the possibility of three one-year extensions to be granted at the pleasure of the Fed.

BANKING IS NECESSARY—
BANKS ARE NOT

▲▼▲

*Why has banking become less and less important to
America? Let us count the ways.*

Twenty years ago, back before he became Ronald Reagan's
first Treasury Secretary, Donald Regan used to give a stock
speech about the future of Merrill Lynch, the firm he ran
throughout the 1970s. The speech centered on a branch office
in Tampa, which had an unusual feature: four entrances, one
in each direction. Those doors were Regan's metaphor for
where Merrill Lynch—and the financial services industry—was
headed. As he saw it, the day was coming when each entrance
would lead to a different part of a true "full service" financial
firm. One door would still open to a brokerage office, but
another would lead to Merrill Lynch Insurance, a third to Merrill
Lynch Realty, and the final one to Merrill Lynch Bank & Trust.

Regan's vision of the future was not only ambitious—it
was impossible under the regulatory strictures of the age. The
Depression-era banking laws, creating barriers separating
banks from investment firms from insurance companies, were
still very much in force. And yet Regan was not the only person in the industry who believed those barriers were doomed.
Walter Wriston, the farsighted chairman of Citicorp during that
same era, had a similar vision.

Now, of course, the day Regan and Wriston foresaw has
arrived—with a vengeance. And though Merrill Lynch is not a
participant, Citicorp is at the heart of it: The $70 billion
Travelers-Citicorp deal, melding as it does banking and investments and insurance, obliterates those old barriers once and
for all. But that's not all it does: More than any other financial
services merger, it signals where the future lies. The essential
fact about banking is that it is an industry in decline. Once
you look past the short-term profit picture, you can see a
long-term problem that is not going away: As bank consultant
Edward Furash puts it, banks used to be at the center of the

intermediation process, and now they're not. In 1975, for instance, the typical American household had 36% of its financial assets in the bank; by 1998 that number was 17%. On the commercial banking side, the decline has been, if anything, even more pronounced. "As a stand-alone business," declares Norwest Chairman Dick Kovacevich, "banking is dead."

What has replaced banking at the center of America's financial life, of course, is the capital markets. In the late 1970s, when interest rates hit double digits, people began turning to a little-known investment vehicle called a money market fund, which paid market rates of interest. Then along came the bull market. A radical shift had begun, as Americans moved toward investment vehicles. "What people want—and what they're going to continue to want—is investment products," says Furash.

There is another part of the story, though. Over the years, nonbanks have had surprisingly little difficulty replicating basic bank services. The money market fund, for instance, has really become, in the minds of most people, a turbocharged savings account. Another example is the cash management account. With it you can borrow against your securities, write checks, and deposit your paycheck. Until recently, banks responded to these and other encroachments mainly by merging. Though that allowed banks to consolidate functions, cut costs, and keep profits growing, it was still a stopgap measure.

The Travelers-Citi merger should work. Travelers has the array of products, in insurance and investments that the people demand, while Citi has the brand, the global reach, and the distribution network. Far more than just about any other bank in the country, Citicorp has long understood that the survival of banking depends on its ability to offer other, nonbank financial services, such as mutual funds and insurance. Citicorp eagerly sought to break down regulatory barriers, knowing that was the only way banking could be saved. Now Reed has done it: The Travelers-Citi deal completes the revolution. "This deal," says Furash, "makes banking relevant again."

—JOSEPH NOCERA

One scenario for Citigroup is that it will eventually have to dispose of Travelers' insurance-underwriting activities. Another scenario is that new banking legislation will relax the restrictions on what banking companies can do.

TWO VERY DIFFERENT CULTURES

On April 3, Citi's directors debated the proposed merger for 7 1/2 hours. In the end, both Citi's board and Travelers' simply decided that the fit between the two companies made the management risks worth taking. "I love this deal because we start off with such a big pile of chips," said a Travelers director recently. "But I know that there is no stack of chips high enough if these two guys can't work together."

Just starting out, Reed and Weill must get accustomed to a board that neither can call his own: The script calls for Citigroup to have 24 board members, half from Citicorp, half from Travelers. This bit of balance is a far cry from what either man is used to. Reed has dominated his board, somehow managing to keep it under control even in the dark days of the early 1990s, when his then approach to managing—we are Citi; we can do anything—nearly brought the company to its knees. Weill, meanwhile, had a board largely composed of close friends, many of whom signed on in 1986 when he took control of Travelers' predecessor, Commercial Credit.

Where the culture clash may first have to be addressed is in the compensation policy for executives, which is starkly different at the two companies. Citi has a relatively conventional compensation structure that leans on grants of restricted stock for people it wants to keep and that incorporates stock-price targets at which option grants become vested. Citi has no general requirements that its executives hang on to their stock or that board members be significant owners. Consequently, the entire cadre of officers and directors at Citi owned less than 0.5% of the company's stock in early 1998.

In contrast, Weill all by his lonesome owned at that time 1.3% of Travelers stock, worth about $950 million, and its officers and directors combined own 2.4%. These stakes have been built by bountiful option grants and by something called the "blood oath"—the sworn promise of Travelers' management team and its directors that they will not sell shares (except to finance the costs of exercising options and the resulting tax bills).

About blood and stock, Reed says, "All or nothing is hard." He points out that Citi has many foreigners in its senior management to whom stock ownership is "a strange thing." So Reed thinks there are big questions about compensation to be ironed out.

A byproduct of the compensation philosophy at Travelers is an impressive amount of teamwork. For example, though cross-selling is not about to take over the world anywhere, including at Travelers, the company has made real strides in getting its divisions to focus on selling the products of their siblings. PFS salespeople—those folk who sell term insurance across kitchen tables—are, for instance, generating a good number of new loans for Commercial Credit. Reed looks at this Travelers talent and admires it, going so far as to suggest that it is important in his thinking about the merger. "I've been struggling for years to try to improve the management and energy levels within Citi," he says. "I think there's an intensity and a sales capability in Travelers that we don't have as well developed. This is going to improve our management DNA."

The problem is going to be getting the cells transferred into a Citi biochemical makeup that has traditionally been resistant to teamwork. Citi is known for a go-it-alone attitude bordering on outright arrogance—which is no sign of promise for cross-selling. Citi has not Played Well With Others.

A reason is the kind of individualists that Citi tends to attract and that co-CEO Weill is now going to have to get used to. Citi is filled with extremely smart people, which is good, of course. But these extremely smart people come equipped with powerful ambitions and frequently tend to protect their baronies (or "silos," in Citispeak) at all costs. The result is an odd cultural mix of supreme talent, bloody political warfare, ponderous bureaucracy, and major collateral damage on the human resources front. The high turnover occurs partly because Reed is constantly reshuffling management, moving people around the world, and generally trying to keep the whole corporation in a never-ending state of revolution. People have been known to leave organizations like that.

Reed has also pursued a controversial strategy of bringing outsiders into the company and putting them into boat-rocking jobs. In January he created a seven-member second tier of lieutenants and gave them all the title of "corporate executive vice president." Of these seven people one rung down from Reed, four weren't even in the company before 1993. And of these four, not one sprang from the banking industry: Lawrence Phillips, who runs Citi's human resources operation, came from GE Aerospace; Mary Alice Taylor, Citi's global operations and technology chief, from FedEx; Edward Horowitz, in charge of Citi's advanced development group, from Viacom; and Bill Campbell, who runs all Citi's consumer businesses, from Philip Morris.

"UNDAUNTED COURAGE"

Reed and Weill will face incredible challenges as they begin their ramble into co-CEO-land. Remember also that sometime in the future they'll have to face the last grand challenge—a succession plan. Here we have a few facts to deal with: The official retirement age at Citi is 65, and at Travelers there is no such thing. That could be because Weill has absolutely no intention, as many of his friends think, of retiring. Put succession down as one of the great imponderables in this remarkable business story about to unfold.

Weill and Reed, and just about everybody else, know the imponderables will include many a rocky moment. But they sat together on the Monday of their blockbuster announcement and displayed, if we may borrow a book title, undaunted courage. You could make a long list, said Reed, of reasons for not doing this merger. But the world, he went on, was not created by people who focus on the "nots." And to Reed's left, his co-CEO nodded in perfect agreement.

MICHAEL DELL ROCKS

BY ANDREW SERWER

▲▼▲

*Actually, he's plain vanilla. But this
billionaire CEO has transformed his
industry and enriched thousands
of shareholders.*

▲▼▲

Michael Dell's company, Dell Computer, is a runaway money train. Measured by growth in sales, profits, market share, or, of course, stock price, Dell seems to defy conventional logic. Over the three years ending in December 1997, sales climbed from $3.4 billion to $12.3 billion (that's 53% compound annual growth). Profits were up from $140 million to $944 million (that's 89% annual growth). Dell grew more than twice as fast as any competitor, and its worldwide PC market share doubled. Never mind merely comparing it with other boxmakers. Among the FORTUNE 500, Dell ranks No. 7 in return on stockholders' equity— ahead of Coca-Cola, Intel, and Microsoft. It is the only FORTUNE 500 company that increased sales and earnings by more than 40% a year in each of those three years. Then there's the stock. Ah, the stock! Over the same period it was up more than 26 times. In fact, Dell stands a good chance of being crowned stock of the decade, as in the best-performing stock of the S&P 500.

After a run like that, the easy money in Dell has been made, right? That's what folks keep saying. But for now, nay-saying seems wrong-headed. Dell's competitive position seems stronger than ever. It's not just that Dell is reshaping its industry by selling made-to-order computers directly to customers, thus bypassing the middlemen and their markups. It's that Dell is leading this revolution with a run of execution and innovation that no competitor has matched. It is more focused than any rival on speedily manufacturing and delivering inexpensive top-quality machines. At the same time, Dell is helping to define Internet commerce—the company could sell over $1 billion on its Website in 1998—and perhaps even the future of commerce in general.

"Think about it," says money manager Graham Tank. "Going directly to customers. Eliminating the middleman. Selling over the Internet. Wouldn't everyone want to do business like that?"

Perhaps. But not everyone has a CEO like Michael Dell, who is looking less and less like a computer nerd and more and more like an awesome manager and competitor. The more time you spend with him, the more you realize how singular and impressive he is. And how impervious he is to the pressures of running a multibillion-dollar phenomenon.

On an April morning in 1998, in a packed-to-capacity ballroom at Manhattan's Pierre hotel, Dell is addressing 270 Wall Street analysts, many poised with cell phones as they listen for the slightest equivocation. If they hear something they don't like, they'll punch up their clients or traders and urge them to dump the stock. Dell pitches them coolly, without notes, answering every question from the technical to the arcane. It's an impressive performance, especially when you realize that Dell is one of the youngest people there. The analysts' verdict comes in at the end of the trading day: Dell's stock is up almost $2 a share.

For that, Wall Street breathes a sigh of relief, because in early 1998 nearly every bellwether tech company—Intel, Motorola, Oracle, Compaq—announced that results would disappoint. The market's response was swift and unforgiving, with each stock blowing up. Back in Austin, Texas, Dell sighed and gave one of his little Dell grins. "Every spring, the analysts say PC growth is slowing to below 10%," he begins. "In the fall, they get too excited and say it's growing 20%. By year-end they get realistic and move the estimate to 15%, which is where it usually ends up. That doesn't much matter to us anyway, because we're looking to grow at a multiple of that rate."

Dell will tell you that his company's growth is the sum of many little things done right. That's in tune with how he thinks: He segments the business into discrete parts to focus his plans of action. So in an effort to answer the question on every investor's mind ("Isn't Dell due for a fall?"), we segmented his business as well. Whether you look at how Michael Dell makes war on competitors, how he's expanding the company overseas, or how he seduces Wall Street, he seems to be making all the right moves.

WINNING THE PC WARS

▼

Making PCs has been, is, and will continue to be a nasty business. It's a business in which competitors cut prices literally every week, where the product you make is obsolete just months after you make it, where customers choose between your boxes and essentially similar boxes made by a slew of rivals. Right now, the market is choosing Dell's. He seems to have the kind of three-yards-and-a-cloud-of-dust game plan it takes to win.

Peter Mojica moved to Charlotte, N.C. some two years ago, to take a job as an IT manager for First Union's capital markets group. The job was great, except for the bank's PCs. The unit generates nearly 20% of the bank's profits, and to ensure that kind of performance, traders need top-of-the-line equipment. "For us, having the right technology is do or die," says Mojica. "We need to have 50 PCs available at any given time for delivery within 24 hours. But our resellers were never able to provide us with that." When Mojica arrived, the unit depended on some 2,500 PCs and 75 Windows NT servers, a mix of various generations of Compaqs and DECs. That meant Mojica had to stock and install a mishmash of peripherals and software. "Imagine networking those babies," he says.

Another bugaboo was taking delivery and installing new machines. "UPS would deliver the PC," he says, "and a purchasing guy would open the box, pull out the machine, tag it, power it up, and program its electronic address. Then he would put the PC back in the box and store it in a holding station. Later another guy would take the PC out of the box again, load in our software, and stick it back in the box. Then it would go to someone's desk to be installed. If we were doing this in an office outside of Charlotte, we'd have to send a guy there for two days. Can you believe how much money we were throwing out the window?"

Mojica called Dell. "They were priced below the other guys, and Dell could tag and address the machines and load our software in its factory," he says. "That alone saves us $500,000 a year." Mojica has now cleaned out the Compaqs and DECs and replaced them with Dell PCs.

SHARING THE DELL WEALTH

▲▼▲

Businesses in Dell's hometown, employees, and investors all benefit from Dell's soaring stock.

So Dell Computer generates billions of dollars of wealth—where does it all go? One beneficiary is the Roger Beasley Porsche dealership in Austin, Texas. Its sales manager, Ken Keys, says Dell employees make up 15% to 20% of his clientele. Dell vice chairman Kevin Rollins is a regular customer, having purchased three cars in two years. When Rollins traded in his 1996 Targa for a 1997 Turbo S, he decided that the Turbo alone (which Keys says cost more than $150,000) was not sufficient. So he came back and also ordered a $40,000 Boxster for the family. Small change to Rollins, who in 1998 owned Dell stock worth $36.4 million, not to mention millions more in options.

It's not just employees and Austin businessmen who cash in. Ordinary investors in Texas and around the country are reaping Dell rewards, and whether they've become millionaires or merely rich, they're spreading the Dell gospel. Donnie Yeagin of Austin wanted for years to buy Dell stock, but his brokers warned it was overvalued. "I finally bought Dell in 1996, and I'm extremely happy. When we had the October correction [Dell dropped to $36 a share], I told my mother-in-law to load up, and she is thrilled pink."

Philip Treick of San Francisco was a Dell customer back in the 1980s, ordering several computers and on one occasion dealing on the phone with Michael Dell himself. When Treick became an analyst at Transamerica Investment Services, the

Dell has dozens of these stories. Such as in the fall of 1997 when it shipped 2,000 PCs and 4,000 servers loaded with proprietary and multimedia software to 2,000 Wal-Mart stores in six weeks—just in time for the Christmas season. Or in October 1997, when it delivered eight customized, fully loaded PowerEdge servers to Nasdaq in a New York minute (36 hours, actually) so first stock he recommended was Dell Computer. "I was a young analyst, and I got shot down." Eventually he did convince his fund manager; he also bought a position for himself, which has financed his lavish house outside San Francisco. "I was so excited about the prospects that I told all these people to buy Dell stock."

Perhaps the most devout Dell-vangelist is Kemble Matter, a high school gym teacher in New Paltz, N.Y., who used to supplement his salary by restoring old houses. In 1996 he bought Dell on the advice of a former student, a broker. Netting a quick ten grand on a day trade of 1,750 shares, he paid off his credit-card debts and gave his wife a ring with five diamonds for their 25th anniversary. Nine months later he reloaded on Dell. His Dell investments have freed him to indulge his passions, which include furnishing his Tudor-style home and landscaping his 13 acres of English gardens with specially designed stone walls. Says Matter: "This whole thing has been a fantasy for me."

When he's not teaching or coaching wrestling—as he still does, after 27 years—Matter studies Michael Dell obsessively, collecting articles in what he calls his Dell bibles. "When I see Michael on TV, I tape him." Matter recalls watching an interview after the October 1997 crash; the expression on Dell's face spoke to him, saying, "I hope you're sticking with me. You'll be sorry if you sell." Matter has persuaded 70 to 80 people to buy the stock, including 13 teachers and four students at his school. "I know you're not supposed to fall in love with a stock," he says, "much less with a man, but I am in love with the stock, the man, and the company." Whatever you say, coach.

—JEANNE LEE

the exchange could handle higher trading volume during the Asian crises.

Still, with its 6% market share worldwide, Dell was only the third-largest PC maker in 1998—behind Compaq and IBM, with Hewlett-Packard breathing down its neck. And in the corporate market, which accounts for the majority of Dell's sales, the appeal of dealing directly with a manufacturer is not universal. Mike Kwatinetz of DMG is a Dell analyst and a raging Dell bull, but even he says resellers have a role to play: "The reseller may be a local company or may specialize in providing PCs to a certain industry. And some companies want to deal with more than one PC maker." Nevertheless, for now Dell Computer seems to be in a pretty comfortable spot.

To really understand Dell's eye-popping numbers, you have to consider how fully it exploits the model of selling custom-made machines directly to buyers. First, Dell has no finished-goods inventory. Second, it ships machines with the latest high-margin components. Almost every computer Dell makes is a Pentium II machine. Third, unlike manufacturers that use resellers, Dell has nothing but direct contact with its customers. If customers start requesting an 8.4-gigabyte drive, Dell knows immediately. Fourth, selling directly means that Dell isn't getting paid by resellers; it's getting paid by the likes of Boeing, Ford, and Shell Oil and by consumers and small businesses using their credit cards.

For Michael Dell, that's what business is all about—milking every edge he has. He now wants to measure parts inventory in hours instead of days. "Seven days doesn't sound like much inventory, but 168 hours does," he says. "In a business where inventory depreciates by 1% per week, inventory is risk. A few years ago no one in this business realized what an incredible opportunity managing inventory was." In 1993, Dell had $2.6 billion in sales and $342 million of inventory. At the end of 1997 it had $12.3 billion in sales and $233 million of inventory. By comparison, Gateway 2000, which also sells directly, had $6.3 billion of sales and $249 million of inventory.

DELL INTERNATIONAL: HOW IT WORKS

It's 7 A.M. at a Dell telecenter in Bray, Ireland, where hundreds of employees, many in extra-smart attire, are lined up outside the cafeteria to meet the CEO. At 7:45, Michael Dell arrives and wanders through the canteen mingling with the staff. At 8:30 everyone files into an auditorium. When Dell strides onto the stage, he receives a standing ovation from the employees, who enjoy the same company stock plan as their brethren in the U.S. Beaming, Dell looks over the crowd. "Gee, I wish I got a reception like this every day I go to work," he says.

The enthusiasm in Bray speaks to Dell's success in overturning a significant image problem for the company. For years, Dell doubters offered a standard line that went like this: Selling directly was a very nice idea for the U.S. But Dell could never become a global power. Dell could never sell PCs directly to customers overseas. There were no 800 numbers abroad. Resellers were too strong in those markets. The cultural barriers would be too great. But the numbers say otherwise: In 1997, 31%, or $3.8 billion, of Dell's sales came from abroad. In Europe, Dell's sales are climbing 50% annually. In Britain, where the company has been on the ground for a decade, Dell has a 12% market share, trailing only Compaq. In Asia, sales were up 70% in 1997, albeit from a much smaller base, and would have been up more had it not been for the financial crisis.

How does Dell sell overseas? Just as it does in the U.S. Hundreds of Dell sales reps court large international accounts such as Deutsche Bank, Michelin, and Sony. U.S. customers like First Union want Dell PCs in their foreign offices. And while it's true that 800 lines are in their infancy overseas, Dell has things arranged so that customers all over the world can dial toll-free to one of six call centers in Europe and Asia. A customer in Lisbon, for instance, makes a local call that is automatically forwarded to Dell's center in Montpellier, France, where he is connected with a Portuguese-speaking sales rep.

Dell still uses some resellers overseas, particularly in Asia, where the regulatory environment or traditional business practices can make direct selling difficult. "But it's changing," says vice chairman Mort Topfer, "and of course there's the Internet, the ultimate direct-sales channel." The fastest-growing segment of Dell's international effort is Internet sales. The company sells $5 million a week on the Net in Europe.

Dell assembles its European PCs in Limerick, Ireland—in an old Atari factory—and its Asian PCs in Penang, Malaysia. (By the end of 1998 the company expects to have added another plant in

Ireland and a new one in China—the next huge PC market, says Dell.) As in Austin, the overseas plants are close to suppliers such as Intel; Maxtor, a hard-drive maker; and Selectron, a motherboard manufacturer, which ship parts just-in-time.

Be they in Limerick or Austin, Dell's plants are a remarkable balance between the cost-saving efficiencies of mass production and the value-added process of customization. An order form follows each PC across the factory floor, starting from when the machine is nothing more than a metal chassis. Drives, chips, and boards are added according to the customer's request. At one spot, partly assembled PCs roll up to an operator standing before a tall steel rack with drawers full of components. Lights flash next to the drawers containing parts the worker must install. When he's done, the machine glides on down the line.

Still, Dell has nowhere near the presence overseas that it has in the U.S. HP, for example, gets some 55% of its PC sales overseas, almost twice Dell's share. Is there, though, a competitor that Dell people fear? The answer, says Adrian Weekes, head of Dell's U.K. corporate accounts, is, "No one. We fear no one."

WAY UP ON WALL STREET

In the past few years, Dell shareholders have been treated to an exhilarating but nerve-racking experience. Every time the stock rises another ten points, any sane shareholder must wonder, "Isn't it time to sell this stock?"

Imagine the questions that must swirl through the head of Scott Schoelzel, a fund manager at Janus in Denver, who has been keeping watch on his firm's 23 million shares of Dell, worth about $1.5 billion. Needless to say, Schoelzel watches Dell like a hawk.

"I remember meeting Michael on one of his early road shows," Schoelzel says. "Back then, Dell seemed just like any other boxmaker." Eventually Schoelzel became a true believer and bought millions of shares, some at a split-adjusted cost in the teens. "I realized Dell was a whole new way of doing business," says Schoelzel. "The more time you spend with him, the more you realize that he is completely focused on the customer and his model."

Actually, there is a third constituency Dell completely focuses on: Wall Street. "Dell management really knows what the Street wants," says Schoelzel. "They are great communicators." Wall Street likes simple. Dell keeps its story very simple, as in "We sell custom-made computers directly to our customers." Wall Street likes stock buybacks. Dell has bought back some $1.5 billion in recent years. Wall Street likes consistency. Dell offers explosive growth consistently; it posted record numbers for 17 out of 18 past quarters, and usually beats analysts' estimates. Wall Street also likes managers it can count on. So over the past few years, Michael Dell has turned himself into a manager Wall Street can count on.

Five years ago his company hit the wall. It was growing out of control, had a crummy line of notebooks, and had made a disastrous foray into retailing. With foresight rare for the young founder of a company, Dell learned from the experience, bringing in top managers like Topfer and CFO Tom Meredith. The execs actually put a governor on growth, and they now watch business units and factories closely as they grow, to ensure they remain manageable.

For long-standing bulls like analysts Kwatinetz, Mary Meeker at Morgan Stanley, and Rick Schutte at Goldman Sachs, covering Dell has become, well, a little boring. "I sound like a broken record," sighs Meeker during a meeting at the Pierre. "The beat goes on." Says Kwatinetz, who figures he has raised his earnings estimates on Dell perhaps 40 times: "I can understand why you might not buy a Dell computer. But I can't see any reason you shouldn't buy Dell stock."

The analysts do have some questions. What about network computers? Dead in the water, Dell replies. Sub-$1,000 PCs? No way he wants to compete in that low-margin segment. Will new software applications be demanding enough to make companies upgrade their PCs? Yes, Dell says, because businesses continue to install rich E-mail systems like Lotus Notes, continue to roll out complex enterprise applications like those made by SAP, and continue to rely more on the Internet. How can Dell compete with full-service companies like Compaq and IBM? We offer all the services our customers need, says Dell, either internally or through partnerships with the likes of EDS and Wang.

What concerns analysts most is pricing. While Dell's machines are still cheaper than comparable ones from Compaq and IBM, it hasn't been lowering prices as fast. "Isn't price Dell's real advantage?" asks one. According to Meredith, the answer is no: "Increasingly, we find that we don't need a discount. We are winning on quality and service." But just in case, Meredith promises the analysts privately that Dell will keep its machines cheaper.

Such answers soothe the analysts. Kwatinetz has said Dell could double its market share in three years. To do so while the PC business grows 15% a year, Dell would have to grow about 40% annually—a slowdown from its current rate. If that came to pass, Dell's sales would grow from $12.3 billion in 1997 to $33 billion in 2000. Extrapolation? Yes. Pie in the sky? No.

How far can Michael Dell go? It's an open question, and his only response is, "Hey, I'm a young guy. I like this game." But think about it this way. Henry Ford transformed the transportation business in the Industrial Age by figuring out how to make a car affordable for every man. Sam Walton revolutionized retailing in the Service Age by making cheaply priced goods available to everyone. Might Dell be considered one of their Information Age heirs? His business is predicated on redefining the information-technology business by streamlining the distribution of cheap, made-to-order computer hardware. How far can you go on something like that? The jury's still out, of course, but the first two guys had pretty good runs.

▲▼▲

THE MICHAEL JORDAN EFFECT

BY ROY S. JOHNSON

▲▼▲

*The world's greatest basketball play-
er is also one of its great brands.
What is his impact on the economy?*

▲▼▲

Words no longer suffice when the subject is Michael Jordan.
You need numbers. Call him the very best basketball play-
er who ever lived, and no one puts up much of a fuss anymore:
five championship rings, five MVP trophies, a record ten scoring
titles. Ask whether he's worth all that money he's paid by Chicago
Bulls owner Jerry Reinsdorf, and you're still not likely to start any
bar fights. Sure, Jordan's salary is some $34 million for the
1997–98 season. But, hey: Between the year after Jordan arrived,
when Reinsdorf bought 56% of the Bulls for $9.2 million, and
mid-1998, the investment grew more than 1,000%—the team is
worth well over $200 million.

So here's a way to ignite a debate about Jordan: Ask the question, What is the bottom-line value of the entire Jordan era?

Beyond his own vast (and growing) personal fortune, if you
add up all the Jordan-influenced business—the sneaker and
apparel sales, the higher television ratings, the increased game
attendance, the endorsement value, the videos, the cologne, and
the rest of it—what is his overall economic impact? What is, in
essence, the Jordan Effect?

It is 14 years since Jordan arrived in the pros as a skinny,
tongue-wagging kid out of North Carolina. Now, the Chicago
Bulls guard may well be dribbling out the clock on one of the
most astonishing reigns in sports history. He has said that
1997–98 could be his final season.

During his time in the NBA, Jordan has parlayed his breathtaking skills and overwhelming cross-cultural appeal into a one-man
global industry, and he's done it more effectively than any sports-
man before him. Says Rick Welts, the NBA's executive vice president
and chief marketer: "If Michael leaves, he leaves having changed the

public's view of what role athletes can play in society—how they can be viewed, how they can be used by corporations, how they can be social icons. He also leaves the sports business a fundamentally different industry from the one he came into."

VIDEOS, BOOKS, COLOGNE, SKIVVIES, AND A MOVIE

Where to begin adding it all up? With the easy stuff: the revenue attributable to the Jordan "brand." His sports videos have sold over four million copies—including the all-time No. 1, *Michael Jordan: Come Fly With Me*. Together, they generated revenue of $80 million. Jordan has inspired about 70 books—*Rare Air*, *The Jordan Rules*, *Hang Time*, and *I Can't Accept Not Trying* are foremost among them. Publishing industry executives estimate that together, those four books generated nearly $17 million in sales. Michael Jordan cologne has had sales of $155 million worldwide. Hanes expects sales of Michael Jordan underwear to exceed $10 million annually. Add those figures to his kids' movie *Space Jam* ($230 million at the box office and another $209 million in video sales), and we've got $701 million in revenues, not including shoes and sports apparel, which we'll get to shortly. Not a bad start. Write it down.

AT THE GATE

What the Jordan Effect has meant for the NBA is a far trickier question. In 1997, professor Jerry A. Hausman of MIT and Gregory K. Leonard, director of the consulting firm Cambridge Economics, conducted an exhaustive econometric analysis that painstakingly charted and analyzed the league's television ratings and attendance records. Using a formula you have no desire to know (trust us), they calculated the lift that Jordan and the Bulls gave to ticket sales and revenues from licensed products around the NBA. What did they learn? Jordan generated $53.2 million for the league during the 1991–92 season.

We borrowed from their methodology to put a value on attendance data for Jordan's entire career. By comparing the league's average attendance (excluding the Bulls) each season with Chicago's road averages, then multiplying the difference by an estimated average ticket price and the number of games, we determined the Jordan Effect on road gate receipts to be $30.5 million during his career.

The impact was even more dramatic at Chicago Stadium, where Bulls games had been lonely affairs before Jordan arrived. We gave Jordan full credit for any home attendance above the average for the season before he was drafted but deleted from the equation the two years when he played for the Birmingham Barons in baseball's minor leagues. Our total for Jordan's impact on home gate receipts is $135 million. Added to the road figure, Jordan's overall impact on NBA attendance is $165.5 million. (Subtotal: $866.5 million.)

FOR THE NBA: TV AND ALL THAT STUFF

To determine Jordan's impact on the league's television revenues, we awarded a percentage of cable and broadcast rights fees paid to the NBA in the '90s to the Jordan Effect. We arrived at the percentage by comparing the average ratings of the five NBA finals in the decade in which the Bulls were participants (16.3) with the three series in which they weren't (12.9). Applying the difference (27%) to the $1.3 billion in rights fees the NBA earned above our baseline season, the Jordan Effect in this category is worth $366 million. (Subtotal: $1.23 billion.)

Another big category is revenue from licensing fees for NBA merchandise—everything from "official" caps and jackets to decorative plates. In 1983, the year before Jordan entered the league, gross retail sales of merchandise were relatively tiny at $44 million. By the time Chicago won its first championship in 1990–91, merchandising sales had reached $1.56 billion—and Jordan and the Bulls were the darling of the retail industry. Gross retail sales peaked at $3.1 billion in 1995–96 (Jordan's first full season after baseball). The league says sales have hovered around $3 billion ever since. Hausman and Leonard figure that Jordan was responsible for 20% of the league's gross retail sales. We granted Jordan the same percentage of gross retail sales for the years he played in since 1989–90 but smaller percentages for his first five seasons. Over his entire career, that works out to $3.1 billion. Write it down. (Subtotal: $4.33 billion.)

AND THEN THERE'S NIKE

When Jordan signed on as a celebrity endorser for Nike in 1984, one of his first questions was, "Who's my designer?" The inquiry signaled something new for the sneaker folks, who thought their new spokesman might be another passive jock waiting for free shoes and a check. Wrong. "It told us we had someone truly committed to the process," says Erin Patton, marketing director for the Jordan brand. David Falk, Jordan's agent, persuaded Nike to spend at least $1 million marketing Jordan, a gargantuan sum at the time. Nike CEO Phil Knight, then hired edgy young filmmaker Spike Lee to shoot the commercials that his ad agency conceived for Jordan. Result: Air Jordans jolted the sports shoe industry. By 1990, Jordan products—shoes and apparel—were generating about $200 million annually for Nike. Overall, Jordan products have grossed about $2.6 billion for Nike.

Of course, Jordan's value to Nike goes beyond just sneaker and apparel sales. What's that worth? Says footwear analyst Jennifer Black: "I've been doing this for 18 years, and I have not seen anything like the power of the name, the ties to the consumer, and the sales generated by him. Is it worth double the number he's done in sales? Maybe." Okay, let's go with it. That multiple places the Jordan Effect on Nike at $5.2 billion. Write it down. (Subtotal: $9.53 billion.)

ENDORSEMENTS

Evaluating the Jordan as Pitchman Effect is maybe the diciest aspect of our exercise. How to measure the impact of a famous face on the consumer's desire to buy your product?

Marketing experts say celebrity endorsers can do any of three things for a company: increase sales, boost awareness, or improve its image. Jordan has accomplished at least one of these for each of the companies he has been aligned with: Coke, General Mills (Wheaties), Wilson, McDonald's, Sara Lee (Hanes, Ball Park franks), Upper Deck, WorldCom, CBS SportsLine (Website), Quaker Oats (Gatorade), Oakley (sunglasses), and Rayovac. Still, even he's a little mystified by how it all worked out. "I never really envisioned myself having any kind of major impact on people," Jordan told FORTUNE. "Even now, when I see kids wearing my shoes, it's kind of wild. Sometimes I still feel shocked. It's fun, but it's also a lot of responsibility, and I don't take that lightly."

Neither do the companies. They typically pay Jordan between $2 million and $5 million annually and boost their marketing budget to take advantage of Jordan's broad appeal. Have the investments paid off? We heard absolutely no complaints. Gatorade controls 80% of the sports drink market, with $1.5 billion in revenues. That's more than twice the $681 million in sales it recorded for 1990, the year before Jordan signed a ten-year deal with the company paying $5 million annually. Jordan's impact is most apparent when Gatorade enters new markets overseas. "We've gone into countries where they don't have a clue about what a sports beverage is, but they know Michael," says Gatorade marketing executive Bill Schmidt. "He's instant validation."

But what's this all worth? To assign dollar figures to Jordan's endorsement value, Stephen Greyser, a professor of marketing at Harvard Business School, suggested that we apply a multiple to Jordan's endorsement earnings, if only because companies wouldn't hire him unless they expected a positive return. To settle on a reasonable multiple, we looked at an average of the change in market share for a range of companies during the years Jordan endorsed their product, then applied the percentage to the companies' revenue growth during the same period. At the end of it all, our multiple was 1.7—a figure generally considered quite conservative. According to published estimates, Jordan has earned about $240 million in endorsement money in the 1990s. Applying our multiple, the Jordan Effect for endorsements is $408 million.

So what's the overall value of the Jordan Effect?

AND THE GRAND TOTAL IS:

Add it all up, and you get a bottom-line number of roughly $10 billion—and still counting. Dazzling indeed.

How much bigger can this one man's economic impact get? Jordan says he is at a stage in life when he can make choices. He talks of spending more time with his family. He says he'll pare back some of his business obligations. Not surprisingly, Jordan will probably focus on the sneaker and apparel businesses when he leaves basketball. He'll also likely launch a line of fashion accessories with Bijan. But not much else, for now. "When people come to me with deals now, I've got no problem saying no," he says. "I've got enough on my plate. I'm not greedy."

In 1997 Nike created a separate division for Jordan's sneaker and apparel lines, which the company expects to generate about $300 million in 1998. Jordan smiles at the number and says he wants to make the division a $1 billion business. The $10 billion man is not greedy, just fiercely competitive—in any arena.

DON'T MESS WITH DARLA MOORE

BY PATRICIA SELLERS

▲▼▲

She's not just Mrs. Richard Rainwater: Outrageous and unstoppable, she's won love, money—and the upper hand at Columbia/HCA.

▲▼▲

Darla Moore fell hard for Richard Rainwater the moment he told her, "I view you like an equity investment."

"It was the ultimate compliment," says Moore, a woman who believes that business and love are similar games.

She was then the highest-paid woman in banking. He was renowned as one of America's most ingenious investors. Since they merged matrimonially, Moore has taken charge of Rainwater's stock portfolio as well as his life. In a $3^{1}/2$-year period as CEO of Rainwater Inc., she nearly tripled her husband's net worth, to $1.5 billion.

What's more, she has eagerly adopted a crucial role that Richard has always loathed—that of the tough-guy, dissident shareholder. When the couple bought into Mesa in 1996, it was Darla who booted the oil and gas company's founder, the once notorious corporate raider T. Boone Pickens. And in the biggest business drama of 1997, it was she who forced out Columbia/HCA CEO Richard Scott after the health-care giant got slammed with a massive criminal investigation.

"I've harassed guys all my life," Moore says, surveying the view from the back patio of the Rainwaters' hillside villa in Montecito, Calif., a few miles south of Santa Barbara. It was here, overlooking their vast gardens, that Darla dished it to old Boone, and where she strategized with Columbia board members to run off Scott. To get a picture of Darla Moore, imagine, say, a cross between the Terminator and Kim Basinger, with a wicked South Carolina drawl. Upon first meeting, she can come across as a prima donna, tough and aloof. As she warms up she can turn fun and flirty, even girlish, though the shift is deceptive. "She's a cutthroat killer underneath," says her friend Martha Stewart, with admiration.

Like most women who reach the heights of corporate America—a rare breed—Moore is paradoxical. She collects 18th-century French furniture and rare books. She also hangs out at hot-rod events with Rainwater, who owns the world's fastest street car. A charming and free-spirited opportunist, Rainwater astutely turned over the heavy lifting to his cunning and stunning queen of capitalism—"Little Precious," he calls her—so that he can focus on the big picture, relaxation, and of course, Darla. (Not just one of capitalism's most powerful couples, they're also outrageously affectionate.) In their unique partnership he remains the investment visionary, choosing industries into which the Rainwater money flows. Darla and Richard together, with the help of only two associates, select the companies. Then Darla, whose ambition seems limitless, executes the deals. "My wife wants to rule the world," says Rainwater, only half facetiously.

SHE'S THE TOUGH GUY

Moore's test of true grit came with Columbia/HCA, a business Rainwater started with Rick Scott in 1987 when each pitched in $125,999 to buy two Texas hospitals. At the time Rainwater was a Fort Worth investor, having just struck out on his own after 16 years with Texas' *Über*-rich Bass family. He had made the Basses billions by acquiring big stakes in distressed companies like Disney and Texaco when their stocks were really cheap. Having helped recruit Michael Eisner to Disney in 1984, Rainwater had made some $100 million for himself and was on the hunt for new ways to invest it. He met Scott, a scrappy 34-year-old lawyer who specialized in hospital mergers and acquisitions, and found they shared a vision—to build a national multiservice health-care chain. To attract the best practitioners, they came up with the idea of selling doctors equity in the business.

Moore got involved in early 1994 when she became CEO of Rainwater Inc. and replaced her husband on Columbia's board of directors. This was Rick Scott's heyday. In two years he nearly tripled Columbia's revenues by merging with four other companies, including Hospital Corp. of America (HCA), a big Nashville chain that Rainwater was a major investor in. Darla and Richard, in fact, persuaded Tommy Frist, the courtly surgeon who was then HCA's chief executive, to let Boy Wonder Scott be CEO of the combined companies.

From Darla's perspective, she spotted trouble early on at Columbia. When she resigned from the board in 1996—because the Rainwaters' investment in Magellan Health Services posed a conflict of interest—she felt uneasy about Rick Scott's management style. The Columbia board meetings were typically limited to two hours; Scott would present a litany of issues—scripted—and leave little time for debate. Darla kept up with the industry scuttlebutt, which was that Columbia was horribly difficult to deal with. And the press started hammering the health-care provider, charging that its cost cutting compromised quality medical care. Yet whenever Moore and Scott talked, which was every few weeks, he always told her not to worry, that "everything's great."

Moore did worry, though. Late in 1996 she started voicing her concerns to Rainwater and Frist, Columbia's vice chairman and largest individual shareholder. Neither of them was losing faith in Scott yet, however. After all, profits were going up some 20% a year. The stock was rising steadily. And Columbia, with $20 billion in revenues, was America's most admired health-care company, according to FORTUNE's annual survey.

But Moore trusted her instincts, which proved to be right. She says, "My single greatest strength is seeing through the smoke into chaos, and operating where everything is exploding." In March 1997, federal agents, suspecting that Columbia was overcharging Medicaid and Medicare, raided company offices in El Paso. The day the news hit the papers, Scott assured Moore on the phone that the company had done nothing wrong. "Rick was disdainful" of the investigation, Moore says, even though the federal government supplies about a third of Columbia's revenues. She adds, "You don't spit on Uncle Sam."

Her wisest strategy, she decided, was to strengthen her ties with Frist, who by this time was feeling completely shut out by Scott and thinking about quitting. Darla urged him to hang on.

Rick Scott didn't know it, but the noose around his neck tightened just before the July 4 weekend. In Montecito, Moore got a surprise visit from Frist, who said he was too angst-ridden to enjoy his holiday in Aspen. They spent all afternoon on the patio devising a plan. Moore wanted to merge Columbia with the industry's No. 2, Tenet Healthcare, and install Tenet's CEO, Jeffrey Barbakow, as chief executive of the combined company. Not only did the deal make sense financially, but it would also allow Scott to depart Columbia with relative dignity—Rainwater's biggest concern. Frist designated Moore as the intermediary for a Columbia-Tenet merger. (The merger did not happen.) It seemed only a matter of time before Scott would be gone. But the moment came sooner than anyone expected. On July 16, the feds seized documents from Columbia locations in seven states. Early the next morning, Scott called her in Montecito. "How ya doin'?" she asked.

"Great," Scott said, true to form. "I'm doing great."

Darla begged to differ. "Rick," she said, "it's over."

Scott resigned, and the board elected Frist as Columbia's new CEO.

Rick Scott wasn't the first guy Darla messed with. Before Scott, there was Boone Pickens. The cantankerous oilman who terrified CEOs during the '80s was by 1996 facing what some might call divine retribution: The stock of Mesa, the company he had founded at age 28, had sunk from $48 a share to less than $3, and Pickens was threatened by proxy fights and possible takeover. Smelling opportunity, Moore and Rainwater offered to help by buying some stock, selling new equity, and refinancing Mesa's out-of-control debt. To Pickens, this was a friendly partnership. He figured he'd stay at the helm for a while.

Before the deal was done, Pickens and his attorney flew to Montecito. On the Rainwaters' power patio, Darla told Pickens that he had to step down, that his reputation was a problem. Pickens says he holds no grudge. Mesa is back on firm ground, and following a merger with another oil company to create Pioneer Natural Resources, Pickens' total holdings doubled in value. The Rainwaters, meanwhile, gained a $161 million profit on their $66 million investment.

"I TREATED DARLA LIKE A BOY"

Either he's naive or he's coy, but Rainwater says the source of his wife's rabid ambition is "a mystery." (Hence her allure.) Really, it isn't so difficult to fathom if you study Moore's past. Darla Dee, as she was known back then, grew up in the tiny tobacco hamlet of Lake City, S.C. (pop. 8,398). She was the first of two daughters born to Eugene Moore, a schoolteacher and coach, and his wife, Lorraine, who worked at the Methodist Church. Eugene Moore, an all-star athlete in college, wanted his eldest daughter to excel at every sport. He had no sons or sisters, and so, he says, "I treated Darla like a boy." He set up a track in front of the house and clocked her 50- and 100-yard sprints. He timed her laps in the swimming pool, and coached her on the basketball court. He took her fishing and hunting. Eugene Moore even made sure that by age 8, his daughter knew how to map a football team's field formations.

Her mother pushed her too, but in other areas like music (piano) and academics. If Darla Dee brought home straight A's— and she did—Lorraine Moore figured she could be a nurse or a teacher, both good professions that allow a woman to follow her husband wherever he moves. "She kept telling me, 'I'll never do that. I'll do anything but that!'" her mother recalls.

In high school, Darla wasn't hugely popular. "I was on the fringe. I rejected what you do to be popular—the beauty queen/cheerleader/sorority thing," she says. "I must have had an air of superiority about me, but I felt destined for bigger things."

Moore's first big thing was a summer internship with Senator Strom Thurmond during college at the University of South Carolina. After college, Thurmond got her a job as a researcher for the Republican National Committee. It was 1976, post-Watergate, and an awful year for the GOP. (Carter beat Ford.) Moore realized that politics wasn't her game. "It dawned on me that this is all borrowed power. The guy who's powerful one day is nobody the next." She opted for business school, at George Washington University in D.C., though she hadn't a clue what she wanted to do with her life.

THE QUEEN OF DIP

Soon after graduating in 1981 with an MBA, Moore entered the training program at Chemical Bank in New York City, choosing a hardball area of banking where few others wanted to go: the bankruptcy business. "A mentor had advised me, 'Find a niche and become the very best at it,'" she explains. "I saw the bankruptcy area as a career opportunity because it had no cachet, no protocols, and no women."

Her boss, Bob Conway, believed Chemical could make a lot of money by actually soliciting business from bankrupt companies and offering them loans at really high interest rates. He sent his 30-year-old protégée knocking on the doors of lawyers, accountants, and investment bankers who specialized in bankruptcies. "Being a woman gave me a competitive edge," Moore says. "They would much rather have lunch with me than with other men."

It was part ingenuity and part luck, but Moore's timing was impeccable. This was the dawn of the LBO era, and when debt-ridden giants like Texaco, R.H. Macy, Federated Department Stores, and Eastern Air Lines went bankrupt, they turned to Chemical, and to Moore, for help. Chase Manhattan vice chairman James Lee, her former colleague at Chemical, remembers FORTUNE 500 CEOs strong-arming Moore to get lower rates on loans. "Darla would turn to the CEO and say, deadpan, 'You are bankrupt,'" Lee recalls. "She's totally fearless."

When Richard Rainwater bounded into Darla Moore's life, she was known in the banking industry as the Queen of DIP (debtor-in-possession financing), she was generating huge profits for Chemical (at least $100 million during her last years there), and she was earning more than $1 million annually. They met in Fort Worth on a deal to finance Farley Industries, an underwear company. Their first two encounters were platonic, but sparks flew. "I thought I was going to hyperventilate and collapse," Moore says. "This was the most intense, complex guy I'd ever met. I thought, 'This cannot be.'" Trouble was, she was in a serious-long-term relationship with a man in New York. Rainwater, little did she know, had just separated from his high school sweetheart and wife of 25 years, Karen. Shortly after that second meeting, Rainwater flew up to New York to see her. Sitting down to dinner that first night at the Regency Hotel, Rainwater told Moore, "I'm not interested in having an affair. I'll go forward with this only if you're interested in marriage."

She shot back, "You're too big. You have too much money. And you're going to ruin everything I've worked for."

Like any smart executive, she wasn't about to be acquired easily. She told Richard and her close friends that she dreaded becoming "Mrs. Rainwater" and losing her identity. "But, says Moore, Richard did "his wooing thing," telling her "When I see a unique and remarkable opportunity, I commit quickly and I invest heavily, because if I don't, someone else will."

"I thought, 'This is my kind of guy. Where have you been all my life? You think just like I do.'"

Since they were married in December 1991, Richard Rainwater has won everything he bargained for and more.

PARTNERS IN LOVE AND BUSINESS

▼

It sounds too California, but Darla and Richard share a particular passion: They're looking for the meaning of success and happiness. Around the time he married Darla, Richard had what you might call a mid-life crisis, or maybe an epiphany. He quit working for a year, wrote reams of poetry to Darla, became quite introspective, and through Crescent Real Estate Equities, a company that he started, bought Canyon Ranch, America's No. 1 campground for the health-crazed rich.

No trophy wife, Moore kept her job at Chemical. The lovebirds' business partnership began in earnest four years ago when Rainwater envisioned a boom in Southwestern real estate and started Crescent. He asked Moore to take charge at Rainwater Inc., which had net assets of about $600 million. She quit Chemical and plunged in, streamlining the business. She sold a bunch of small investments and partnership interests and redirected the money into publicly held companies where she could make a big impact—which, as we now know, she did. She also became famous as the woman who detonated Rick Scott's career, one of the most meteoric entrepreneurial careers of the decade.

Of Darla, Rainwater says "She's the best investment I've ever made. She wants to do not just a little more, but a lot more." Yes, her plan is to hunt bigger prey and do tougher deals and stage more audacious power plays. Asked what she'd like etched on her tombstone, she replies, "Darla Moore never let a problem overwhelm her—not even Richard Rainwater."

▲▼▲

COKE'S DOUG IVESTER IS IT

BY BETSY MORRIS

▲▼▲

*Coke's new CEO is as driven as they
come—and he shows signs of being
a prototype boss for the 21st century.*

▲▼▲

It is nighttime in Shanghai, and by rights Doug Ivester should be in bed. He arrived here from Atlanta late at night, having spent a good part of his 51st birthday in an airplane. He was up early to christen a new bottling plant, attended meetings all day, and hosted a dinner for his Chinese bottling partners. But as the dinner ends, instead of heading upstairs, he heads out the front doors of the Ritz-Carlton and down Nanjing Road, in what has become one of his favorite pastimes—walking the streets to see for himself what is really going on out there.

This is Shanghai's main shopping artery, and on Saturday night it is still hopping. Ivester heads down the street toward the Mei Long Zheng Square, an upscale shopping mall, to see how many people have turned out for the World of Coca-Cola, a traveling multimedia exhibit. The place is jammed, and Ivester is pleased.

But not for long. Heading up the street, he ducks into a little store called Shanghai Cosmetics Club, scans the odd mix of ladies' cosmetics and household cleansers, and looks perplexed. "Why wouldn't you put Coke in here?" he asks George Chu, the Shanghai regional manager, who is at his side. At the Shanghai Children's Food Shop, a tiny, jam-packed grocery, he finds that the Coke has been stacked on the floor, behind the checkout clerk. "You have to reach for it," he says. "You have to ask for it." In the little Bai Yu Lan flower shop, amid the orchids and lilies, he points to a shelf filled with bottles and cans, and quizzes the shop owner. How much do you sell in a week, Ivester wants to know. What does it cost? Which of the array of soft drinks sells the best? (Coke is No. 1; Sprite is No. 2.) That should make Ivester happy, but he frowns at a fountain machine in the corner that is turned off. The shopkeeper assumes that customers won't want cold drinks until the weather gets warmer. "Since we left the hotel," Ivester says with some frustration, "there has not been a single place to buy a cold Coca-Cola."

Now, why on earth does Doug Ivester feel compelled to walk the streets of Shanghai in search of Coke? Coke is, after all, in the bigger picture nearly everywhere. It has 50% of the global soft drink market. No other competitor, including Pepsi, comes even close. Coca-Cola, 112 years old, has the brand to beat all others— last year it became the best-known foreign brand even here in China. In overall market value, it ranks No. 3 on the FORTUNE 500, surpassed only by General Electric and Microsoft. Ivester could, one would think, relax a little. Go to bed. Get a life.

DON'T UNDERESTIMATE IVESTER

▼

But that's not Doug Ivester. Doug Ivester is the guy who for nearly two decades worked unflaggingly to provide critical support for Roberto Goizueta as he turned Coca-Cola into a powerhouse. If you want to know just how driven Ivester is, know that more than a decade ago he set for himself the goal of becoming the CEO by Nov. 1, 1996 and chairman of Coca-Cola by Nov. 1, 1998.

He was not far off. In October 1997 he took on what has to be one of the toughest jobs in corporate America: succeeding Goizueta, one of the great wealth builders of the 20th century. From the time Goizueta became chairman and chief executive of Coke in 1981 to the time of his death in 1997 from complications of lung cancer, Coca-Cola's market value grew from $4.3 billion to $147 billion. And Goizueta himself had become an almost larger-than-life figure, not just because of his proficiency at rewarding shareholders but also because of his warm Latin charm, his funny Cuban proverbs, and his inspirational journey—the refugee from Castro's revolution who became CEO of the company that for the last two years of his tenure was corporate America's most admired.

By comparison, Ivester seemed an obscure understudy. He is an accountant by training, an introvert by nature. He worked systematically to obtain the breadth needed to be a modern chief executive—getting media coaching and spending three years of Saturdays, six hours at a shot, being tutored in marketing. He is a straight arrow, constantly exhorting his executives to "do the right thing"; yet he is fascinated with Las Vegas, which he visits once a year, gambling some and people-watching a lot. He is an odd mix of Protestant work ethic and New Age motivational technique. He is big on discipline, which to him means, Be where you're supposed to be. Dress the part. Return phone calls promptly. Set "aspirations." He is a capitalist missionary who believes in teaching the world not to sing but to sell—Coke, preferably. That's a byproduct of a Southern Baptist, rural Georgia upbringing that he's never totally left behind.

And it would be a big mistake to underestimate him. This is the man who continued and accelerated the difficult, sometimes messy consolidation of the bottling process at a breathtaking rate and on an astounding scale. It is not that Ivester is a brute so much as a relentless force. "Ivester has been proving himself for the past 20 years at a variety of jobs," says Herbert A. Allen, CEO and managing director of Allen & Co. and a board member since 1982. "Everything he has touched has improved dramatically. Whatever target he sets, he hits."

And he's tough, which is a good thing because it's not the easiest time to be taking over at Coke. The company's underlying business is very solid. But Coca-Cola's bottom line, usually the picture of nice, steady, predictable earnings growth, has been ravaged by the strong dollar. Weak foreign currencies are playing havoc with the dazzling 15% to 20% earnings-per-share gains Coke likes to report. But is Ivester flinching? No. He has said repeatedly he sees no reason whatsoever to change the course he helped to set. "Look," he says bluntly, "if our shareholder base said, 'We want to manage this business for the short-term results,' I could do it. I know how all the levers work, and I could generate so much cash I could make everybody's head spin. As long as you know I could do that, I don't need to. We won't take any short-term actions that are reactionary in nature. We won't change our fundamental course. We are not managing for the next quarter."

ONE OF THE FIRST OF A
NEW GENERATION OF CEOS

And as his recent tour of Shanghai shows, he's not wasting a lot of time worrying about it. If Goizueta was a man obsessed with the success of Coca-Cola, Ivester is even more so. If Goizueta will go down in history as the quintessential late-20th-century CEO, Ivester may give us a glimpse of the 21st-century CEO, who marshals data and manages people in a way no pre–Information Age executive ever did or could. He is among the first of a new generation of CEOs to take over from the handful of charismatic business leaders who defined corporate ingenuity in the latter part of this century—the Andy Groves, the Jack Welches, the Roberto Goizuetas—and he is already redrawing the map.

Hierarchy is out—it slows everything down; he communicates freely with people at all levels. The conventional desk job is also out. Ivester prefers that employees think of themselves as knowledge workers—their office is the information they carry around with them, supported by technology that allows them to work anywhere. This really matters when your business is as far-flung as Coke's, which gets some 80% of its profit from overseas. Three years ago Ivester hired a chief learning officer, Judith A. Rosenblum, to figure out how to institutionalize the sharing of experiences and outcomes, country to country, executive to executive, and how to turn Coke into a "learning organization." Ivester is even down on old-fashioned notions of time—namely, the time it takes to get a job done. He has played with all sorts of ways to avoid doing things sequentially, pushing instead for what he calls "viral growth." Say you want to open 200 sales offices in China, which he does. Don't open first one and then the next. Use each new office to help open several more—pyramid-like.

At Ivester-era Coke, business planning is no longer an annual ritual but a continual discussion—sometimes via voice mail—among top executives. Technology is not just nice; it's crucial. Huge volumes of information don't intimidate Ivester; he insists that they are necessary for "real time" decision-making. A CEO on a pedestal is definitely out; a CEO as platoon leader is in. With past-generation executives, the style was more "don't bring me your problems, bring me your solutions," says Tim Haas, senior vice president and head of Latin America. "Doug thrives on finding the solutions." In a world this complicated and fast-moving, a CEO can't afford to sit in the executive suite and guess, Ivester says. He believes that many of America's executives "are getting terribly isolated."

THOSE CHILDHOOD VALUES

Ivester is the son of factory workers from a tiny Georgia mill town on the eastern edge of Gainesville. He was raised in New Holland, a stone's throw from the local Milliken textile plant where his father, Howard "Buck" Ivester, worked a variety of jobs while Doug was growing up. When he was in high school, his mother, Ada Mae, went to work at a small motors factory. His parents were children of the Depression, he recalls, "strong savers, very strong religious values," and had very high expectations for their only son. If he got an A, his father would say, "They give A-pluses, don't they?" On Sundays, Ivester played the organ at the Pleasant Union Baptist Church.

From the time he was 8 years old, he worked after school—cutting grass, doing construction work, raising chickens. He attended North Hall High School, where kids tended to come from either factory families or farm families. There wasn't much time for extracurricular activities or team sports. After school and on weekends, Ivester worked 35 hours a week. When his boss refused to let him move to a job working the cash register, Ivester volunteered to do it on his days off, for nothing, to learn the skill. For four months he did that, working seven days a week, until his boss relented.

Just as Goizueta had been profoundly influenced by the sudden confiscation of his family's wealth by Fidel Castro, so too was Ivester shaped by his childhood. He has a belief in plowing through barriers, in imagining opportunities even when there don't appear to be any. "One thing I learned in Gainesville was to never let my memories be greater than my dreams," he says.

Ivester went on to the University of Georgia in Athens, 48 miles from home but what seemed a world away at the time. He majored in accounting and then got a job with Ernst & Whinney, where eventually he headed up Coke's audit team. Along the way, he eloped with his high school sweetheart, Victoria Kay Grindle. He joined Coke in 1979 as assistant controller and soon became the executive assistant to John Collings, the chief financial officer who would become a trusted adviser to a green and uncertain new president, Roberto Goizueta. In 1981, Collings died of a heart attack. Four years later, Ivester became Coca-Cola's chief financial officer at the tender age of 37.

CREATIVE SOLUTIONS
FOR A TROUBLED COMPANY

▼

The events landed Ivester in the heart of the action at a critical time: Goizueta and Don Keough were trying to straighten out a soft drink company that had badly lost its way, and much of what they had to do in the 1980s was financial reengineering—right up Ivester's alley. Ivester provided a dazzling array of creative financial solutions to their problems. There is a lot of tension now over who should get credit for Coke's big acts during the '80s. Ivester won't touch the subject, possibly because he feels he deserves more of it. But here's what happened in the 1986 creation of Coca-Cola Enterprises, which put Ivester on the map. The idea was mostly Keough's; he had long been seeking a way to force consolidation of Coke's many small bottlers. The opportunity came when two independent bottlers came up for sale; Keough advocated taking them public. Ivester followed up, and with his team acquired the two billion-dollar bottlers, merged them with some Coke holdings, then took the whole thing public in what, at the time, was one of the largest initial public offerings ever. Normally, the job would have taken three years. Ivester got it done in 99 days—one day ahead of his goal.

By the late 1980s, Ivester had endeared himself to Goizueta and proved himself to Keough, who was determined to put him through the paces. What followed was a crash course in line management. In a year in Europe, Ivester made quick work of a recalcitrant French bottler, reclaiming that country's Coke business. When the

Berlin Wall fell, he pushed into Eastern Europe, persuading Goizueta to take a huge risk on local currency in order to be first.

But his performance was even more noteworthy when he returned to the U.S. in 1990 as president of Coca-Cola USA. Like so much of the rest of the beleaguered consumer-products industry, Coke had come to believe that the U.S. market was mature. "I think there was a belief that we could only grow at 2% to 3%, and it had become a self-fulfilling prophecy," recalls Charley Frenette, Coke's chief marketing officer. But if Ivester had accepted conventional wisdom, he never would have gotten out of Gainesville. He rolled up his sleeves and began challenging assumptions. "I asked people to get into a helicopter and mentally rise up above where they were and change their perspective of how they looked at things," he says.

He and his team walked through stores and walked down streets, identifying all the spots where Coke couldn't be found. Coke had become too focused on supermarkets and had let up on vending machines and all those odd places one finds a Coke. One Saturday Ivester drove from Atlanta to Rome, Ga., with a video crew, identifying all the missed opportunities along the way to make his point. Coke needed to get more micro.

By the time Ivester was done, Coke and its bottlers had installed thousands of new vending machines, coolers, and fountains. Ivester had brought back Coke's marketing star of the '80s, Sergio Zyman. By 1994, Coke USA's unit volume was growing at a 7% clip, and Ivester had shown the world that there is no such thing as a mature market. In the process he had created a model that would later work in all sorts of markets—Shanghai; Nairobi, Kenya; Barranquilla, Colombia.

ALERT ON ALL FRONTS

Goizueta's death propelled Ivester onto center stage and into circumstances that would have been daunting for any rookie CEO. Goizueta had been revered, and he was badly missed. Ivester says, "I am not competing with his image. He was a unique person at a unique point in the company's history. It is not something I need to spend a lot of time thinking about."

Nor has he. Since October 1997, he has set about doing things his way. For starters, he doesn't believe in an office. Ivester spent nearly a third of the first half of 1998 on the road, visiting eight countries. "Whenever I take one of these trips, I get great clarity," he says. "A lot of people need command central. What we are trying to do is to make the *person* command central, so that your office is not a place with a desk and a telephone. Your office is the intellectual capital you carry with you and the technology that supports it."

Which is possible because of a technology revolution inside Coke over the past 15 years, driven almost single-handedly by Ivester. He has insisted the company be wired globally, and now he runs the place by two-minute voice mails, using them to disseminate key news. Employees know to listen up. But voice mail isn't the half of it. As a new Coke recruit, Ivester couldn't understand why it took $2^{1}/_{2}$ months to collect the financial results from Coke's far-flung operations. He collapsed the process to five days, then forced a redesign of as many other sources of information inside the Coke system as possible. Today, Coke marketers in much of the U.S. can know how a particular package of a particular brand did in a particular outlet two days ago, which allows them to detect and respond quickly to Pepsi's pricing moves. "The place is terrific on information. A machine," says board member Warren Buffett.

All of which leads to some rather unorthodox, if effective, marketing. "What we're trying to do are things that connect with consumers," Ivester says, "and the way we read the data, our bonds are just getting stronger and stronger." Advertising, he says, is a very small part of a big marketing picture, which includes the signs at the ballpark, the Spencerian script, billboards, contour bottles, philanthropic efforts, and the 27 personal letters he wrote back to schoolchildren one week.

He is constantly after his subordinates to be on the alert on all possible fronts. Jack Stahl, senior vice president and president of Coke's North America Group, says he gets six or seven notes from Ivester a day, often attached to something Ivester has read. Recently one of them was an article from a furniture magazine that ranked the 12 best places to eat in High Point, N.C. Attached was a note from Ivester: "What's our availability in these 12 restaurants?"

Stahl knows the question isn't meant to be rhetorical. In what bemused executives call Ivester's "lock-solid follow-up system," there is usually a little date in the corner of such communiqués, by which he expects a reply. If he doesn't hear from you, you'll most certainly hear from him.

IVESTER'S GOAL

So far Ivester is managing to stay on top of it all. In fact, he says he doesn't want a No. 2 right now. Coca-Cola under Ivester is a flat-topped affair, with Ivester in the big job, then 14 senior vice presidents (including his six operating heads), and nobody in between. Says Ivester: "There is no need to pick a No. 2 right now. I've got six operating executives performing very, very well, who are very motivated in their relationship with me. If I tried to put somebody between me and the six, it wouldn't be a very good job."

Ivester has pushed the global consolidation of the company's bottlers faster even than some board members thought possible. It's a delicate business. As some competitors like to point out, the Ivester-era Coke runs the risk of appearing too aggressive. Yet, says Leenie Ruben, marketing consultant for Cadbury Schweppes, "Coke is the No. 1 icon in the world; it has to be a good corporate citizen. They are not in a situation where they can create shareholder value by being a bully."

On his trip to China, Ivester goes out of his way to convey just how good a global citizen Coke really is. China is an important market, for obvious reasons—Coke's eighth-largest market and one of its stars. The company needs continued cooperation from a Chinese government that is in transition and that has lately been nudging Coke to allow it a bigger stake in some of the bottling ventures.

There is a lot of ceremony to this part of his job, and Ivester appears to take to it less naturally than to the other parts. In a formal chat with the mayor of Shanghai, Ivester delivers Coke's message: We want to be good guests in China. We want to help the economy. Each Coca-Cola job creates ten more jobs to support it. In the days to come, in meeting after meeting, Ivester will deliver the same message to Chinese officials. We want to help China.

We want to help your schools. Frequently, he will invite them to come to Atlanta. Sometimes he talks sports.

But he seems to have a lot more fun in the trenches with his troops. "Did you understand the relevance of the egg?" he asks several days after his night tour of Nanjing Road. "We are competing against that egg." He is referring to a woman running a kiosk who was selling very few soft drinks and lots and lots of tea eggs—eggs marinated in tea and soy sauce that sell on the street like hot dogs in New York and that have much lower margins than Coke. "We have to get in there and show that lady that she will make more money selling Coke than selling eggs."

By the time he leaves China for his next stop, Taiwan, it doesn't matter much that Ivester isn't the natural statesman that Goizueta was. By the end of his meetings, he has delivered his message: explaining what Coke needs to be able to operate successfully. And he has gotten back the message, "We love Coke; we want to stay in this business." He says he has succeeded in "calming the waters."

There's no telling now just what kind of legacy Ivester will leave at Coke. But it's hard to argue with his track record. I asked him at one point whether he had written down somewhere his goals for the company, just as he wrote down so long ago his goal of becoming CEO. He demurred, saying, "I'm not real sure I'd be willing to share that. I'm not sure I want to read about that. It gives away too much." In other words, of course he has written down his goals for the company. Pressed further, he said, "My goal is on the cover of the annual report."

The cover of the 1997 annual report refers to a major milestone the company reached: selling a billion drinks a day, which amounts to 2% of all the world's daily beverage consumption. The cover has 48 Coke bottles on it, representing the 48 billion beverages consumed in the world in one day. One of the bottles is colored red, for Coke's share. Ivester says his goal is for two of the Coke bottles to be red—to double worldwide consumption.

So, Doug, have you written down a deadline? "It won't take us another 112 years" is all he will say.

THE BILL & WARREN SHOW

BY BRENT SCHLENDER

▲▼▲

*In a meeting of incomparable
minds, Buffett and Gates muse
about success, innovation, the
global scene, valuing stock, mergers,
and decisions. The result: something
pretty darn close to wisdom.*

▲▼▲

The queue of students stretched through the lobby and out the door of the University of Washington's Husky Union Building in Seattle on a balmy Friday afternoon in late May 1998. The group was staking out prime seats for, of all things, a lecture—albeit a very special lecture. The students and a few lucky guests were to be treated to a rare public dialogue between the two richest businessmen in the solar system: Microsoft founder and CEO Bill Gates and Warren Buffett, chairman of Berkshire Hathaway Inc.

(For the record, on that day the 42-year-old Gates' net worth hovered around $48 billion, compared with Buffett's $36 billion.)

Here are some excerpts:

How did you become richer than God?

Buffett: How I got here is pretty simple in my case. It's not IQ. The big thing is rationality. I always look at IQ and talent as representing the horsepower of the motor, but the output—the efficiency with which that motor works—depends on rationality. A lot of people start out with 400-horsepower motors but only get a hundred horsepower of output. It's way better to have a 200-horsepower motor and get it all into output.

Pick out the person you admire the most, and then write down why you admire them. And then put down the person that you can stand the least, and write down the qualities that turn you off in that person. The qualities of the one you admire are traits that you, with a little practice, can make your own, and that, if practiced, will become habit-forming. Look at the behavior that you admire in others and make those your own habits, and look at what you really find reprehensible in others and decide that those are things you are not going to do. If you do that, you'll find that you convert all of your horsepower into output.

Gates: I think Warren's absolutely right about habit. I was lucky enough when I was quite young to have an exposure to computers. Some friends of mine and I … didn't see any limit to the computer's potential, and we really thought writing software was a neat thing. So we hired our friends who wrote software to see what kind of a tool this could really be—a tool for the Information Age that could magnify your brainpower instead of just your muscle power.

By pursuing that with a pretty incredible focus and by being there at the very beginning of the industry, we were able to build a company that has played a very central role in what's been a pretty big revolution. Now, fortunately, the revolution is still at the beginning. It was 23 years ago when we started the company. But there's no doubt that if we take the habits we formed and stick with them, the next 23 years should give us a lot more potential and maybe even get us pretty close to our original vision—"a computer on every desk and in every home."

How you define success, personally?

Buffett: I can certainly define happiness, because happy is what I am. I get to do what I like to do every single day of the year. I get to do it with people I like, and I don't have to associate with anybody who causes my stomach to churn. I tap-dance to work, and when I get there it's tremendous fun. They say success is getting what you want and happiness is wanting what you get. I don't know which one applies in this case, but I do know I wouldn't be doing anything else. When you go out to work, work for an organization of people you admire, because it will turn you on.

Gates: I agree that the key point is that you've got to enjoy what you do every day. For me, that's working with very smart people and it's working on new problems. The competition, the technological breakthroughs, and the research make the computer industry, and in particular software, the most exciting field there is, and I think I have the best job in that business.

Both of you are innovators in your given industries. I was wondering what your definition of innovation is?

Buffett: I don't do a lot of innovating in my work. I really have just two functions: One is to allocate capital. And the second one is to help 15 or 20 senior managers keep a group of people enthused about what they do when they have no financial need whatsoever to do it. If I do those two things, they do the innovation.

Gates: The technology business has a lot of twists and turns. No company gets to rest on its laurels. That makes you wake up every day thinking, "Hmm, let's try to make sure today's not the day we miss the turn in the road. Let's find out what's going on in speech recognition, or in artificial intelligence. Let's make sure we're hiring the kinds of people who can pull those things together, and let's make sure we don't get surprised."

Sometimes we do get taken by surprise. For example, when the Internet came along, we had it as a fifth or sixth priority. But there came a point when we realized it was happening faster and was a much deeper phenomenon than had been recognized in our strategy. So as an act of leadership I had to create a sense of crisis. Eventually a new strategy coalesced, and we said, "Okay, here's what we're going to do; here's how we're going to measure ourselves internally; and here's what the world should think about what we're going to do."

That kind of crisis is going to come up every three or four years. You have to listen carefully to all the smart people in the company. That's why a company like ours has to attract a lot of people who think in different ways, it has to allow a lot of dissent, and then it has to recognize the right ideas and put some real energy behind them.

How do you as businessmen take your companies global?

Buffett: [At Berkshire Hathaway] we don't take our businesses global directly. Our two largest commitments are Coke and Gillette. Coke has 80% of its earnings coming from abroad, and

Gillette has two-thirds of its earnings coming from abroad. So they are participating in a worldwide improvement in living standards, and we go global by piggybacking on them. I can sit in Omaha and let Doug Ivester [CEO of Coca-Cola] fly all over the world.

Gates: Our business is truly global. The PC standard is a global standard. Our market share is much higher outside the U.S. than it is inside. Since most of our competitors are from the U.S. and aren't as good at doing international business, we thrive even better in these other countries. Most of our growth will come from outside the U.S. Here it will get to the point where it is largely a replacement market. That doesn't mean U.S. customers don't want better software that can see, listen, and learn. But outside the U.S. we still have that early-growth-slope phenomenon.

Which countries and companies are best prepared to take advantage of the Information Age that is revolutionizing society?

Buffett: When you think about it, 15 years ago this country almost had an inferiority complex about its ability to compete in the world.

Gates: Everybody was talking about how the Japanese had taken over consumer electronics and that the computer industry was going to be next, and that their system of hard work somehow was superior, and that we had to completely rethink what we were doing. Now, if you look at what's happened in personal computers or in business in general, or at how we allocate capital and how we let labor move around, the U.S. has emerged in a very strong position. And so the first beneficiary of all this information technology has been the U.S.

The whole world is going to benefit in a big way. There will be this shift where, instead of your income level being determined by what country you are from, it will be determined by your education level. When we get the Internet allowing services and advice to be transported as efficiently as goods are transported via shipping, then you'll get essentially open-market bidding for [an] engineer in India vs. an engineer here in the U.S. And that benefits everyone, because you're taking better advantage of those resources. So the developed countries will get the early benefit of these things. But in the long run, the people in developing countries who are lucky enough to get a good education should get absolutely the biggest boost from all this.

Buffett: The technological revolution will change the world in dramatic ways, and quickly. Ironically, however, our approach to dealing with that is just the opposite of Bill's. I look for businesses in which I think I can predict what they're going to look like in ten or 15 or 20 years. That means businesses that will look more or less as they do today, except that they'll be larger and doing more business internationally. So I focus on an absence of change. That doesn't mean I don't think there's a lot of money to be made from that change. I just don't think I'm the one to make a lot of money out of it.

Take Wrigley's chewing gum. I don't think the Internet is going to change how people are going to chew gum. I don't think it's going to change the fact that Coke will be the drink of preference and will gain in per capita consumption around the world; I don't think it will change whether people shave or how they shave. So we are looking for the very predictable, and you won't find the very predictable in what Bill does. As a member of society, I applaud what he is doing, but as an investor, I keep a wary eye on it.

Gates: I agree strongly with Warren. I think the multiples of technology stocks should be quite a bit lower than the multiples of stocks like Coke and Gillette, because we are subject to complete changes in the rules. I know very well that in the next ten years, if Microsoft is still a leader, we will have had to weather at least three crises.

Mr. Buffett, I was told that you have a policy against splitting stock, and I wondered if you might comment on Microsoft's history of splitting stock?

Buffett: I've never felt that if I went into a restaurant and said, "I want two hat checks instead of one for my hat," I'd really be a lot better off. But I also don't have any quarrel with companies that do split their stock, and I don't think Microsoft's been hurt by it.

I think that our policy fits us very well. I happen to think that by not splitting Berkshire stock, we attract a slightly more long-term-oriented group of investors. What you want to do is attract shareholders that are very much like you, with the same time horizons and expectations. We don't talk about quarterly earnings, we don't have an investor relations department, and we don't have conference calls with Wall Street analysts, because we don't want people who are focusing on what's going to happen next quarter or even next year. We want people to join us because they want to be with us until they die.

Mr. Buffett, what's your response to those who say that traditional methods for valuing companies are obsolete in this market?

Buffett: I think it's hard to find companies that meet our tests of being undervalued in this market, but I don't think that the methods of valuation have changed. There's no magic to evaluating any financial asset. A financial asset means, by definition, that you lay out money now to get money back in the future. If every financial asset were valued properly, they would all sell at a price that reflected all of the cash that would be received from them forever until Judgment Day, discounted back to the present at the same interest rate. There wouldn't be any risk premium, because you'd know what coupons were printed on this "bond" between now and eternity. That method of valuation is exactly what should be used whether you're in 1974 or you're in 1998. If I can't do that, then I don't buy. So I'll wait.

What do you think of the recent wave of mergers? And at the end of the day, is the shareholder better off after a merger?

Buffett: There truly are synergies in a great many mergers. But whether there are synergies or not, they are going to keep happening. As long as our economy works the way it does—and I think it works very well—you're going to see a lot of it. A generally buoyant market tends to encourage mergers, because everybody's currency is more useful in those circumstances.

In most acquisitions, it's better to be the target than the acquirer. The acquirer pays for the fact that he gets to haul back to his cave the carcass of the conquered animal. I am suspicious of people who just keep acquiring almost by the week, though. If you look at the outstanding companies—say, a Microsoft or an Intel or a Wal-Mart—their growth overwhelmingly has been internal. Frequently, if some company is on a real acquisition binge, they feel they're using funny money, and it has certain aspects of a chain-letter game. I'd like to see a period where merged companies just run by themselves after a deal, rather than moving around the accounting and putting up big restructuring charges. I get suspicious when there's too much activity. I like to see organic growth.

Gates: I think it's good to have a healthy skepticism. But General Motors was created out of a restructuring of the automobile industry from a specialized orientation to companies that did the whole job. And anybody who missed that was basically wiped out.

We've bought a lot of small companies, and I'd say that's been vital to us. These are companies that on their own probably wouldn't have made it, but when their abilities were combined with ours, both of us were able to create a much better set of products than we could've otherwise.

I think in banking today, if you're a medium-sized bank, you're probably going to need to participate in all this stuff that's going on. It doesn't make that much sense to have so many banks in this country, and so there will be certain ones going after scale. But there are a lot of silly mergers too.

What was the best business decision you made?

Buffett: It was just jumping in the pool, basically. The nice thing about the investment business is that you don't need very many deals to succeed. In fact, if when you got out of business school here, you got a punch card with 20 punches on it, and every time you made an investment decision you used up one punch, and that's all you were going to get, you would make 20 very good investment decisions. And you could get very rich, incidentally. You don't need 50 good ideas at all.

I hope the one I made yesterday was a good one. But they've always been kind of simple and obvious to me. The truth is, you know them when you see them. They're so cheap. When I got out of Columbia University, I went through the Moody's manuals page by page—the industrial manual, the transportation manual, the banks and finance manual—just looking for things. And I found stocks at one times earnings. One was Genessee Valley Gas, a little company up in upstate New York, a public utility selling at one times earnings. There were no brokerage reports on it, no nothing, but all you had to do was turn the page. It worked out so well I actually went through the book a second time.

Gates: In my case, I'd have to say my best business decisions have had to do with picking people. Deciding to go into business with Paul Allen is probably at the top of the list, and subsequently, hiring a friend—Steve Ballmer—who has been my primary business partner ever since. It's important to have someone whom you totally trust, who is totally committed, who shares your vision, and yet who has a little bit different set of skills and who also acts as something of a check on you. The benefit of sparking off somebody who's got that kind of brilliance is that it not only makes business more fun, but it really leads to a lot of success.

▲▼▲

WHY WOMEN FIND ESTÉE LAUDER MESMERIZING

BY NINA MUNK

▲▼▲

*Selling cosmetics works best if you
get intimate with the customer.
Estée Lauder knew that; so does her
son Leonard.*

▲▼▲

The year is 1950. Harry Truman is President. *Father of the Bride*, starring Spencer Tracy and the 18-year-old Elizabeth Taylor, has opened in movie theaters. And Mrs. Estée Lauder, fortysomething years old, is determined to get her creams and lotions into Neiman Marcus. "She came to see me late one afternoon as I was on my way home, and she introduced herself," recalls Stanley Marcus, then president of Neiman Marcus. " 'I'm Estée Lauder, and I have the most wonderful beauty products in the world and they must be in your store.' "

"Well," Marcus continues, "we already had Elizabeth Arden and Germaine Monteil and Charles of the Ritz. We didn't need another line. So I said to her, Why don't you go and talk to so-and-so, who was our merchandising manager at the time. And Estée replied, 'I have done that, and he said that I should come back another day. But you see, Mr. Marcus, I don't have time for that because my products must be in your store right away.' "

Marcus, over 90 and chairman emeritus of Neiman Marcus, remembers the day perfectly. "I asked her, 'How much space do you need?' 'That's not important,' she replied. 'Four or five feet will do.' 'When can you have your merchandise here?' I said. Well, by God, she had it all with her. She had brought a big bag filled with merchandise, and the very next day she set it up and she was in business at Neiman Marcus. Stopping everyone who came in the door, she said, 'Try this. I'm Estée Lauder and these are the most wonderful beauty products in the world.' "

"Yes," says Marcus. "She was a very determined salesperson; she pushed her way into acceptance. She was determined—and gracious and lovely through it all. It was easier to say yes to Estée than to say no."

Determined, gracious, and lovely Estée Lauder began life as Josephine Esther Mentzer, living above her father's hardware store in Corona, Queens. The company she founded in 1946 controls over 45% of the cosmetics market in U.S. department stores—three times the volume of its closest competitor, L'Oréal, which owns Lancôme and holds fragrance licenses for Ralph Lauren and Giorgio Armani, among others. According to market researchers at NPD Beauty Trends, the four best-selling prestige (industry rhetoric for "expensive") perfumes in the U.S. belong to Estée Lauder. When it comes to prestige makeup (mascara, lipstick, foundation, you name it), seven of the top ten products are Estée Lauder's. Of the ten best-selling prestige skin care products, eight belong to Estée Lauder. Overseas, Estée Lauder products are sold in 118 countries. In Japan, Estée Lauder's Clinique brand outsells Shiseido in the 110 doors, or outlets, it's sold in. The British and the Germans adore Estée Lauder. In Eastern Europe and Russia, it is said that Estée Lauder is as well known as Coca-Cola.

In the fiscal year that ended in June 1998, Estée Lauder Cos. earned $236 million, after taxes, on revenues of $3.6 billion. The Lauder family—including the "ageless" Estée, who, it is rumored, has turned 90—controls 77% of the common stock and 96% of the votes; the family's stake is worth some $6.2 billion.

A LIPSTICK WILL CHANGE YOUR LIFE

Most people assume that cosmetics are an easy sell, that women are suckers for anything that promises to make them look better, younger, more attractive. But the truth is, selling cosmetics is a tricky business, in part because you're selling a product that no one really needs. That's why Estée Lauder Cos.' performance is so remarkable: Few companies are as canny at persuading women to spend and spend and keep spending on the unessential. Selling cosmetics is a subtle art; to do it well, you have to tap into something bigger, wider, more abstract than the product itself. A lipstick is more than a lipstick; it'll change your life.

And perfume? It's a stairway to paradise. No one understands this better than Estée's eldest son, Leonard Lauder, who has turned his mother's cream and lotion business into a global cosmetics empire.

While Estée strove to make her eponymous brand a giant used by all, Leonard has recognized that cosmetics are personal, intimate; that increasingly the trend is toward specialization, toward brands that make a woman feel she's buying something that's made just for her, that conforms to her unique style, her "very special" look. Leonard Lauder's goal is to own not one single brand with mass appeal but instead a collection of dozens and dozens of brands—including the original Estée Lauder brand, Prescriptives, Clinique, Bobbi Brown Essentials, M.A.C., and Origins—each targeting a different kind of customer.

Each of these brands—and more—is owned by Estée Lauder Cos. Of course, hardly anyone knows that. A 23-year-old who's loyal to M.A.C. would never dream of buying a gold-cased Estée Lauder lipstick (uncool). There's no way she knows that for all that choice she's being offered, there is virtually no choice at all.

But there is a difference: If you go to Walgreens for a Revlon lipstick, you'll leave with a $6 lipstick and maybe a roll of Life Savers. On the other hand, if you go to Saks for an Estée Lauder lipstick, there's a pretty good chance you'll leave with a $16 lipstick, a $13 lip liner, a $15 lip gloss, and maybe even a $25 tube of LipZone to help prevent your new lipstick from "feathering." The sales technique is called "link selling." You ask the salesperson for a foundation; you wind up with foundation, plus concealer, plus powder. You ask for eye shadow; you wind up with eye shadow, plus eye shadow remover and maybe an eyeliner.

Nobody is better at link selling than Estée Lauder. Which helps explain why, in a relatively stagnant industry, Estée Lauder's revenues increased 50% in five years. Link selling is partly why earnings have grown at a compound annual rate of 22% over five years. To persuade any woman to buy three products when she intended to buy just one is an art. If the salesperson gets pushy, even for a moment, she's finished. That's why Estée Lauder Cos. places so much emphasis on training.

In March 1998, at a Marriott hotel in Maryland, Clinique organized a three-day seminar for its consultants. Working on a volunteer, Leslie demonstrates Clinique's skin assessment technique. "Using these three fingers, touch the skin on her face—her forehead, her cheeks, her chin, her eye area—but be sure to ask for permission. Share your observations with her. Bring up her good features before you discuss the trouble spots. Customers may be intimidated, so if you point out one or two things that are terrific, they'll feel good about themselves."

FLOWERS, PUPPIES, SMILES

Teaching saleswomen to sell is pointless if you don't first drive customers to the counter. To attract busy women, you must convince them that what you're selling is more than just another cream. You have to offer a little escapism, make women hope, believe, even for a moment, that they can look like Elizabeth Hurley. Here's where "aspirational marketing" comes in. You must have seen Estée Lauder's advertisement for its fragrance Pleasures, the one where Elizabeth Hurley, curled up in a pale-pink twin set, sitting in a field of pink flowers, two golden Labrador puppies at her side, smiles sweetly at the camera. It's an aspirational ad: Apparently women aspire to certain identifiable things, and that is largely the reason Pleasures is the No. 1–selling prestige perfume in America. "Pleasures is a lifestyle aspiration," explains Robin Burns, 45, who heads the Estée Lauder brand. "It's about family, children, outdoors, the puppy dog, the sunshine, relaxation, the hammock. It's about pleasure, it's about the one thing that people don't have enough of."

So important is the power of imagery in this business that in its last fiscal year Estée Lauder Cos. spent $980 million, or almost 30% of sales, on advertising and promotions. (As a point of comparison, the firm spent just $35 million on research and development.) Revlon, by contrast, spent only $397 million, or 17% of sales, on advertising. Such sums help explain why Estée Lauder's net income for the last fiscal year was just 5.8% of sales. The creams and lotions and lipsticks that Estée Lauder sells cost very little to make—so little that last year the company reported an awesome 77% gross profit margin. But Lauder spends so much on advertising, on training, and on luring customers with free samples that at the end of the year there's almost nothing left. From that splendid gross margin, Lauder is left with an unimpressive net margin. That's the nature of the business. And it helps explain why Estée Lauder rules the prestige cosmetics market. Who can compete with that budget? "They have such deep pockets that we can't fight them [in advertising and promotions]," sighs an executive at Lancôme who prefers to remain nameless. "Our only option is to be more strategic."

The bad news for competitors, however, is that few companies are as strategic as Estée Lauder. The word on the Street was that the company in 1997 was going nowhere fast. Analysts had two major concerns: One, Lauder's products were primarily sold in department stores; and two, Lauder's competitors in the cheap mass market were stealing market share.

TIMES CHANGE

For years Leonard Lauder had scoffed at the idea of selling his products anywhere but in department stores (and, overseas, in classy perfumeries). But in department store retailing, things have turned on their head. In the old days, the '50s and '60s, say, cosmetics companies benefited from customer traffic: A woman might buy a Charles of the Ritz lipstick, maybe an eye shadow, on her way to the fur department.

Today the situation is reversed, and cosmetics companies, namely Estée Lauder Cos., drive most department store traffic. Now, after buying a new face cream or lipstick, a woman may visit the shoe department. But attracting women to department stores gets harder all the time; it's the mass market and specialty stores that draw them in now. And when you already control over 45% of cosmetics sales at department stores, how much room is left for growth?

Like his mother, Leonard Lauder is a relentless, determined promoter with no tolerance for failure. He makes his ambitions clear: "Every time I talk to our people, every time I go to a sales meeting, every time I meet with beauty advisers, I say to the peo-

ESTÉE'S MANY FACES

▲▼▲

Seducing the hip, the old, the eco-correct: Lauder collects brands that appeal to women (and men) of all tastes.

▶ **ARAMIS** *Sales: $135 million. Sold in 100 countries.* The classic Father's Day gift. Musty. Other Aramis scents: Tuscany, New West, and Havana.

▶ **AVEDA** *Sales: $120 million. Sold in 18 countries.* For the New Age in you. Lauder says Aveda's sales will hit $1 billion–plus.

▶ **BOBBI BROWN ESSENTIALS** *Sales: $50 million. Sold in ten countries.* Her customers want to be just like Bobbi, the ultimate working Mom. It's a cult thing.

▶ **CLINIQUE** *Sales: $1.3 billion. Sold in 80 countries.* The basic. Middle America. For the mom in the GMC Suburban.

▶ **CRÈME DE LA MER** *Sales: Tiny. Sold only at Neiman, Saks, and Bergdorf Goodman.* Believers say it's a miracle product. At $155 for two ounces, it had better be.

▶ **DONNA KARAN** *Sales: $50 million. Sold in 17 countries.* Now Estée Lauder plans a properly executed relaunch of Karan's line.

▶ **ESTÉE LAUDER** *Sales: $1.6 billion. Sold in 118 countries.* The classic. Pretty. Perfect for Junior Leaguers.

ple, 'Listen, I simply want this to be the best company in the world. The best means being the best in everything.' "

Being best means making it easier for people to buy your product. Cosmetics are impulse purchases. To encourage women to be more impulsive, Estée Lauder Cos. is replacing traditional glass counters in department stores with open displays that let women browse, touch bottles, and test products without having to ask for help. In the first year this new open format was intro-

▲▼▲

- ▶ **JANE BY SASSABY** *Sales: $30 million. Sold in the U.S. only but expected to be a hit in developing countries.* Every product is $2.99. Gum-snapping teens say, Jane rules!
- ▶ **KITON** *Sales: Tiny. Sold in 19 countries.* Licensing agreement with Italy's high-end men's wear line, Kiton.
- ▶ **LAB SERIES FOR MEN** *Sales: Tiny.* Men are vain, but persuading guys to buy this stuff still ain't easy.
- ▶ **M.A.C.:** *Sales: $100 million. Sold in 13 countries.* Edgy. You'd expect only the hip to buy M.A.C., but it attracts nice girls too.
- ▶ **ORIGINS** *Sales: $100 million. Sold in seven countries.* If you wear Birkenstocks and like wheat germ, Origins is for you.
- ▶ **PRESCRIPTIVES** *Sales: $170 million. Sold in seven countries.* Poorly positioned for years, Prescriptives is now getting its act together. New ads scream: fresh, cool, young, urban.
- ▶ **TOMMY HILFIGER TOILETRIES** *Sold in 51 countries.* The all-American fragrance. A giant hit. First came Tommy, then Tommy Girl, and now Tommy Athletic. Watch for Tommy makeup next.

duced at Macy's in Paramus, N.J., sales increased 22%. To reach new customers and niches, Clinique has placed counters in 18 college bookstores and is now infiltrating the workplace in innovative ways like setting up temporary stalls in offices. The Estée Lauder brand has opened two freestanding stores, including one in Las Vegas. In 1998, an Estée Lauder spa opened on Long Island. Origins now has a catalog. M.A.C. has 30 stand-alone stores. Sales in airports are growing fast.

CRACKING THE MASS MARKET

But none of these initiatives are big enough to wow analysts who fret about the future of department stores. So at Halloween in 1997, Lauder's company bought Jane by Sassaby, a scrappy little makeup line sold in Wal-Mart, Target, and Rite Aid. A modest purchase, yes, but hugely significant, for it suggests that Estée Lauder Cos. is determined to crack the mass market. Then a few weeks later Lauder announced that it had paid $300 million cash for Aveda, an ecologically correct line of shampoo, hair conditioners, perfume, scented candles, and makeup. Aveda is sold through thousands of independent hair salons and through its own freestanding "lifestyle stores." In one short month Estée Lauder Cos. had jumped into two new, big channels of distribution.

At the Estée Lauder headquarters in Manhattan's General Motors Building, at the elevator banks, near entranceways, you'll find little frosted squares of pale-green glass engraved with a motto: "Bringing the best to everyone we touch." That motivational cliché is to be interpreted literally. Estée Lauder herself understood that selling cosmetics works best if you can get intimate with the customer. Intimacy means not groping but touching—lightly placing those three fingers on someone's forehead, smoothing lotions on her cheeks, applying gloss to her lips.

Leonard Lauder is his mother's son. Joseph Gubernick, who is head of research and development for Estée Lauder Cos., has worked for the company for 26 years. So I asked him, What has changed since Leonard took over from Estée? Without hesitation he replied, "Nothing. There has been no change, because Leonard and Estée are the same person. Leonard is just a transformation of Estée. He learned from her. Everything she did, he does." Touching people, becoming intimate with customers, charming everyone he comes in contact with—no one does it better than Leonard. Bobbi Brown, of Estée Lauder's Bobbi Brown Essentials line, praises Leonard Lauder in these terms: "When Leonard gives speeches, he talks about his close relationships with people, and everyone in the room thinks he's talking just about them."

That skill gives Leonard Lauder an edge over his competitors. Soon after Estée Lauder Cos. bought Jane by Sassaby in 1997, Leonard Lauder started going out on sales calls with Jane's president and co-founder, Howard Katkov. Merchandising managers at drugstores and discount stores, where Jane is carried, were astounded, thrilled, that Leonard Lauder himself—a man worth billions—would take his valuable time to visit them in person on behalf of such a little brand. It was an honor and a privilege. "When I visit stores with him," says Katkov, "it's like I'm taking the Pope around. Everyone clamors to meet him. We now get calls from accounts who used to turn us away, and they ask, 'So when are you bringing him to our store?'" Thanks to Leonard Lauder's sales calls to discount stores and drugstores, Jane will in 1998 almost double the number of outlets where it is sold, from 9,200 to 15,000.

"I CARE, PERSONALLY"

One of Leonard Lauder's sales techniques must be the oldest in the book: Within 24 hours or so of meeting someone, he invariably writes that person an intimate, often handwritten, note. In fact he's famous for his notes, for his ability to always say just the right thing and to touch people just that way. Like his mother before him, Leonard Lauder knows that business is about relationships. It's about making people feel important. He travels compulsively, greeting the women who sell his makeup, checking up on cosmetics counters everywhere. "I'm in department stores all the time," he says. "I am the only person in the cosmetics industry that the retailers around the world know. Because my competitors don't care. I care, personally."

Touching people, building relationships, is a sales technique that Leonard Lauder expects every person in his company to perfect. On March 6, 1998, at Saks Fifth Avenue in New York City, Bobbi Brown made a personal appearance to meet her customers. Dozens of women lined up, and Bobbi Brown greeted each one, taking five minutes or so to recommend a new makeup palette. Karen, a 35-year-old account manager from Hackensack, N.J., told me she'd made an appointment one month earlier to meet Bobbi Brown. What was so special about Bobbi Brown's make-up? I asked. "Bobbi is so down to earth," Karen explained. "There's no glitz or phoniness. I mean, she's just like us." While a makeup artist was giving Karen a new face, a video about Bobbi Brown looped around and around on a Panasonic television. There was Bobbi talking about fragrance, Bobbi talking about life, Bobbi on being a woman. An hour and 45 minutes after she'd arrived for her appointment, Karen was finished. She had a new look, a $566 new look. She had bought Bobbi's eye shadows in Taupe, Sable, Bone, Charcoal, Shell, Pale Silver, and Pale Pink. She'd bought Bobbi's lipsticks in Burnt Red, Soft Rose, Cranberry Stain, and Plum Stain. She'd bought Bobbi's lip shimmers in Berry and Beige Gold, and Bobbi's lip gloss in Aubergine and Petal. She'd also bought Bobbi, a $75 bottle of perfume, signed for Karen by Bobbi herself. "I didn't expect to spend this much," said Karen, a little apologetically. "But they definitely didn't push it on me."

Bobbi Brown was in Saks that day for three hours, from 10 A.M. to 1 P.M. In that time she sold $27,000 worth of product. Estée herself would have been proud of the performance. Leonard probably wrote her a thank-you note.

▲▼▲

CHAPTER THREE

▲▼▲

MANAGEMENT AND CAREER
IDEAS WORTH A FORTUNE

OVERCOMING A STUBBORN CORPORATE CULTURE

BY ANNE FISHER

▲▼▲

*Once, you weren't considered a
real Georgia-Pacific mill guy unless
you were missing a few fingers.
Now, after a corporate makeover,
safety comes first.*

▲▼▲

The forest-products business is definitely not about glamour. Paper mills, sawmills, and plywood factories are dangerous places, full of constant deafening noise, gargantuan razor-toothed blades, long chutes loaded with rumbling tons of lumber, and giant vats full of boiling water and caustic chemicals under tons of pressure. People working around all that stuff tend to sweat a lot.

People used to bleed a lot too. Eight years ago the 241 plants and mills operated by Georgia-Pacific, the Atlanta-based forest-products giant with $13 billion in annual revenues and more than 47,000 employees, had an unenviable safety record, pretty bad even for a notoriously hazardous industry. There were nine serious injuries per 100 employees each year, and 26 G-P workers had lost their lives on the job between 1986 and 1990.

All that began to change when A.D. "Pete" Correll, a former boss of forest products at Mead, took over as president and chief operating officer of Georgia-Pacific in 1991. (He became CEO two years later.) Soon after settling into the president's job, Correll called in Mike Skinner, G-P's director of workers' compensation, for a chat about safety. Skinner recalls the meeting all too vividly: "He said, 'So, Mike. What are we going to do about this?' It was one of those bet-your-career moments."

Skinner still has his job, and plenty of other people have managed to keep their arms, legs, fingers, and lives as well. For four years Georgia-Pacific recorded the best safety record in the industry. By 1996 fully 80% of its plants operated without any injuries at all. Best of all, nobody died anywhere. The company's mill in

Brunswick, Ga., a vast, hot, clamorous place that produces more fluff pulp than any other place in the world, was recording injuries of 0.7 per 100 workers annually. According to OSHA, that is about one-third the injury rate at the average bank—a place where the scariest piece of machinery around is most likely a photocopier.

TEN POWERFUL IDEAS

How did Georgia-Pacific pull this off? The work itself hasn't changed. But the way people think about it, and do it, has. Barry Geisel runs the company's plywood factory in Madison, Ga. He says that most mistakes in any industry aren't caused by the nature of the equipment itself—such as, for instance, the 55-inch knife blade in his plant that, whirling like a giant's pencil sharpener, peels a 30-year-old tree down to thin air in just eight seconds. Rather, the trouble comes from people's attitudes and behavior—like, for instance, hauling that blade around without wearing protective gloves, or trying to clean it while it's running. Workers routinely attempted both procedures in the past, often with bloody results.

G-P people are a little sheepish when they talk about it now, but a macho factor operated in the past as well. Before 1990, workers sometimes took deadly chances as a way of proving their mettle. "People now understand that the same actions that used to make you a hero are just going to get you in trouble around here," says Geisel, who has fired people for ignoring safety rules. "The biggest challenge has been trying to change everybody's old habits and assumptions."

Georgia-Pacific's safety crusade has worked so well that the company has begun applying the same principles to improving other areas of its business, including quality and customer service. Any company—even, say, a bank—that wants to learn how to alter a stubborn corporate culture could do a lot worse than to ponder how Georgia-Pacific got safer. It boils down to ten ideas.

1. Realize that you can change how people work. "Everybody in our industry always paid lip service to safety, but nobody ever did much about it," says Mike Skinner. Why not? "We all assumed we had no control over whether accidents happened or not." As recent experience has proved, that's just wrong.

2. Whatever you do, don't call it a program, if you want results. "Programs don't work," says CEO Correll, "because nobody, believes they're for real." Make it clear that the new order of things is not a passing phase but a pervasive and permanent commitment.

3. Understand why you have a problem in the first place. "In the old days," recalls Ray Powell, director of human resources at the Madison plant, "we would ask: 'Why did this idiot stick his hand in this machine without shutting it off first?' Now we ask the same question but in a very different way: 'Why did he do that?' People do not generally do things without a reason that to them looks pretty good. So if you really want to solve the problem, find out what the reason was—then fix that."

As in any commodity business, one big reason workers took dangerous risks was to keep the line moving. Now any worker at Georgia-Pacific can shut down any production line rather than take a chance on an injury (or worse).

4. Be consistent. Go to any Georgia-Pacific division meeting, read any internal how-we're-doing memo, or listen to any speech Correll or any manager under him ever gives, and the first thing on the agenda is always safety, safety, safety. Steve Church, a senior manager at headquarters in Atlanta, observes, "But what would be the point in saying something is your No. 1 priority if you're not really going to treat it that way?"

5. Reinforce your message every way you can (humor helps). On top of formal training sessions and weekly safety meetings at all its plants, Georgia-Pacific hammers home its "safety first" message in a way that is extremely thorough, not to say obsessive. Posters, stickers, buttons, T-shirts, jackets—exhortations about safety turn up on every available surface. All this may sound a little too much like life in a Stalinist regime, but people have learned how to have fun with it. Says Skinner: "There's no good reason why just because something is important, it also has to be boring."

6. Reward good behavior, if you really want to change how people work. Georgia-Pacific's supervisors and managers are evaluated, and compensated, based on how they do in four areas. Safety is now one of the four and carries the same weight as production.

7. Take advantage of people's natural urge to compete. Alan Ulman, Georgia-Pacific's director of internal communications, was surprised by his annual (anonymous) employee surveys: Even more than not wanting to be hurt or killed, workers want to avoid letting down their team, which compete company wide to claim the fewest accidents. Every plant keeps track of how many consecutive hours it has gone without an injury, and those figures are posted at plant entrances and publicized elsewhere. Nobody wants to be the bozo who resets his plant's clock at zero.

8. Don't let a "right sizing" distract anybody from the task at hand. A cyclical business, buffeted by the vagaries of pulp and paper prices, Georgia-Pacific had to cut about 2,500 salaried jobs, including dozens of first-line supervisory slots. Yet safety performance in the plants continued to improve, because after six years of constant emphasis, employees had bought into the new ways of doing things—even without a boss on hand to remind them.

9. Share success stories throughout the company. The company's SafeTV network beams question-and-answer sessions via satellite to about 350 Georgia-Pacific sites around the U.S. It also produces and distributes documentary videos filmed by Georgia-Pacific employees for use in safety meetings at the plants. If your company does not have a TV network, fax reports all over the company and post them on bulletin boards.

10. Never let up. "We know we can't ever stop emphasizing and reinforcing this, because if we do, our safety record could start to slide again real fast," says Alex Hopkins, who heads up the company's lumber group. Chief Executive Correll agrees: "Our goal is zero accidents. We haven't reached our destination yet. We're on a journey." Aren't we all?

GOIZUETA'S SECRET FORMULA

BY JOHN HUEY

▲▼▲

*One of the greats has left the field
for the last tine. I'm not certain I'll
see the game played this way again,
and I'll miss the pleasure.*

▲▼▲

In almost a quarter-century as a business journalist I have logged a lot of time in the company of CEOs, a few of them great—Sam Walton, Andy Grove, Jack Welch, Michael Eisner—and others, well, not so great. It's easy to tag most of the stars with some dominant characteristic that sets them apart. Walton was the world's greatest motivator. Grove's intellect towers over his peers'. Welch is the ultimate social architect. Eisner is a unique blend of business and entertainment genius. Such labels may not tell the whole story, but they make it easy to think and write about these leaders in interesting, instructive ways.

Roberto Goizueta of Coca-Cola, who died in October 1997, was altogether different. He was the CEO I knew longest and best, and yet the one I still find most puzzling. I was saddened by Roberto's death, feeling a sense of both personal and professional loss. If you caught any of the many eulogies published upon Roberto's death, you already know about his record as a wealth builder: He took Coke's market value from a mere $4.3 billion in 1981 to as high as $180 billion in 1997. So his place in the pantheon of truly great chief executives is forever secure.

Yet I remain puzzled. After years of interviewing the man, traveling with him, exchanging correspondence with him, arguing with him, and reading his essays, I still don't understand exactly how he managed to take a company written off by most people as a spent bullet in a mature industry and transform it into one of the glamour stocks of two decades. To try to get at an answer, I have excavated my old notes and tapes, and I have quizzed his close associates and confidants. What follows is an attempt to unlock Roberto Goizueta's "secret formula" for being a superb chief executive. Warning: The quest uncovered a good bit of paradox and no small amount of contradiction.

THE DEVIL IS IN THE DETAILS, BUT HAVE A REAL STRATEGY

For starters, there's the question of whether Goizueta was a hands-on detail man or an above-the-fray, clean-hands CEO. And the answer is clearly—both. When he first came to power at Coke in 1981, many journalists and Wall Street analysts quickly concluded that Roberto was a boring engineer who was bogged down in the details of his company and seemingly uninterested in all the problems on which they were focused, like, say, some super-duper ad campaign Pepsi had just launched. They were half right, of course. He was immersed in the details of his company. He knew the per capita soft drink consumption rate in remote countries. He could quote the price-escalation clauses in high-fructose corn syrup contracts. And most important, he knew the cost of every cent of capital Coke had invested anywhere in the world and its expected rate of return.

What few of us realized was that while Roberto was marinated in all those details, he had no intention of attending to them himself. In fact, rarely has there been a CEO who delegated more of what we normally think of as the "work" involved in running a company. Nor did anyone appreciate just how brilliant his strategic plan for Coke was—even though he talked about it incessantly and passed it out in pamphlet form.

I'll never forget my first meeting with the man, very early in his tenure. He summoned me, a young Atlanta bureau chief for the *Wall Street Journal,* to his office, where I found him sitting behind his desk, suit jacket on, smoking a cigarette. He introduced himself, took polite exception to my beard (he hated facial hair, I think, because of its associations with Fidel Castro, the man who robbed his family of its home and wealth), and said in his thick Cuban accent, "You and I need to get to know one another. You seem to be quite interested in the Coca-Cola Co., and things are going to be very different around here from now on."

Then he told me about his plan. Basically, he said, the company now had a strategy that would focus entirely on increasing long-term share-owner value (he hated the word "shareholder" because, he said, it wasn't precise enough). He planned to reduce the percentage of earnings paid out in dividends from almost 60% to around 35%, he explained, and for the first time Coke would take on debt. This would free the company to explore new opportunities and—very important—lower its cost of capital. He would divest businesses that weren't likely to pay off for shareholders. Performance would be rewarded; perfect attendance would not. It was the only time a CEO ever explained to me a strategy so simple that it seemed almost naive, and I, along with everyone else outside the company, was skeptical.

At the time, remember, Coke was in disarray. It had lost significant momentum to hard-charging Pepsi and had yielded only a 1% compound annual return to shareholders for an entire decade. Its culture was one of entitlement and arrogance. And it was locked in a paralyzing war with its own bottlers. To compound these problems, the company had no communication with Wall Street and hostile relations with the business press.

Not surprisingly, the announcement that a shy, 49-year-old patrician Cuban virtually unknown to the outside world was assuming the helm of this famous but seriously screwed-up company had underwhelmed practically everyone. With the résumé of a competent general administrator, he had no credentials as either a marketer or a finance man, yet he was planning to revive probably the greatest consumer brand in history?

Of course, it all worked. Those who believed—a group that eventually came to include Warren Buffett—and those who signed on as soldiers in Roberto's crusade became wealthier off soda pop than they ever dreamed they could, watching their stock multiply over and over and over for 16 years.

The simplest explanation of why it worked is that Goizueta was so diligent at performing the few primary duties he assigned to himself, the most important being the proper allocation of the company's capital. It's a job that doesn't require much heavy lifting—if you know everything there is to know about your company and you're very smart.

Roberto's calendar was remarkably uncluttered. Journalists and analysts were amazed at how much time he took to respond to the things they wrote or said. He was often available for a chat on the phone, a drop-by interview, or even lunch. His classically appointed office suite rarely showed any sign of activity. Usually when a guest arrived, "the Chairman," as he was known, was down the hall checking his stock ticker. And most afternoons he headed home around 4:30—riding up front with his driver and listening to country music—for a quiet evening with family.

PROMOTE THE BEST
AND SHOWER THEM WITH STOCK

One reason Roberto could keep banker's hours was the decisiveness with which he made executive choices and the extraordinary trust he placed in those chosen. Shortly after assuming office, for example, he made two characteristic decisions. He quickly purged from the company one of the men who had been his rival for the top job, then anointed the other, Don Keough, as his right hand. Keough was everything Goizueta wasn't—gregarious, motivational, in-your-face, peripatetic. And for the next decade he would circle the globe in his Gulfstream, starting fires for Roberto and putting others out. He inspired the troops, fought Pepsi, launched invasions of new territories, bought and sold divisions, ran off underperforming executives, confronted recalcitrant bottlers, and schmoozed big customers. For these efforts Goizueta was happy to pay Keough more than many CEOs earn.

Herein lies an essential ingredient of Roberto's formula. Once he felt he had the best possible people in executive jobs, he rewarded them lavishly with a stake in the game: Coke stock. "The compensation system was the key to driving shareholder value," says Herbert Allen, chairman of the Coke board's compensation committee. "It completely aligned bottom-line productivity with the stock price."

And while Roberto was happy to delegate many typical CEO responsibilities to others, he reserved for himself the annual award of stock options. Thus when Coke's 35 or so top executives would gather periodically for a dinner at, say, Atlanta's Capital City Club, everyone in the room was a millionaire several times over, and they all knew from whom their wealth had come.

THINKING IS WORTHWHILE

O kay, we've identified a few of the duties with which Roberto occupied his time. So what else was he doing? "Thinking" seems to be a big part of the answer. As Keough puts it, "He believed a big part of his role was to make sure he had a viable long-term strategy for the company, and he wanted to have time to think."

What kind of thinking? According to Doug Ivester, it was consistently linear, based on his Jesuit training as a boy in Cuba. "He always began with the broadest possible statement everyone could agree on," says his successor, "and you never moved on to step two until you had exhausted the possibilities of step one."

As Warren Buffett puts it, "Roberto was super-strategic. He wasn't ever focused on anything other than getting results at Coca-Cola over a long period of time." I once stood with Roberto on a stage in New Orleans in front of a roomful of CEOs, gathered for the FORTUNE 500 CEO conference, and heard him exclaim for the 10,000th time, "A publicly traded company exists for one purpose and one purpose only: to increase share-owner value. If it does that, all the other good things will follow."

Roberto Goizueta was way ahead of his time in adopting this point of view. He was also a pioneer in figuring out how to do it. Early on in his CEO tenure, he spotted Ivester, a former outside auditor for Ernst & Whinney, and enlisted him as his collaborator in the financial reengineering of the company to enhance share-owner value. Before anyone had ever heard of EVA, they were examining the underlying cost of the company's capital and redeploying it. When he sold Coke's wine business in the early '80s, Goizueta explained the move in terms even I could understand: "If we earn 3 cents for every dollar of capital we have invested, this is fundamentally a bad business to be in," he said. "We would be better off to take the $250 million we have invested in the wine business and put it in the bank."

While Keough was out strong-arming Coke's bottlers into accepting new rules of the game or selling their franchises to Coke, Goizueta and Ivester were back home figuring out ways to boost Coke's stock by spinning off the capital-intensive bottling assets into a new company. And long before stock buybacks became all the rage, they decided Coke stock was a great investment for the company. Ultimately, they bought around a third of the company back for an average of about $11 a share.

There was one other important ingredient of Roberto Goizueta's formula, a hard one to acquire if you don't already have it: a taste for risk. As Keough puts it, "He had a hell of a lot of guts."

ROLL THE DICE

Think about it. Goizueta was the first person ever to stick the Coke brand on a derivative product, bucking years of company orthodoxy that said it would destroy the franchise; Diet Coke went on to become the most successful consumer product launch of the '80s. He changed the sacred formula of Coca-Cola, a move that would have been previously unthinkable; New Coke blew up in his face and became the biggest consumer product disaster of the '80s, but he quickly reversed his decision and, in fact, capitalized on all the attention it got.

Maybe none of these ingredients really hold the secret of Roberto Goizueta's extraordinary success. But what the man did is worth studying. He was born rich, lost everything, did something he loved at one company for his whole life, and made a billion dollars for himself and more than $175 billion for others. His greatest skill, says Keough, was "the ability to focus the entire Coca-Cola system, including me, for 24 hours a day, on building shareholder value." Buffett puts it another way: "Coca-Cola was Roberto's painting. It was never finished, and he was never totally satisfied with it. But he had that Sistine Chapel ceiling in his head, and he was always working on it."

▲▼▲

A NEW WAY TO THINK ABOUT EMPLOYEES

BY THOMAS A. STEWART

▲▼▲

*Employees are not assets; they are
investors in a company. Here's how
to ensure a payoff for everyone.*

▲▼▲

Employees are not simply human capital or company assets. They are investing themselves in an enterprise, and that means they should expect an equitable return.

In 1988, D. Quinn Mills, a professor at Harvard Business School, published *IBM: The Profitable Art of Full Employment*. The book celebrated the no-layoffs policy at IBM, one of the most successful companies in capitalism's history. On its payroll that year: 387,112 people. By 1993, IBM had shed 123,000 employees. That year FORTUNE published a now famous article in which Carol Loomis analyzed the decline of IBM, Sears, and General Motors. Perhaps, the article suggested, these formerly grand enterprises might have become dinosaurs—big, brain-dead, and doomed.

The next year, 1994, I attended a seminar that focused on human capital. IBM came up. Most of us in the room bemoaned the downsizing, the job loss—what decent folk wouldn't?—and said that IBM was poorer for it: Look at the wealth, in the form of human capital, draining from that once great company as an army of the world's brightest workers were driven out of it.

In 1996, Mills published *Broken Promises: An Unconventional View of What Went Wrong at IBM*, which argued that IBM got into trouble because it disregarded its customers and misled employees. In 1998, ten years after the appearance of *The Profitable Art of Full Employment*, Mills is bringing out a new book. Its title is *The Big Blue Bottom Line: The Story Behind the Turnaround at IBM*.

I'm not making fun of professor Mills, who is very good and whose books are too. Also, the difficulty Mills has had describing the reasons for IBM's success, tribulation, and rebirth is common.

It's the difficulty we had at that seminar and the difficulty most of us have thinking about intellectual assets in general, and especially human capital. IBM was indisputably richer in human brains when it employed more than a third of a million people than it is today, with its much smaller payroll. But it was performing dreadfully back then—as dreadfully as you would have expected it to perform if it had half again as many factories as it needed or if it stocked 50% more inventory than it really had to.

EMPLOYEES ARE NOT CHAIRS

▼

Business isn't about amassing assets; it's about getting a return on them, whether the assets are bricks and mortar or cap and gown. Head count is no way to tally human capital. As I quipped in my own book, *Intellectual Capital: The New Wealth of Organizations*, if physicians reported the results of physical examinations according to generally accepted accounting principles, fat would go on the asset side of the balance sheet.

In fact, we should not confuse human beings with human capital at all. Surely people are not assets in the same way that their desks and chairs are assets, or that factories or bank balances are. A school of "human capital accounting" foundered in the 1970s partly because it seemed inappropriate—and in any event impossible—to put a dollar value on people. It's more accurate—and more useful—to think of employees in a new way: not as assets but as investors. Shareholders invest money in our companies; employees invest time, energy, and intelligence. Just as shareholders who put their money into Sara Lee cannot put it into Norwest Corp., employees, when they hitch their wagon to one star, forgo the chance to ride with another. "I've given the best years of my life to XYZ Corp.," people say. That statement shows an instinctive grasp of this view of employees: not wage slaves, not assets, but investors, who are investing their personal human capital.

Sometimes a great deal of value is produced by investor-employees: Think of the wealth of ideas that have turned into new products and sales for 3M, Hewlett-Packard, or Merck. A research chemist or an investment banker, who puts in brains, schooling and training, creativity, may produce the knowledge equivalent of a machine tool or some other piece of capital equipment: a molecule, say, or a financial product, or a methodology that can be used again and again to make money.

Increasingly, we are all expected to be knowledge workers. Today's factory hand may spend much of her day in a control room, monitoring screens and dials that tell her about the performance of the robots she commands, or in meetings with other workers, planning how to use time or materials more efficiently. Dana Corp., for example, has used an enthusiastically managed suggestion system to harvest millions of dollars' worth of ideas, mostly from blue-collar workers.

WHY WORK FOR A COMPANY?

That leads to a fundamental question: Why do companies exist? Why work for one? There is just one reason, says Gerhard Schulmeyer, CEO of Siemens Nixdorf, the giant European computer maker: "The corporation exists insofar as it provides a place where the individual can do what he is good at, at a lower cost than he could do it alone." In traditional industries, corporations exist because they aggregate capital that allows them to buy machinery workers couldn't afford on their own— steel mills are beyond the means of most individuals. But in the New Economy, entry barriers have collapsed in many industries or have nothing to do with financial capital. Overall, U.S. companies today need 20% less in tangible assets to produce a dollar of sales than they did a quarter-century ago, according to Lowell Bryan, who is (still) a McKinsey partner. Many knowledge workers need little more gear than a laptop and a phone.

Take away the capital-magnet role; then what are the other ways in which a company can enable people to do what they are good at more cheaply than they could do it alone? Three come to mind. First is to be a magnet for intellectual capital—that is, to provide a place, a purpose, a culturing medium, and a culture: a community of practice. I work for Microsoft because the presence of so many bright code writers stimulates and challenges me, gives me help when I need it, provides easy access to experts in graphics, allows me to work faster and better than I could in a garret. The existence of a talented community is, in turn, a magnet for customers. Add a few techies to link our laptops in a LAN, and voilà! The company has gathered human, structural, and customer capital, lowering the transaction costs I would pay to attract them myself. That's worth something.

Function two is a warranty function. The company's brand and reputation are umbrellas under which I shelter. The company vouches for me to suppliers and customers. Because I write for FORTUNE, people return my phone calls who might not if I freelanced or worked for a scandal sheet. Recently an investment banker told me why he stayed with his company rather than set up a boutique of his own. His revealing reason: "I'm not famous enough yet." Similarly, the company warrants colleagues to one another: The engineer in the next cubicle is, just like me, working at Hughes Space & Communications, so I can presume she is talented and trustworthy. The warranty function can work in both directions—hiring hotshots can give a company credibility—but usually it's the company that vouches for the person. That's worth something too.

Third, the company performs various insurance and other financial services. "It evens out the swings," Schulmeyer says. It limits our liability, annualizes our income, tides us over during unproductive patches, collects money owed by our customers, borrows on our behalf. Employees, then, work for a company for any or all of these three reasons: It provides purpose and community, warranting, and insuring.

IS IT TIME TO BAIL FROM BIG-COMPANY LIFE?

BY EILEEN P. GUNN

▲▼▲

Should you trade in your mega-company pay and perks for the risky world of startups?

▲▼▲

Pacific Bell President David Dorman wasn't happy. When SBC Communications bought his company's parent in 1997, he faced his third corporate move in four years. His family was grumbling at him about their imminent departure for San Antonio. So after a bit of soul-searching, he summoned the courage to jump ship. He became the CEO of a small Bay Area Internet information services company called PointCast, earning about 30% of his former salary, but with a pile of stock options that could make him a multimillionaire someday. "The business model for phone services is proven," he says of the move. "But no one knows where the Internet will go. I thought this would be fun."

A growing cadre of corporate defectors like Dorman are thinking small these days, and many are finding a ready market for their services. That shouldn't be surprising. In 1997 alone, reports San Francisco research firm VentureOne, venture capitalists invested $6 billion in about 1,100 PointCasts—young companies founded by engineers and software gurus who know nothing about running a business. Not long after (sometimes before) their patents are filed, they need CEOs, financial officers, marketing experts, and other management types, so these bootstrapped, fast-growth companies are seriously courting corporate refugees. Dorman, for example, got at least 30 inquiries from small companies after the SBC takeover.

For managers being wooed by the startups, some of the attractions are obvious. The pay and perks may be relatively skimpy, but there are compensations: the psychic value of being in on the ground floor of a new venture, plus the possibility of a massive payoff if it pans out. As John O'Neil, a San Francisco consultant who often advises executives on jobs, puts it, "There are very few companies where people feel they have security anyway, so why not try a job that offers adventure and equity?"

ARE YOU ENTREPRENEURIAL BY NATURE?

▼

Still, executive coaches regularly warn that such a leap into the unknown is not for everyone. The financial risk is chillingly real; stock options in a startup are typically worthless for years, and many never pay off at all. Also, a lot of corporate managers aren't as ready as they imagine for the uncertainties of a smaller outfit. Experts say the corporate defectors happiest at small companies are those who took the time to find partners they could get along with and a company that's doing something that stirs their passions. And it goes without saying that job jumpers have to be entrepreneurial—committed to the idea of having a personal stake and a hands-on role in building a company.

Jesus Leon is a classic big-company expat. He gave up a senior-executive slot at Alcatel Alsthom Group, the global telecom giant, that came with a $200 million budget, two assistants, six weeks of vacation, a luxury car, and a posting in Madrid. He became co-head of product development at Ciena, a recently public Baltimore-area company with products that increase the capacity of fiber-optic cables already in the ground. Leon took a 25% pay cut and agreed to only one week of vacation and virtually no budget or staff. He hopes his stock options will make him rich someday, but meanwhile he revels in the entrepreneurial challenge. "I love it," he says. "Instead of looking after 1,200 people whose names I don't know, I get to be an artist. I get to paint what Ciena will be."

Sound good? Well, if you're a corporate type yearning to be free, it may be time to figure out if you've got what it takes to make the move. In some cases, such as Leon's, a firm grasp of specific technology issues is mandatory. More commonly, what you need is a set of general entrepreneurial skills. Jon Bayless, a general partner with the Dallas venture capital firm Sevin Rosen, says he likes "nuts-and-bolts people," those who know how to work within a small budget and how to bring a new product into the market-place. Along those lines, the successful corporate candidate often has "intrapreneur" experience, such as a key role at a division that's strategically or geographically separate from the parent.

THERE'S MORE THAN ONE WAY TO GO

Another strong plus is a corporate background in the markets that a startup's trying to crack. Take, for example, Myra Williams, the new CEO of a Palo Alto startup called Molecular Applications Group. The company sells software that can expedite certain drug research, and Williams' former job, director of R&D information resources at Glaxo Wellcome, made her a prime candidate. Explains Molecular Applications Group director Gary Morgenthaler: "She had a high-level position within the customer group we were targeting. She understood them and how to craft a product that would meet their needs."

As the Internet puts a high-tech edge on just about every industry, recruiters are also beginning to see demand for people who can adapt their low-tech job skills to electronic commerce. Bill Feeley was a traditional investment banker, a managing director at Bankers Trust, until the firm's merger with Alex. Brown left him jobless. Since he no longer had a fat six-figure salary holding him back, he figured the time had come to indulge his entrepreneurial interests. Rather than signing on with another big organization, he parlayed his financial savvy into a job at a much smaller firm. He became the director of capital markets at Wit Capital, an online investment bank founded with the goal of making traditional initial public offerings and private venture equity offerings available to the masses via the Internet. "Not a day goes by that we're not doing something that's never been done before. It's exciting," he says with obvious satisfaction.

In today's tight labor market, skilled corporate managers interested in taking a small-company plunge shouldn't have much trouble putting themselves in play. "You'd be amazed at how accessible venture people are," says Bayless. "Just pick up the phone, and be ready to explain what your skill set is." Or skip the middleman, as Feeley did, and get in touch with companies you'd like to join. Small-business people, without assistants to screen calls and mail, tend to be accessible.

Say you lack firsthand knowledge of how small companies operate; you just know you don't like the way big companies do. You might consider a gradual transition. Kathryn Gould, a former recruiter and a general partner with Foundation Capital in Silicon Valley, suggests targeting midsized businesses for jobs while seeking out seats on small-company boards. You'll probably face a less dramatic salary cut, and you can establish yourself as a company builder before landing in a high-pressure startup situation. "Startups are hard," Gould says. "For people who walk right out of AT&T or IBM to a startup, there's a history of disaster."

If you're one of those lucky corporate types who are already getting three or four calls a week from headhunters, consider quitting your job and taking a few months to explore the possibilities more closely. Gould sees this move as a gut check: "If you can't deal with the insecurity of being unemployed, you probably can't deal with the insecurity of working at a startup."

In any event, you should stare hard at the financial risks involved. Lonnie Smith did just that before abandoning his high-level executive job at Indiana conglomerate Hillenbrand to become CEO of Intuitive Surgical, a Silicon Valley firm that makes a computer-assisted minimally invasive surgical system that allows a wider range of major "open" surgeries to be done through tiny incisions. Smith was not about to trade his $1.2 million annual salary for $300,000 and a hatful of options without thoroughly exploring the market for his new company's products. "I asked surgeons what the implications were if they could do this, and the feedback was very good. I wouldn't have taken the job otherwise," Smith says.

At the very least, say executive recruiters, don't quit corporate life without understanding your new company's culture and the specifics of your role. Take time to get to know the founders, key investors, and other executives. Ask yourself if these are people you want to trust with your career and your fortune. These days if you decide to pass on an offer, there are likely to be plenty more.

DON'T BLOW YOUR NEW JOB

BY ANNE FISHER

*Managers are switching companies
like never before, but a startling
number don't last 18 months.
Here's why.*

Been getting a lot of calls from headhunters lately? Thinking about moving on to a new job? If so, you're part of a huge, restless crowd. Executive recruiters report a record number of new searches, and the upper-middle reaches of U.S. corporations are coming to resemble a vast game of musical chairs, with a constant stream of new faces and new nameplates on the doors. Increasingly, companies are looking outside for fresh talent rather than promoting from within. A survey of 700 companies by New York–based search firm Thorndike Deland Associates found that 70% are turning more than ever before to other companies for managers. These are heady times.

But before you leap into anything, be warned: About 40% of new management hires fail within the first 18 months, say studies by the Center for Creative Leadership in Greensboro, N.C., and by executive-search and coaching firm Manchester Partners International. Manchester defines failure as "being terminated for performance, performing significantly below expectations, or voluntarily resigning from the position"—maybe with a little push from above. There are ways to avoid becoming what some HR types call a revolving-door hire. But as with every other aspect of managing your career these days, you have to work at them.

First, an intriguing question: Whose fault is that 40% washout rate? Considering how costly it is to keep recruiting, training, and then replacing managers, there's no shortage of finger pointing—and plenty of blame to go around. Bill Morin, who left Drake Beam Morin a few years ago to start WJM Associates, a New York–based executive-coaching firm, is in the sizable camp that blames careless or overworked headhunters: "When the job market is booming like this, traditional search firms can't do quality work. Some of these people are handling 17 searches at a time. How can you do a really good job at any of them?" Not surprisingly, recruiters get pretty defensive about this. "We verify people's references, education, and background, and we try to present candidates' weaknesses as well as their strengths. But the client company does far more face-to-face screening and evaluating of candidates than we do, and that's as it should be," says Michael Kirkman, a managing director at Korn/Ferry International who heads the firm's Washington, D.C., office. "If someone doesn't work out, we take umbrage at the notion that it's our fault." Says Gerald Roche, CEO of Heidrick & Struggles: "Getting the right fit between a candidate and a given job is never simple or easy." Roche hires people for his own firm by relying on "gut instinct. I ask myself, 'Would I want to fly from New York to Los Angeles with this person? Could I stand him or her for seven hours straight?' "

THAT OLD BLACK MAGIC

If that sounds like a frivolous criterion, think again: Hordes of consultants, coaches, and other gurus of various stripes have been studying the question of why new managers fail, and their unanimous conclusion is that personal chemistry and cultural compatibility—the soft, people-skills stuff that makes up that old black magic called fit—are all-important. Asked to identify the reasons freshly hired managers flame out, 826 human resources honchos in a Manchester Partners survey said that failure to build good relationships with peers and subordinates is the culprit an overwhelming 82% of the time. The three other big stumbling blocks: confusion or uncertainty about what higher-ups expect (58%), a lack of internal political skills (50%), and inability to achieve the two or three most important objectives of the new jobs (47%).

Once you've disappointed on those scores, the game may be over. Jean-François Manzoni, who teaches at the business school Insead in Fontainebleau, France, has written extensively on what he calls the Set-Up-to-Fail syndrome. At its core is people's tendency, well documented by psychologists, to live up—or down—

to others' expectations of them. Manzoni's research shows that many bosses quickly group their subordinates into "in" and "out" groups, treating the "out" folks like outcasts, dismissing their every move and idea until a kind of paralysis sets in. "It becomes a vicious circle," says Manzoni. "Neither person realizes it, but the boss, with his very negative unstated assumptions, has set the employee up to fail, and the employee then fulfills the boss' worst expectations, even as he tries desperately not to."

Sometimes the fit between a given culture and a new manager is so bad—usually because of unclear signals at the outset about just what the new manager is supposed to be doing—that people get sacked for doing exactly what they thought the job required. Bill Morin had one search client who spent $280,000 finding and hiring a "change agent" and then canned the guy because he wanted to make too many changes. Often what works beautifully in one company, or at one stage of a manager's career, becomes the kiss of death at another job. Michael Wakefield, a senior executive trainer at the Center for Creative Leadership, gives the example of a driven, ambitious person who succeeds in one place by pushing others hard—and then goes to a different company and finds his style is considered so abrasive that nobody can stand working with him. "The strengths and skills that got you to the dance may not get you danced with once you're there," Wakefield notes. "It's insidious, too, because once the source of your old confidence is taken away, you start to get very disoriented." You may also get very fired.

In an effort to prevent this kind of calamity, a growing number of firms, Manchester Partners and WJM Associates among them, are now combining executive searches with extensive personality screening and then—once the new manager is in place— following up with continuous coaching for six months to a year. For example, Byron Woollen, WJM's chief psychologist, uses detailed aptitude testing at the start of a search to pinpoint where a candidate may need special help during the coaching phase. "A very reserved, analytical person might be viewed in some cultures as a cold fish," Woollen says. "So we need to know that going in, and then work with him or her to address that." Does altering your style to fit a particular environment really work? Woollen thinks so:

"I believe people can depart successfully from their natural tendencies, if they're aware of what they need to do."

THE TWO BIG MISTAKES

A h, self-awareness. Now we come to the crux of the matter. Lois Frankel, a psychologist who is a partner in Los Angeles–based Corporate Coaching International, notes that many job changers make two big mistakes. First, they don't stop to analyze what they want out of the new position: balancing family and career, developing new areas of expertise, achieving whatever it was that made them want to change jobs in the first place. "How do you know if a new job will meet your expectations—and hence whether you're likely to succeed in it—if you don't analyze what your expectations are?"

After failure to assess honestly what you're looking for, the second big mistake, experts say, is not doing enough homework—including not asking enough hard questions in interviews. Debbie McClister, a former corporate controller at Philips Electronics who later became chief operating officer of the company's North American software business, forced herself "to ask a lot of questions in interviews and to listen very hard to the answers." She wanted: a high-powered finance job in a company where she would feel comfortable. With one prospective employer, McClister went through a series of ten interviews for a chief financial officer post before realizing that "the culture was just not right. I don't want a job where I only see my kids on weekends."

McClister asked between ten and 20 questions in a typical one-hour interview, and that is probably the right number. In the Manchester Partners survey, human resources people gave specific clues as to what kinds of questions are likely to help you identify the best fit; 76% urge you to find out what results will be expected of you in the first year, and 64% say you need to ask for a timetable spelling out what is supposed to happen when. You should also ask how potential higher-ups will measure your performance (62%). And finding out how often the people above you want progress reports and provide feedback (45%) couldn't hurt. At the same time, gather as much hard information as you possibly can about a prospective employer by scrutinizing the company's annual report and Website, hunting down press clips and securities analysts' reports, and chatting with current and former employees. The more diligent your research, the less likely you are to encounter nasty surprises later. Randy Harris, a senior vice president at Sodexho Marriott Services in Bethesda, Md., got six tempting job offers in the space of three months before deciding to leave Dun & Bradstreet in 1997 for his current position. "In each case, I looked especially hard at three factors—the CEO, the overall organization, and the industry," he says. At one company, he liked what he saw, except that the CEO underwhelmed him. So Harris turned down that offer and, three weeks later, read that the CEO had been fired: "If I'd taken that job, I'd have been walking into a situation full of turmoil, with a totally new and untested boss, on my very first day." Not a promising way to start.

Adds Harris: "A crucial question is, Am I going to have the resources to do what I'm expected to do here, including the time it will take to do it? The kind of disconnect that causes failures is, the CEO is expecting a certain result within three months, but you suspect it will take a year. If you're trying so hard to make a good impression that you neglect to hammer out a workable plan right at the outset, you've already doomed yourself."

Whatever you do, make very sure you understand what Ray Harrison, practice leader for executive development at Manchester, calls the CFOs, for critical few objectives. Says Harrison: "Any management job has 101 responsibilities, but there are usually only two or three that you absolutely must excel at. People often go in with an amazingly vague and foggy idea of just what those really are." He says most managers who make up the aforementioned 40% failure rate start to go off the rails in their very first week in the new job. How? By not asking enough questions of bosses, peers, and underlings who know what the critical few objectives are—or by not listening carefully enough to the answers. Explains Harrison: "Many successful people, unfortunately, think they already know everything. This is where failure begins."

ARE YOU READY FOR A PAY RAISE?

BY RONALD HENKOFF

▲▼▲

*You probably haven't seen a
substantial one for some time.
Yet they're available—if you can
face the dreaded prospect of asking.*

▲▼▲

What a splendid time this should be for you—and your paycheck. You, the great American worker, are in demand. You've got something valuable to sell—your skills, your education, your experience, the power of your brain cells, the sweat of your brow. You've got it, they want it, and by golly, they should pay for it. Basic rules of supply and demand tell us that the price you charge for your services should be heading up—way up.

But right about now you may be asking a pretty basic question, something like: Where's mine? The sad fact is that big raises haven't been nearly as widespread as one might expect. For most Americans, including white-collar professionals, raises in the '90s haven't even kept pace with inflation. While wages have started to perk up, they're hardly flying off the charts. And if you're just an ordinary, smart, talented, hard-working, dedicated middle-level business person, then it has probably been a very long time since you have received a very big raise. Says Marilyn Moats Kennedy, president of Career Strategies, a Wilmette, Ill., counseling firm: "You wouldn't believe the number of people who come in here and say they haven't gotten an increase in two years. It's pitiful. People should be out there fighting for more money."

She's right. In a bounteous economy, it is time to demand your due, time to claim your piece of prosperity, time to get mad as hell. You've got a mortgage, kids to put through college, retirement to worry about. You need a big bump-up in your base pay. For too long you've worried that your job would be merged, purged, downsized, outsourced, or reengineered. Now you're in the driver's seat.

DON'T GET MAD. GET THE MONEY.

A nd there are big raises to be had, for the lucky and the bold at least. Kate Wendleton, president of the Five O'Clock Club, a career management organization based in New York City, has said: "People are leaving their employers and getting jobs so fast it makes your head spin. And they're getting enormous raises too."

But you don't have to jump to another company to juice up your paycheck. In some industries, employers are so keen to keep workers from defecting that they are handing out double-digit raises even to people who don't ask for them. Cellular One, a South San Francisco wireless company, for example, jacked up the salaries of 125 customer-service reps by an average of 11% after it decided the reps' compensation hadn't kept up with their new and expanded responsibilities.

Yet relatively few workers seem ready to take strong action to get their due. White-collar workers aren't storming into the boss' office, pounding on the desk, demanding a raise, and threatening to quit. But they are quietly seething with discontent. Of the more than 87,500 managers queried in 1997 by International Survey Research (ISR), a Chicago workplace polling firm, just 37% think their companies are doing a good job of keeping salaries in sync with the cost of living. A mere 30% believe their employers are adequately matching pay to performance.

Fortune teamed up with Exec-U-Net, a career-information and networking group based in Norwalk, Conn., to canvas a national sampling of Exec-U-Net members who earn at least $75,000 per year. We found that only 39% felt they were being paid their true market value. A resounding 93% said the best way to get a significant raise was to move to another company.

DON'T BE SCARED. BE PREPARED.

S o what's holding them back? There are many explanations for why people aren't making more of a stink over pay. Inflation has been tame, and more households now have two breadwinners. Then there's the lack of peer pressure. If you're not getting good raises, your colleagues and your friends probably aren't either. But the real reason workers aren't storming the ramparts over raises is far more elemental. It all has to do with fear.

When it comes to pay, many otherwise capable, intelligent, and courageous people are still basically scared out of their wits. Memories of downsizing die hard. Anyone who has been forced on to the job market in the '90s is probably leery of landing there again—no matter how much that market may have changed.

Talking to your boss about money is one of life's most dreaded encounters. To get what you want, you need adroit planning, a keen sense of timing, and guts. It's hard to overcome that knee-buckling sensation of powerlessness. Says Lee Miller, a New York employment lawyer and the author of the new book *Get More Money on Your Next Job*: "Most people are terrible at negotiating salaries. They get too emotional." So before you approach your boss, gather your facts, plot your strategy, and force yourself to stay cool. The whole process of compensation has become much more complicated than it used to be. Here are a few key pointers:

Figure out your market value.
Don't try to compare yourself with your colleague in the next office. Even if she'll tell you what she's earning, you'll be plunging into risky, politically charged waters. Instead, gauge your worth on the open market. You don't need a job offer to do this. Professional associations, trade publications, and organizations like Exec-U-Net do regular salary surveys. You can also use the Internet. One information-packed site is JobSmart, a service run by the Bay Area Library and Information Service in California that has links to salary surveys on the web (www.jobsmart.org).

Negotiate your position, not your paycheck.
No matter how much you think you're being underpaid, don't kvetch about it. Instead, talk about what you've achieved for the company and offer to slay even bigger dragons in the future. The same sort of approach makes sense if you're moving to a new employer. Cindy Leonard recently took a job as Midwest regional sales manager for Trefethen Winery. Before she flew to

California for a round of interviews, she spent hours prepping. She consulted colleagues at a former employer, read up on negotiating tactics, and pumped her career counselor at the Five O'Clock Club in Chicago for advice. She came up with a list of items to put on the table—including salary, bonus, expenses, severance, and vacation.

But when she sat down to talk with executives at Trefethen headquarters in Napa, she emphasized the big picture—her experience, her abilities, and what she hoped to accomplish in the new position. Says Leonard: "The main thing is not to talk too much about money. I actually left compensation to the last thing." She didn't get everything she asked for. But she did come away with a package that with bonuses could net her as much as $90,000 a year, 20% more than she made at her previous job.

Sharpen your skills, but do your homework first.

Take courses, attend conferences, expand your expertise. But don't expect to make more money just because you have more schooling or you're good at what you do or you're pursuing your dreams. Ask Robert Lane, who has yearned to fly airplanes since he was a kid. After he earned a degree from Embry-Riddle Aeronautical University, he landed a job as a flight instructor, but was making only a small fraction of what pilots at major airlines get. Says he: "I found out this was a tough field to be in. I saw lots of people in their mid-40s who were still waiting for their big break."

Lane decided he didn't want to tarry that long. So in June 1995 he parlayed his math skills and his teaching experience into a job as an instructor at New Horizons Computer Centers in Michigan. The company paid for his training and offered him a starting salary of $25,000. The more Lane learned, the more he earned. By the end of his first year he was making $34,000. Once named manager of New Horizon's 25 technical software instructors, he found hinself, at 29, making $70,000.

Become a vacuum cleaner.

"Sweep up projects that are not being done by anyone else," advises John Challenger, president of Challenger Gray & Christmas, a Chicago outplacement firm. Edward Mills has been

THE DISCONTENTED

▲▼▲

▶ Are you being paid the true market value for someone with your experience and responsibities?

Yes: 39%   *No: 61%*

▶ Was your most recent raise, as a percentage of your annual base pay, bigger than your previous raise?

Yes: 40%   *No: 60%*

▶ Do you believe you would have received a bigger raise if you had asked for one?

Yes: 12%   *No: 88%*

▶ Do you believe the best way to get a significant raise is to switch employers?

Yes: 93%   *No: 7%*

▶ Do you expect a bigger raise this year than last?

Yes: 49%   *No: 51%*

Sources: FORTUNE; Exec-U-Net

doing just that for most of his career. Formerly a software project manager at IBM, Mills, now a consultant, completed an 11-year stint at the U.S. Committee for Unicef, a fundraising and merchandising arm of the U.N. organization for children. Hired on to manage the group's computers, Mills oversaw the introduction of word processing and E-mail. Ever eager to broaden his skills, he persuaded his boss to send him to an executive education program at Harvard.

When the director of Unicef's catalog business departed unexpectedly, Mills volunteered for the post. He did the job, plus his regular job, for nine months, reviving a moribund operation by, among other things, instituting a toll-free phone number. By taking on extra tasks, Mills managed to secure increases beyond Unicef's normal low-single-digit increments. In 1996, his last year there, his compensation climbed 11%, to $115,000, including bonus and tax-deferred pay. Says Mills: "The lesson is to always look for opportunities to expand the scope of your assignments. And then make sure you let the organization know exactly what you've done for them."

Threaten to quit.

Of course, nothing quite gets your boss' attention like dangling another job offer in front of him and telling him you plan to accept it if he doesn't pony up more cash. But be careful what you wish for, because your boss just may call your bluff. Says Lee Miller: "If you deliver an ultimatum, which I advise against, you have to really be ready to walk out the door. Even if they offer you more money to stay, they may start looking for your replacement. Once you've made a threat, who's to say you won't do it again? So even if you win, you can lose."

But sometimes you do win, and so do your co-workers. One woman we talked with was earning $70,000 as a database manager at a major financial services company. A consulting firm offered her a job paying $20,000 a year more, plus a $10,000 signing bonus. When she notified her current boss, he counteroffered with a promotion, a $15,000 raise, a $15,000 retention bonus and a pledge to pay for training in the latest database technology. Ms. Data decided not to leave after all.

Employers can be notoriously slow learners. Says author and lawyer Miller, who recently became an executive at a major retailer: "I don't think it has quite dawned on some companies how much the job market has shifted. There's going to be a rude awakening." Your boss, of course, may still be slumbering. There's a right way to rouse him or her: work hard, measure your value, test the market, seek new skills, ask for more assignments, take a deep breath, hold down your breakfast—and go for the gold.

ASK ANNIE

▲▼▲

Everyday advice on what employers
want, dealing with conflicting job
offers, unexpressed love, instinct,
and office politics.

▲▼▲

WHAT EMPLOYERS
ARE REALLY LOOKING FOR

▼

Dear Annie: I am a teacher in a work-study program at a suburban high school, and I try to teach my students realistic lessons about the business world. In your opinion, what is the most crucial thing I should teach them about building a solid career? *Sarah*

Dear Sarah: Your students may want to think about what human resources consulting firm Caliper discovered in a survey of 1,000 U.S. executives: People who do the serious hiring in companies these days are desperate for candidates with two traits:

(1) A talent for problem solving. By which they mean: If I give you a Serious Situation to fix, can you figure it out? Assuming that you have the technical skills and we give you the resources, do you have the imagination—and the dedication—it takes to worry this thing like a dog with a bone until it works? And (2) conscientiousness. That is, do you know how to meet a deadline? Do you understand your responsibilities to other people? Will you try to do a good job even when you're having a bad day?

Problem solving and conscientiousness were selected by these 1,000 executives more than twice as often as any other quality, although "open to new ideas" and "versatile" ranked pretty high too. "Ability to handle stress" is also a must-have. Says Harold Einstein, CEO of Caliper: "Employers don't want to hire managers just to carry out routine tasks. Computers can do that." The more sophisticated the technology we utilize, in other words, the more fully human we have to be. With that in mind, the best advice you could give your students might be pretty good advice for anybody at any age: Always do your best.

DEALING WITH CONFLICTING JOB OFFERS

Dear Annie: I, a junior person in a FORTUNE 500 financial services company, am being actively recruited by two senior managers who run other departments here. My current boss has encouraged me to consider moving but also wants me to stay where I am. How do I manage disappointing the other two senior people? *Flattered*

Dear Flattered: It seems to me that the real question here is not how but whether. With all the emphasis these days on gaining cross-functional skills, wouldn't it be to your advantage to accept one of the two offers? Harvey Mackay, CEO of Mackay Envelope and author of how-to-succeed bestsellers, including *Swim With the Sharks Without Being Eaten Alive* (Ivy, $6.99 paperback), believes you ought to go for it. "Sometimes the biggest risk is not to take a risk at all. You need to learn as many new things as you can," he says.

Mackay urges you to set a goal so that you have some idea of where you want to be in a year, or five, or eight. Then take whichever of the two jobs seems more likely to move you in the right direction. Two factors to look at when comparing in-house opportunities: Which department is more essential to the company? And second, in which job are you likely to learn more? To get a sense of this, Mackay suggests that you interview both of the senior managers who are after you and see how they describe what your new responsibilities would be. Pick the less familiar (read, more challenging) option.

LOVING YOUR (MARRIED) BOSS

Dear Annie: I have a problem that is the opposite of sexual harassment. What would you do if you were me (young, single, female) and you had been in love with your boss (older, male, married) for several years? He doesn't suspect how I really feel about him. Should I tell him that I love him? Quit and then tell him? Or what? *Heartsick*

Dear Heartsick: First of all, let's clear up a big misapprehension. If you tell your boss you're in love with him and this news is unwelcome to him, it very well might be considered harassment, regardless of the fact that he outranks you. Do you want to take that chance? And beyond the harm such a decision could do to your career, just think how uncomfortable it would be for the two of you to work together once you have bared your soul.

So do not tell him. If you really feel you can't stand to suffer in silence, then quitting (without revealing why) might be your only option. But before you do anything rash, Susan Leeds, a managing director in human resources at the Ayers Group in Manhattan, suggests that "you need to get back in control of your own life and get over this—possibly with the help of some short-term professional counseling." Good luck.

TRUSTING RESEARCH—OR GUT INSTINCT?

Dear Annie: What do you do if you have an important business decision to make and there are as many facts supporting one choice as the other? Do you try to stick to one set of facts, or go with your instinct? *Under the Gun*

Dear Under: To help me find an answer to your fascinating question, I called Michael Ray, who teaches creativity and innovation in the graduate business school at Standard and is co-author, with Rachel Dyers, of a great book called *Creativity in Business* (Doubleday, $12 paperback). Of particular relevance here is a chapter on "Practical Intuition," wherein Ray dispels some common myths about intuition—one being that it is based on emotion and is therefore unreliable.

"Another word for intuition is 'recognition,' which literally means 'to know again,' " says Ray. "When you've worked long and hard to build experience in any given area, the right decision often comes quickly as a sort of emotionless recognition" of factual information that has perhaps been partially forgotten by your conscious mind. Ray also says that in situations such as you describe, where key facts are contradictory, intuition is "mistake-free."

OFFICE POLITICS?

Dear Annie: My boss is disliked and not respected by his boss, who is the top guy in our division. The big boss likes to find fault with everything the little boss and his team touch, so my pay and career prospects are being affected. Can I get around this? *Goodbye Without Leaving*

Dear GWL: There only one boss here: It's you. You can take your talent elsewhere, of course: a different division, a new company. Try thinking about what you have accomplished in very specific terms: Whom did it please? (The client, the audience, the tax accountants ...) Why was it great? (What did they like about it? If you don't know, go find out.) How much money did it bring in? (If the answer is a negative number, stop right here.) And then: If I try to sell this someplace else, who will jump at it? (Exclude bosses who don't count at this point.)

Nancy Friedberg, a career coach at the Five O'Clock Club in Manhattan, says this: "There are people watching you all the time—people in your business, your peers, your boss' peers, his boss' peers, your opposite number at some competing company. You may know who some of these people are right now, or you may not. But figure it out—and once you do, make sure you meet these people." Come up with an eight- to 20-word summary of your best stuff, your latest triumph, your real interest, and get it out there—over lunch, in an elevator, at a conference, in a trade-association meeting. "Once you have built a reputation apart from your company, your company sees you as more valuable," says Friedberg. "And in fact, you are."

CHAPTER FOUR

▲▼▲

INVESTMENT STRATEGIES FOR A SECURE FUTURE

HOW THE REALLY SMART MONEY INVESTS
page 120

WHY RISK MATTERS TO YOUR PORTFOLIO
page 127

AVOIDING THE TAXMAN
page 131

HOW TO MANAGE YOUR STOCK OPTIONS
page 139

DIGITAL INVESTING
page 147

HOW THE REALLY SMART MONEY INVESTS

BY SHAWN TULLY

▲▼▲

At DFA investing is a science,
not a spectator sport.

▲▼▲

Suppose you made a list of the smartest people alive in finance—those who have done the most to advance our understanding of how the stock market really works. Somewhere near the top you'd surely place Eugene Fama of the University of Chicago, the leading champion of the efficient-market theory and a favorite to win a Nobel Prize one day. You'd obviously want to include Merton Miller of Chicago, who earned a Nobel by analyzing the effect of a corporation's capital structure on its stock price, and Myron Scholes of Stanford, who won his Nobel by explaining the pricing of options. You'd also pencil in Fama's collaborator Kenneth French of MIT, as well as consultant Roger Ibbotson and master data cruncher Rex Sinquefield, who together compiled the most trusted record of stock market returns going back to 1926.

What would you give to know how these titans invest their own money? Well, don't give too much, because all you have to do is look at the funds of one Santa Monica money management firm, Dimensional Fund Advisors. Sinquefield and partner David Booth, both former students of Fama, founded DFA and now run the funds. Fama and French map out many of the investment strategies (and earn royalties for doing so). Miller, Scholes, and Ibbotson are directors. All except Miller, who believes directors should not invest in their own funds, have large chunks of their own money in DFA.

If you want to invest like these giants, however, you may have to check one of your most cherished investment notions at the door. Unlike any other money management firm, DFA insists that each of its funds must follow a strategy based on rigorous academic research. And for the past three decades, that research has squarely challenged the industry's fundamental assumption—namely, that a stock picker, given enough smarts and enough research, can consistently beat the market. To the *Über*-intellects at DFA, the genius stock picker is a myth. And they have the numbers to back this view up. Sinquefield and Booth will be happy to share the reams of academic research supporting the theory that stocks are, with a few exceptions, an efficient market, in which prices fairly reflect all available information and stock pickers can't really add much value. They can also point to the wildfire spread of indexing among professional and retail investors, an investment strategy they helped pioneer.

Sinquefield and Booth might also bring up the success of their own firm. After being hooted at by Wall Street 20 years ago, the pair went on to manage $29 billion in 22 funds, making their firm the ninth-largest institutional fund manager in the country, managing pension funds for major companies and institutions. The firm also became the most popular choice of the mutual fund industry's fastest-growing retail distribution channel, fee-only financial planners. (If you want to invest your own money in DFA funds, you'll need to go through one of them.) DFA collects fees averaging about a quarter of a percent on that asset base, for a gross of some $70 million a year.

THE GENIUS STOCK PICKER IS A MYTH

If nothing else, DFA's success is a measure of how deeply the once thorny theories of academic finance have taken hold in mainstream investment practice. And that is due in no small part to the two founders' own tireless proselytizing. Sinquefield and Booth met in 1971 at the University of Chicago Graduate School of Business. Booth, a Ph.D. candidate, was grading papers and advising students in Fama's finance course. Sinquefield, an MBA student, regularly bombarded Booth with doctorate-sized questions. Both were already ardent believers in the efficient-market hypothesis, a theory that Fama first espoused in 1964 in his Ph.D. thesis and elaborated on in subsequent articles and academic confabs. Booth, a Midwestern computer jock, moved to Chicago to study under Fama after coming across Fama's thesis as a master's candidate in computer sciences at the University of Kansas.

For Sinquefield, it was a case of one theology replacing another. Raised from age 7 in Saint Vincent's Catholic orphanage in St. Louis, he went on to study for the priesthood but left the seminary after three years. Sinquefield first encountered Fama's theories at the University of Chicago and, like Booth, had an epiphany. "It reminded me of studying Aristotle and Thomas Aquinas," he says. "The theories were so ordered and logical."

The object of their devotion is Eugene Fama. While other thinkers had long questioned whether stock prices were really predictable, Fama's work gave the efficient-market hypothesis its most rigorous intellectual grounding (as well as its name). Fama argued that the stock market is a matchless information-processing machine, whose participants collectively price shares correctly and instantaneously. Unlike the market portrayed in mutual fund advertisements and personal-finance magazines, it is not a place where the smartest managers outwit the less smart. Instead, the market is so full of well-trained, well-motivated investors avidly gathering information and acting on it that not even Nobel Prize–winners can hope to beat it consistently. Sure, some managers will outpace the market for a few years, but it is impossible to prove that those runs are more than just sheer chance.

SOME HARD SELLS: INDEX AND SMALL-CAP FUNDS

The efficient-market theory still raises hackles on Wall Street, for obvious reasons. But in academia the debate is all but over, and among pension fund fiduciaries Fama's theories are now so accepted that an estimated 24% of the trillions of dollars in pension assets is invested in index funds.

When Sinquefield and Booth joined the work force after leaving Chicago, however, the efficient market was a revolutionary idea. While working as a trust officer at American National Bank in Chicago, Sinquefield evaluated the bank's money managers and discovered just what Fama had predicted: Funds that actively pick large-company stocks do no better collectively than the S&P—worse, in fact, once you count their fees of 0.5 to 1.5 percentage points a year. Why not create a fund that simply tracked the index? asked Sinquefield. As long as fees were low, it would be all but certain of beating most professional stock pickers over time.

The new concept was the ultimate hard sell. "You think John the Baptist had it tough!" recalls Sinquefield. But he finally persuaded New York Telephone to invest in an S&P 500 fund if American National started one. So in 1975 Sinquefield and American National launched one of the first index funds to mimic the S&P.

Meanwhile, at investment firm A.G. Becker in New York City, Booth was advising pension fund managers on where to put their money. He noticed that almost all the managers invested in big companies. Booth pleaded to start a small-cap index fund, but his colleagues guffawed at his presentation. The next day Booth started DFA in his Brooklyn apartment, ripping out the sauna to put in a Quotron machine.

As Booth began looking for clients, another of Fama's graduate students, Rolf Banz, was researching the performance of small stocks vs. large. Banz's research proved for the first time what most professional investors take for granted today: that small-cap stocks produce higher returns than big ones over long periods. The reasoning is pretty straightforward. Smaller companies are riskier than larger companies and have a higher cost of capital. No one would invest except in expectation of earning a commensurately higher return.

Sinquefield, who had been following Banz's research, immediately proposed a small-cap index fund at American National. The bank nixed the idea. By coincidence, Booth called shortly afterward to say his fledgling firm was hatching a product just like the one Sinquefield's employer had deep-sixed. Sinquefield quit his job and joined Booth. DFA was in business.

In keeping with Banz's research, the fund would own all the stocks that made up the smallest two deciles, measured by market capitalization, of the companies on the New York Stock Exchange. (The name, the 9-10 fund, derives from the two deciles.) True efficient-market believers, Sinquefield and Booth made no effort to sort the winners from the dogs among the fund's holdings. Thus, there would be no research department or celebrity money managers, and costs could be held to a modest half percentage point, a third of what the average small-cap fund charges today. The result was a fund with the efficiency of an S&P indexer but the promise of higher returns in the long run.

One of DFA's first moves was to recruit Fama, Miller, Scholes, and Ibbotson as advisers. Fama was delighted with the idea of a fund based on his principles. "In class he kept telling us that the efficient-market theory was the most practical thing we'd ever learn," recalls Booth. "I think Rex and I were the only people who believed him."

At first things went splendidly. From July 1982 to mid-1983, DFA's small-cap fund gained nearly 100%, and pension funds rushed to sign up. Then Sinquefield and Booth experienced a corollary of Banz's research: When small stocks fall, they fall harder than big ones. From 1984 to 1990, small caps went through the worst seven years in their history, returning just 2.6% a year, vs. 14.7% for the S&P. "At least it discouraged the competition," muses Booth.

What saved DFA during this period was that Sinquefield and Booth had not overpromised when selling the fund. They never told clients that small stocks would outpace big ones in any given period, even one lasting seven years. They did pledge that DFA would beat most competing small-cap funds, saddled as they were by high fees. And so it did: All small-cap funds underperformed the S&P, but DFA did better than most. Moreover, since the small-stock dry spell ended in late 1990, the 9-10 fund waxed the S&P 500, the Russell 2000 small-stock index, and the average small-company mutual fund.

Then as now, DFA owed much of its outperformance to a fierce attention to costs. After all, in an efficient market, costs are the one thing you can control. In addition to charging low management fees, DFA gains on the competition by sharp trading. Part of its advantage is size: As the nation's largest market maker in small caps, DFA is the first stop for active managers desperate to buy or sell blocks of small stocks. Says Robert Deere, the head of trading: "We make it as painful for them as possible."

ANOTHER BREAKTHROUGH: A VALUE FUND

<hr />

While the 9-10 fund remained a moderate success, it took another breakthrough by Fama to really push DFA into the big time. The study, conducted with Kenneth French, then of Yale, confirmed Banz's small-stock effect but also showed convincingly that the lower the company's ratio of price to book value, the higher its subsequent stock performance tended to be. No other measures had nearly as much predictive power—not earnings growth, price/earnings, or volatility. While "value" managers such as Warren Buffett and Michael Price had long maintained that it was smarter to buy companies when they were out of favor—thus trading at low price-to-book ratios—Fama and French proved the point with statistical rigor. According to Fama and French's most recent data, downtrodden "value" stocks have outpaced high price-to-book growth stocks annually by an average of 15.5% to 11% over the past 34 years.

What makes the numbers so dramatic is that growth stocks—the Coca-Colas and Gillettes—are inevitably the most highly regarded issues, with the most predictable earnings streams. The only problem is that you have to pay for that reliability. That leaves less room for future appreciation. Value stocks, by contrast, have low prices but big upside potential. They have to offer investors higher return to compensate for the extra risk of owning them. In a way, the value effect is similar to the small-stock effect: Bigger risk pays off, in aggregate, with higher returns. In fact, small stocks that also trade at low price-to-book ratios provided the best results of all in Fama and French's study, returning an annual 20.2% over 70 years, eight points more than big growth stocks.

DFA was quick to launch a small- and a large-cap value fund based on Fama and French's research. The funds buy only stocks that fall into low price-to-book deciles, and they make no attempt to distinguish "better" value stocks from worse ones. Partly on the strength of Fama's research, the two funds have proved enormously popular and now hold some $8 billion. One believer is Robert Boldt of Calpers, which invests $1.7 billion with DFA. "I'm convinced the value effect is real," says Boldt. "You have to expect higher returns for investing in beaten-down companies."

<hr />

PUMPING RETURNS WITH SMALL-CAP VALUE

▲▼▲

Had you invested in small-company stocks in 1964, you'd have beaten the S&P 500's 11.9% annual gain through last year with a 14.5% annual return. Had you focused on small stocks trading at low price-to-book ratios, your return would have jumped to 18.5%.

COMPOUND ANNUAL RETURNS, 1964–97

S&P 500	11.9%
Small company stocks	14.5%
Small company value stocks	18.5%

FORTUNE CHART

With a certain amount of academic prudence, the DFA sages are careful to warn that their research is no substitute for a balanced investment plan. They don't, for example, recommend that you invest only in small-cap and value stocks; the two strategies sometimes badly underperform. For stability, they recommend holding about 45% of your equities in an S&P index fund. None of that diminishes their evangelical attachment to their strategies. The zealots at DFA believe that their methods have not only the weight of evidence behind them but the force of history as well. "Today the only people who don't think markets work are the North Koreans, the Cubans, and the stock pickers," says Sinquefield.

Who could argue, given all the brainpower at DFA? Still, hope springs eternal in investors' hearts. The temptation to try to pick the next Microsoft or Peter Lynch is—let's face it—pretty hard to overcome. And besides, at least one DFA giant thinks it's okay to indulge such guilty pleasures as long as you recognize them for what they are. "I choose a few stocks myself," says Nobel laureate Merton Miller. "But I do it strictly for entertainment."

▲▼▲

WHY RISK MATTERS TO YOUR PORTFOLIO

BY DAVID WHITFORD

▲▼▲

How important is a fund's risk profile? This important: It can tell you more—and sometimes a lot more—than past performance.

▲▼▲

Even if you are only a casual follower of mutual funds, you have probably heard of "standard deviation." This statistical measure, which has become a very popular yardstick lately, measures a fund's volatility.

Simply put, standard deviation tells you how much a fund's short-term results vary from its long-term average; the higher the standard deviation, the more the fund's results jump around. If investing is like a roller-coaster ride—and that's as good as any analogy—then standard deviation tells you what to expect in the way of dips and rolls. It tells you how scared you'll be.

The fact is, standard deviation can be an important tool for investors—one that can offer some insight not only into how risky a fund is but even into how it might perform in a given market environment in the future.

That, at least, is what Morningstar found in a 1994 study that used standard deviation to examine risk and returns in successive five-year tranches. The study showed that a fund's past standard deviation was a very reliable indicator of its future standard deviation. The study also found that the higher the fund's standard deviation between 1984 and 1988—that is, the riskier the fund— the higher its return over the next five years. But all of this occurred within the context of the bull market, causing the study's author, John Rekenthaler, to note, "More risk doesn't always equal more returns—in a bear market just the opposite is true—but in one form or another, a discernible relationship between past risk and future returns usually appears. The same cannot be said of [past and future] returns."

THERE'S BEAUTY IN AN ABSOLUTE NUMBER

How can standard deviation offer a clearer window into future performance than a fund's past performance can? Well, for one thing, as has long been known, you can't judge a fund solely on how it has performed in the past—which is why the SEC insists on that stilted disclaimer we've come to know so well: PAST PERFORMANCE IS NO GUARANTEE OF FUTURE RETURNS. A fund at the top of the heap can quite often be there because the manager took outsized risks that paid off last year but might not next year. And particular investment styles are not always in sync with market conditions. When, say, growth stocks slump even the best growth fund managers suffer. Only the rare fund managers top the charts year after year.

Risk and volatility, however, are things a fund manager can control no matter what the investment climate. Especially in recent years, controlling risk has become an ever bigger part of what defines fund strategy. That's why, by and large, a manager's risk strategies—and hence the volatility of his fund—don't change from year to year.

During the long bull market, many investors forgot about risk, but they have been learning anew that investing is inherently risky. Sooner or later, you will lose money in the market. And while you may think you have the stomach to swallow big losses, history suggests you don't. "Immediately following periods of serious market decline, mutual fund investors have become net redeemers," says David Katzen, who manages Zweig's domestic stock funds. "That's happened during every major bear market decline since they've been keeping statistics on this stuff. There are very few things that have occurred frequently in market history without exception. This is one of them." Can paying close attention to a fund's standard deviation help soften the blow—or at least help you prepare for it? In a word, yes.

Standard deviation is not, of course, the only measure of risk out there. Beta is another measure—it tracks how closely a fund hews to the broader market. A stock fund with a beta above 1 is likely to be more volatile than the S&P 500; below 1, less volatile.

The problem with beta is that it only tells you how risky the fund was in comparison with a market index. If the index (the S&P 500, say) doesn't really apply to the fund (a precious-metals fund, for example), then beta can be terribly misleading.

The beauty of standard deviation is that it's an absolute number. It has nothing to do with any index or benchmark. It therefore allows for perfectly valid volatility comparisons among funds and across asset classes. It can tell you, for example, that a corporate bond fund with a standard deviation of 10.8 is more volatile than a high-yield bond fund with a standard deviation of 4.9 and less volatile than a global stock fund with a standard deviation of 20.7. Knowing that, you can begin to make rational decisions about how much risk you're willing to accept for the returns you're trying to get.

THE TORTOISE AND THE HARE

▼

Standard deviation—for our purposes—defines a band within which a fund's total returns tend to fall. The higher the standard deviation, the wider the band. Take, for example, PBHG Growth—a top-performing fund that had a five-year average annual adjusted return of 24.8%. The only problem is, to stick it out for the full five years, you would have enjoyed stretches when the fund performed brilliantly—up 50% or more in the space of 12 months—while enduring other stretches, just as long, when it lost money for investors. The bone-jarring nature of the ride that PBHG delivered is captured in the fund's dizzyingly high standard deviation of 29.0.

PBHG's standard deviation is derived by annualizing the fund's monthly returns over the past five years and comparing those numbers with its annualized average monthly return over the whole period. A standard deviation of 29.0 tells you that PBHG's performance was so uneven that the normal spread of monthly returns (that is, the band within which about two-thirds of them fell) ranged 29.0 percentage points above—and below— the five-year average. As a potential investor in PBHG Growth, it's that range—at least as much as the average annual total return—that you need to respond to. You must ask yourself, as Catherine Voss Sanders, publisher of *Morningstar Investor*, puts it, "Is that the kind of variability I'm willing to deal with?"

But there's another question too: In order to have even a chance at that nearly 25% gain PBHG has delivered over five years, do you have to accept its extraordinarily high risk? Plainly, that's the theory—that investors willing to risk big losses are also the most likely to reap big gains. Fund manager Gary Pilgrim, as an avowed momentum investor, embraces risk. He looks for fast-rising earnings growth—finding it most often in skittish high-tech companies. He makes no apologies for the volatility of his fund. "What an investor has to figure out," Pilgrim argues, "is, how hard does he want to try for higher returns?"

But comparing the standard deviations of funds with similar returns suggests an appealing alternative: Over the long haul, some tortoises have kept pace with the hares. Look at Legg Mason Value Trust, which had an average annual total return of 24.4% over five years and carried its shareholders to roughly the same happy place that PBHG did. Yet Legg Mason Value Trust has a standard deviation of just 16.9, so its ride has been a whole lot smoother. Legg Mason Value Trust fund manager Bill Miller outperformed the S&P 500 for six straight calendar years, in part by keeping a close eye on variables that affect standard deviation. Miller favors a value approach (his P/E is half Pilgrim's 40), takes on risk sparingly, and uses the whole portfolio to offset a handful of volatile selections. While it's pretty unlikely Legg Mason Value Trust will ever zoom up without warning, the way Pilgrim's fund has, it is also much less likely to crash than is PBHG Growth.

Is that important to you? It is if you're not sure how much volatility you can handle—especially if you happen to believe, as Miller does, that the stock market is entering a "new era." Not the "new era" of the optimists, which coincides with the longest-running bull market in history. "We think that's over," says Miller. "We're seeing it right now. The new era now is more volatility." And more reason to pay close attention to standard deviation.

AVOIDING THE TAXMAN

BY SHELLY BRANCH

*The 1997 tax law is a jumble. But
amid the mess, there are a few
ways to make it work for you.*

If you thought the tax code was complicated and silly before, consider the Taxpayer Relief Act of 1997: Its new Hope Credit for education can't be used by convicted drug felons, but a similar tax break in the same measure, called the Lifetime Learning Credit, can. Why? No one knows. Welcome to the wacky world of tax legislation.

The 1997 tax bill is chock-a-block with such baffling twists. Its many tax cuts aren't available to everyone, but figuring out exactly who's eligible is a little like trying to solve Rubik's cube. There are a half-dozen new tax rates for capital gains alone (including a higher rate for collectibles). "From a planning perspective, it's just a terrible law," complains James Shambo, a partner with accounting firm Sanden Shambo & Anderson in Colorado Springs.

But plan we must, so FORTUNE decided to call some of the smartest tax minds we know and compile their cleverest—and least widely known—tax tricks. We found some goodies, like when not to convert your regular individual retirement account into a newfangled Roth IRA and how best to protect your children's college fund. Here is what our tax pundits recommend.

YOUR INVESTMENTS

Now more than ever, it pays to make sure your investments are in their proper places. Tax-favored accounts—such as 401(k)s and IRAs—are the safest harbor for any investment that throws off interest and dividends, since both are taxed at ordinary income tax rates as high as 39.6%. Growth stocks, on the other hand, are best kept in taxable accounts. Gains on those come mainly from price appreciation, which are taxed at the lower capital gains rate of 20%, assuming you hang on to the shares for 18 months or longer.

Individual investors have the most control over their tax situations, of course, since they get to choose when to buy and sell. If you have your own equity portfolio, you can keep more money in your pocket by being methodical about when and how you dump your shares. Not long ago, when tax rates were simpler, it didn't much matter when you unloaded losers—as long as you had some type of gain to offset the losses. But under the new law, the kind of losses and gains you have can be important. Net long-term capital losses, for instance, can be used to offset net short-term capital gains. Say, for example, you have a long-term loss of $2,000 and an ordinary tax rate of 28%. By offsetting it with $2,000 in short-term gains (taxed at your 28%), you'd save $560. On the other hand, if you offset it with long-term gains (at 20%), you'd stand to save only $400.

For people who invest in mutual funds rather than playing the market themselves, the trick is to choose a fund that provides the gentlest tax treatment. One way to do this is to check a fund's so-called turnover rate, which signals how long the manager typically hangs on to stocks. The lower, the better. A modest rate of 50% or less indicates that the portfolio changes, on average, every two years, which minimizes short-term capital gains. Also, keep your eyes open for "tax-managed" funds.

Unfortunately, there are precious few tax tricks for anyone who's bullish on bric-a-brac. Investments in all types of collectibles (which, says the Internal Revenue Service, include Picassos and wine collections, as well as flea-market finds) are still taxed at the old top capital gains rate of 28%, never the new 20% rate. One idea: When you're thinking of giving to charity, says Lisa Osofsky, an accountant and financial planner with M.R. Weiser & Co. in New York City, consider giving from your gallery instead of your investment portfolio. That way you're giving up a more heavily taxed item instead of a more lightly taxed one. Charitable donors get a deduction for the full market value of their gifts of collectibles—to the extent the gift doesn't exceed

30% of adjusted gross income. The gains from stock sales can be taxed at the much more preferable 20% rate.

YOUR HOME

Sell now!! Well, at least think a bit harder about selling if you have lots of profit in your property that you might want to recoup. The new tax law permits sellers to keep, tax-free, up to $500,000 of the gain on the sale of a principal residence. That exclusion was exactly what Ed and Carolyn Williams of Oshkosh, Wis., were waiting for. Over the years they have moved six times and avoided taxes on their gains by rolling them into their next house. They've been ready for a while to sell again, hoping to move into more modest digs. The recent tax change made that much more attractive. Not only will they collect a tax-free profit when they sell their $262,000 home, but they can also pocket the gains they carried over from their earlier sales.

Here's how good the new law is for them. Under the old law they would have had to wait another five years until they could keep any of their gains without paying taxes. (They are both 50 years old.) Even then, their unencumbered profit would have been limited to $125,000. Now they can cash in and redeploy their capital tax-free. Good move, says Tom Ochsenschlager, a tax partner with Grant Thornton. He explains, "The new law opens up a whole new world for a lot of our clients who can put that money to much more productive use."

Many homeowners may be tempted to take advantage of a new tax provision, meant to apply in 1999, that makes it easier to write off a home office. Under the measure, you won't become automatic bait for an audit anymore, as long as you can prove that you do most of your administrative work at home. But, says Ed Slott, an accountant in Rockville Centre, N.Y., "this is one deduction that's highly overrated." Here's the hitch: When you sell your house, you're stuck with what's called a mixed-use transaction, which means that you'll have to add to your gain the sums you wrote off as depreciation for the home office. Worse, that "depreciation recapture" exposes you to a nasty 25% tax.

Take the instance of a $200,000 residence in which the office makes up 10% of the space. If you sell the house in just four years for $250,000, you'll owe taxes on one-tenth of the gain ($5,000), plus the depreciation you must add back ($2,908), for a total of $7,908. The five grand is taxed at 20%, and the rest at the higher 25% rate. Your tax bill at the sale weighs in at a hefty $1,727. "If you'd left the thing alone and hadn't taken the write-off, you would have been better off," asserts Slott, who figures the home-office deduction, over four years, would have been worth only about $814, assuming your tax rate is 28%. So when will the home-office deduction pay off? When you stay in your home for the long term or, even better, when you rent.

YOUR RETIREMENT

▼

Much of the excitement over the 1997 tax law has swirled around the fancy new variations on the traditional IRA. The most innovative, the Roth IRA, is named for Chairman William Roth of the Senate Finance Committee; it lets savers put away nondeductible dollars and withdraw money from the IRA tax-free. We could do nifty math to show that investors in the Roth IRA won't do any better than folks in a regular, deductible IRA. Realistically, though, a lot of people won't have the chance to choose, since the tax advantages of the regular IRA disappear for couples who have adjusted gross incomes above $60,000 a year. The new Roth IRA is more widely available, allowing taxpayers with incomes of up to $160,000 to participate.

The more common conundrum will be whether to convert an existing IRA into the Roth variety—an option for taxpayers with adjusted gross incomes of $100,000 or less. The answer for most people who qualify is yes, assuming that you expect your tax bracket to be the same, or higher, when you retire. If you think otherwise, you'd be better off staying in a regular IRA. But then again, "the caveats are almost endless," says Andrew B. Lyon, a tax consultant with Price Waterhouse in Washington, D.C. Among them: the size of your rollover, the performance of your other savings, and most important—how you plan to pay your tax bill at the time of the conversion.

That's right: The funds you withdraw from a deductible IRA when you convert it to a Roth IRA will be taxed at your ordinary rate. Helpfully, the IRS initially will give converters four years to include those sums in income. But there are still plenty of pitfalls. For example, don't even think about using funds from the deductible IRA itself to settle your tax liability. You'll rack up taxes and an ugly 10% penalty if you do so before age $59^1/2$. Instead, remove money from a savings, money market, or mutual fund account. According to an analysis by Lyon of Price Waterhouse, if you settle your tax bill with IRA proceeds, your Roth IRA would yield you less in the end than if you had kept your money in the regular IRA. Another danger is that the extra income from the conversion will throw you into a tax bracket so much higher that you could erase the advantage of the entire exercise. For example, what if you get an unexpected raise or collect bonus pay? "If any one of those events pushes you into a higher tax bracket, it may defeat the advantages of the Roth," warns Shambo of Sanden, Shambo & Anderson. Anybody whose rate jumps by eight percentage points as a result of a Roth rollover—even in just one tax year—could see the long-term benefits vanish.

YOUR EDUCATION

Congress has removed the penalty from early IRA withdrawals that are used to pay for education. While this may help you finance your children's college years, you will have to pay ordinary income taxes on earnings and any deductible contributions you take out. And many financial planners say you should never pay for education from a retirement account unless you plan to repay the money.

There's also a new IRA, the Education IRA, for post-secondary schooling. These tax-deferred custodial accounts let certain taxpayers put away up to $500 a year for a child's education. But they can't be used together with any of the other new—and often more valuable—education tax credits that were also created in the 1997 legislation. If you start contributing when a child is born, you could net $22,000 when the child turns 18—not nearly enough to pay the

CHOICES, CHOICES EVERYWHERE

▲▼▲

In the wake of the 1997 tax legislation, there are so many new tax-saving gimmicks that they're hard to keep straight. Some of the most intricate involve retirement accounts and tax credits for education. Here are some of the variations:

	EDUCATION	
	Lifetime Learning Credit	**Hope Credit**
How it works	Gives families the chance to reduce their tax liability by up to $1,000 per return on $5,000 of post-secondary educational expenses.	Allows families the chance to slice their tax liability by up to $1,500 a year per student enrolled in post-secondary education programs.
Who can use it	The credit is available to married couples with AGI up to $100,000; $50,000 for singles. Effective for expenses paid after June 30, 1998.	Eligibility is the same as the Lifetime Learning Credit. Effective for expenses paid after December 1997.
Withdrawal rules	Not applicable.	Not applicable.
Advantages/pitfalls	It's available for four years of post-secondary education expenses. Parents as well as their children are eligible to use the credit to offset education expenses.	The credit can be used only to offset the first two years of study. Also, the credit can't be used in conjunction with the Education IRA or the Lifetime Learning Credit.

$60,000 a year that private colleges may then charge. Even worse, "Money in these accounts might screw up a child's chance of receiving college aid," says Lynn Ballou, a financial planner in Lafayette, Calif. Until financial aid administrators indicate otherwise, Ballou

RETIREMENT		
Deductible IRA	**Roth IRA**	**Education IRA**
Allows you to contribute up to $2,000 a year and defer taxes until withdrawal, typically at age 59 1/2. Contributions are tax-deductible.	Permits savers to put away up to $2,000 a year in a tax-deferred account and withdraw the proceeds at retirement tax-free. Contributions are nondeductible.	This so-called IRA is not for retirement but for post-secondary education expenses. Contributions are limited to $500 a year and aren't tax-deductible.
Available to people not covered by an employer's retirement plan, or who are eligible for such plans and have an adjusted gross income below $60,000 if married, or $40,000 if single.	Available to married couples with AGI up to $160,000, or singles up to $110,000. Filers with AGI as high as $100,000 are eligible to convert their deductible and nondeductible IRAs into Roth IRAs.	Contributions can be made by anyone (parent, other relative, or friend) who has an AGI up to $160,000 for married filers or $110,000 for singles.
Principal and earnings are taxed at ordinary income tax rates. Withdrawals prior to age 59 1/2, with certain exceptions, are also subject to a 10% penalty.	Withdrawals are tax-free. Sums rolled over from other IRAs are treated as taxable distributions, although the tax may be paid over a four-year period, if rolled over in 1998.	Withdrawals that are used for higher-education expenses are tax-free.
The new law allows for penalty-free—but not tax-free—withdrawals prior to age 59 1/2 for specific expenses, including college tuition and purchases of a first-time home.	You don't have to start taking money out of this account when you turn 70 1/2, which can leave more in the account to accumulate post-retirement, and for your heirs.	The account must be emptied by the time the student reaches age 30; otherwise, the earnings will be taxed at the student's ordinary income tax rate, plus an additional 10% penalty.

suggests salting away college money the old-fashioned way: in the parent's name, using long-term-growth mutual funds.

For families whose adjusted gross income is under $100,000 ($50,000 for singles) and who have children enrolled in post-sec-

IF YOU CONVERT TO A ROTH IRA ...

▲▼▲

A traditional IRA with $55,000 today will yield a retiree $116,894 in 15 years, assuming an 8% annual return. The table below shows your options for how to pay the $18,150 in taxes to convert to a Roth IRA. Paying the tax over four years instead of one yields a higher end amount because that $18,150 works longer for you.

IF YOU PAY THE TAX FROM...	Your nest egg will be
Savings over four years	$178,025
Savings, all at once	$174,469[1]
IRA proceeds (funds withdrawn before age 59 ½)	$114,953
IRA proceeds (funds withdrawn after age 59 ½)	$121,120
If you keep your regular IRA and invest the $18,150	$160,392

Results assume a combined 33% federal/state tax rate before and after retirement, and that the taxes are paid over a four-year period.

[1]This example assumes you pay the taxes in one year.

FORTUNE CHART /SOURCE: PRICE WATERHOUSE

ondary education programs, there is a new pair of tax credits. The Hope Credit is worth up to $1,500 per student, but only for two years of post-secondary education. The Lifetime Learning Credit can be used for four years of schooling and decreases a family's tax liability by up to $1,000 annually, but doesn't apply for each child. You get only one Lifetime Learning Credit per return. That means that couples with several kids would profit more from the Hope Credit. But if you have one child and wish to receive credits the entire time he or she is in a four-year college, the Lifetime Learning Credit makes more sense for you. Got that? Things could be worse. As we said, if you're a convicted drug felon, it gets really complicated.

HOW TO MANAGE YOUR STOCK OPTIONS

BY JUSTIN FOX

▲▼▲

*There are some simple rules, but
also some surprisingly complex
questions to ask, such as: Do you
really know what they're worth?*

▲▼▲

A decade ago it mattered only to corporate kingpins and a few lucky people in Silicon Valley. Now it has become a nagging question for millions of Americans: What do I do with all these stock options my company keeps giving me?

As hard choices go, this surely falls in the category of dilemmas we all wish we had. But the rapid growth of employee stock option programs means that before long it could be a dilemma many will face. It's one more way—of a piece with the 401(k)'s triumph over traditional pension plans—in which regular people are having to make the investment decisions that will determine whether they retire to Hilton Head or to a job at the local Wendy's. With stock options especially, making the wrong choice can hurt a lot. Cashing in options too early can mean missing out on large, possibly huge, future gains. Holding on too long can mean losing it all if your once promising company slides into oblivion. So what to do? There are a few simple rules—like not letting your options expire unused (it happens more often than you'd think) and making sure you aren't caught unawares by the tax code.

TWO APPROACHES

▼

The question of whether to cash in your options early or late or somewhere in between is one for which reasonable people can come up with wildly different answers. Witness, for example, the cases of Miguel Jardine and David Southwell:

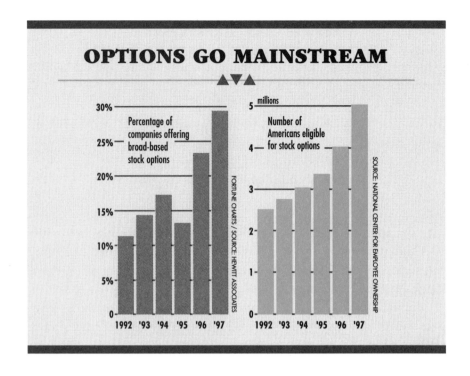

OPTIONS GO MAINSTREAM
▲▼▲

Percentage of companies offering broad-based stock options

30%
25%
20%
15%
10%
5%
0

1992 '93 '94 '95 '96 '97

FORTUNE CHARTS / SOURCE: HEWITT ASSOCIATES

Number of Americans eligible for stock options

millions
5
4
3
2
1
0

1992 '93 '94 '95 '96 '97

SOURCE: NATIONAL CENTER FOR EMPLOYEE OWNERSHIP

Jardine is a twentysomething engineer who in August 1996 got a job at UUNet, a Virginia-based Internet service provider. With the job came a modest helping of stock options, exercisable at the then market price of UUNet's stock. A few days later, phone company MFS acquired UUNet, a deal that converted Jardine's options into MFS options and made them start looking like more than a modest helping. Then, in December 1996, telecom giant-killer WorldCom bought MFS. After that, WorldCom's stock price continued to rise, and before long Jardine's once-modest package—now consisting of options to buy WorldCom stock—was worth between $150,000 and $200,000.

This meant big decisions for someone who just three years previously had dropped out of the University of Southern California to work on the White House Website, a guy who until recently had a negative net worth. With the just over 20% of his options that had vested by the end of 1997, Jardine opted to spend the money: to pay down student loans and credit card debt; to buy insurance, a new Volvo, and a diamond engagement ring for his fiancée (and now wife), Catherine. Jardine says he knows he might miss out on future gains, but that's okay with him. "I've still got almost four years of vesting," he says. "If WorldCom does a tremendous job, I'll still benefit. But if WorldCom doesn't do so well, I'll know my family's taken care of."

Up in suburban Boston, thirtysomething David Southwell was making enough as chief financial officer of Sepracor, a small pharmaceuticals company, to afford a Volvo—and a Land Rover and a house—without dipping into his options stash. So he chose not to dip, even with his options worth about $13 million. Instead, he's holding out for an even bigger jackpot.

Southwell, a former Lehman Brothers investment banker who took a pay cut to join Sepracor three years ago, acknowledges that "I'm totally undiversified; if a financial planner was to look at me, he'd say I'm crazy." But he figures it was a calculated gamble to come to Sepracor in the first place, so why not play out his hand? "I don't understand young people who gradually exercise stock options as they come out," he says. "If you're older, I can understand, but hey, if you're in your mid-30s, you don't need security."

TRADING RISK AGAINST REWARD

Not everyone in Southwell's age bracket would agree, obviously. And in the end, any decision on options has to take into account just how much security you need and just how much risk you can take. But before getting to those kinds of judgments, it helps to know just what you're dealing with.

Here's how the stock options granted to Jardine, Southwell, and millions of others work: A company gives an employee options to buy a certain number of shares of the company's stock at a set price, usually the market price at the time the options are handed out. The options come with an expiration date and a vesting period. The expiration date is in most cases ten years from when the options are granted; after that, they become unusable. Vesting usually takes place over a period of three to five years. Some companies use "cliff vesting," in which all the options become exercisable at once; more common is a vesting schedule in which the first group of options becomes usable after a year and the rest on a monthly or yearly basis after that.

Because of the way the Internal Revenue Service treats most options—when the options are exercised, it taxes the profit made as ordinary income—it is customary to sell the stock immediately after exercising the option to buy it. In fact, most companies have deals with brokerage firms in which employees can exercise their options and then sell the stock without putting up a penny. They simply receive the cash, minus brokerage fees and income-tax withholding.

That's how an option works. A more complex matter is figuring out what it's worth. The obvious solution (used in the examples above) is to subtract the exercise price from the current market price of the company's stock. That is, if you were granted 1,000 options to buy stock at $20 a share, and the stock is now at $100, the options are worth $80,000—and if the stock is at $15, they're worth nothing. But it's not really that simple. "Suppose you have options that are out of the money," says Mark Rubinstein, a finance professor at the University of California at Berkeley. "The intrinsic value is zero. Would you be willing to give them away? No." That's because while the option has no value if exercised today, it doesn't have to be exercised today—and the price of the stock could go up before it does.

The stock options that companies grant their employees can't be bought or sold (they can be willed and, at some companies, given away). But if you exercise an option for a profit that's less than that option would be worth to a buyer, you are still in a sense leaving money on the table. And since Rubinstein and other finance experts have come up with reliable mathematical models for pricing options—Stanford's Myron Scholes and Harvard's Robert Merton just won a Nobel Prize in economics for their pioneering work on options models—it's possible, if you have a math whiz at your disposal, to estimate just how much money you've left behind. The models, or sets of equations, use the option's exercise price and time to expiration, together with the underlying stock's market price, volatility, and dividend yield, to calculate a theoretical present value for the option.

TO EXERCISE OR NOT TO EXERCISE

$\blacktriangledown$

For those who don't have time for the math, it's enough to remember this: The further away an option's expiration date, the greater the gap between what somebody would be willing to pay for the option and what you could make by exercising it. Which means that, according to options pricing theory, it makes no sense to exercise your stock options early.

So why is it that, according to a 1996 study by accounting professors Steven Huddart of Duke University and Mark Lang of the University of North Carolina, most employees exercise their options well before they expire? Do these people not understand how options work?

A lot of them don't. If you're a relative peon at a big corporation, with just-vested options that can be exercised now for a gain of $5,000 or $10,000—and you don't need the money—you'd be nuts not to hold on for a few years (unless you're convinced your company is run by nincompoops who are about to drive it into the ground). But according to Huddart and Lang's study, lower-level employees are most likely to exercise options the moment they vest. Bad move.

If, on the other hand, you're a big wheel at a big company, or any kind of wheel at a smaller company with a hot stock, your options could easily dwarf your other assets in value. In that case, exercising at least some of your options well before they expire can be the only sensible thing to do. "If your net worth is 25% in one company, you need to start looking at doing some diversification," says Michael Beriss, a Bethesda, Md., senior financial adviser with American Express. "There's nothing inherently wrong with exercising stock options early, as long as you've got something to do with the money."

Beriss and other financial planners have come up with a pretty standard strategy for people with outsized options hoards: Put yourself on a calendar and exercise your options bit by bit over a period of years. "You need to get the emotions out of it and treat it as a systematic way of unwinding a large position," says Mark Spangler of Seattle's MFS Associates. This averts the danger that one bad quarter for your company can take a huge swipe out of your net worth.

The problem with such risk-minimizing advice is that the people who've had the most phenomenal success with options are the ones who have ignored it. The best-known examples of this are the multitudes of Microsoft millionaires. At Microsoft, the main determinant of wealth is not your rank at the company but how long you hold on to your options. Spangler tells of a client who left Microsoft a few years ago and cashed in her options for an after-tax gain of $2 million. Four years later another client— one of that first client's former subordinates, who had gotten the same number of options at virtually the same time—decided to sell. Her options netted her $7 million after taxes.

THE GRADUAL SELLOFF

Not every company, however, is a Microsoft. Employees of Oxford Health Plans, Ascend Communications, and Silicon Graphics all would have been much better off cashing in their options early, before their companies' stocks tanked. At Silicon Graphics, CEO Edward McCracken, who could have exercised his options for a gain of more than $70 million when the company's stock price peaked in mid-1995, held tight to see the value of his options drop to about $10 million by the end of 1997.

Like all investment decisions, this one is a matter of trading risk against reward. The rewards of holding on to your stock options can be huge. So can the risks. Says William Baldwin, an attorney who heads Tax & Financial Advisors, a Lexington, Mass., planning firm: "If you held on to the dear end and made good money, you took an unreasonable risk and won." The smartest strategy is the gradual selloff that the financial planners recommend—although you should always bear in mind that, as a rule, the longer you hold on to your options, the more you get out of them. That's not exactly a simple formula for options success. But there are some simple things you can do to get the most out of whatever options strategy you decide upon. And most important, you should be well versed in the terms of your options—whether

FIVE THINGS TO REMEMBER

▲▼▲

*1. **Know the terms:*** Don't miss out on gains by not knowing when your options expire, or how long you can keep them after quitting your job.

*2. **Keep track:*** Always know approximately how much your options are worth; otherwise you can't make intelligent decisions about what to do with them.

*3. **Get tax advice:*** If your options are worth more than a few thousand dollars, you need to talk to an options-savvy tax lawyer or accountant before you cash them in.

*4. **Don't be too timid:*** Options aren't hot potatoes— they're investments. Don't unload them all early just because they make you a little nervous.

*5. **Don't get emotional:*** Yeah, you think your company's great. But that doesn't mean you have to bet your every penny that its stock price will keep rising.

you can give them to family members or charities, how long you're allowed to hold on to them after you retire or leave your company for another job, and when they expire.

Another, less obvious way to maximize the value of your options—once you've decided you want to unload some of them—is to pick the right ones to sell.

If you own company stock as well as options, it's almost always better to sell the stock first, because options have vastly more upside potential. If you've got $20,000 of company stock (1,000 shares at $20 a share) and the stock price doubles, your stake rises to $40,000. If you've got $20,000 of options (2,000 options exercisable at $10 a share, with the stock price at $20) and the stock price doubles, your potential options gain grows to $60,000. If you must unload options, always exercise the oldest, cheapest ones first. If the oldest options aren't the cheapest, you have to run an options pricing model to know for sure which ones are best to sell—if your options hoard is big enough, it's worth paying your friendly neighborhood finance professor or options trader a couple of hundred dollars to figure this out for you.

Finally, there are taxes. Federal income taxes on options are pretty simple, although it's a good idea to plan at least a year ahead to see if you can tweak the timing of your options exercises to keep yourself in a lower tax bracket. State income taxes can be more complicated: They sometimes aren't automatically withheld from your options check, as federal taxes are, and if you wait until April 15 to pay them, you may regret it. The problem comes when you try to deduct that outsized state tax bill from the next year's federal taxes. "You could run into the alternative minimum tax or not be able to deduct it at all," says Greg Sullivan, a financial planner and CPA with the McLean, Va., firm of Sullivan Bruyette Speros & Blayney. "It's much better to pay the state taxes the same year as the federal taxes."

So what to do about all those options? Pay uncompromisingly close attention to the little things, like terms and taxes. And when you get to the big thing—deciding when to cash them in—compromise.

▲▼▲

DIGITAL INVESTING

▲▼▲

*The path to wealth, comfort, or just
peace of mind winds its way
through the Web's collection of
investment information and trading opportunities. Here's how to use
the Internet to manage your financial portfolio and make it grow.*

▲▼▲

You're looking for a technology stock that's well positioned for long-term growth but that hasn't been trading at stratospheric levels. You could try your brother-in-law's broker or the gadget freak down the hall at the office. Or you could tap the almost unlimited amount of financial information available on the Internet with the click of a mouse. Click.

Good choice. And indeed there is choice—too much choice is one of the few drawbacks to searching for financial information on the Net. The online world has vastly enhanced your opportunities to improve your financial health. The Net is a superb research tool, not just for investing but also for all aspects of finance, from insurance to car and home loans to planning for college and retirement. The diversity of the online world also makes it perfect for finding information tailored to your individual needs or interests. There's a new group of financial sites aimed at very specific audiences. One of the newer entrants, for example, is Condé Nast's CNCurrency, which caters to women's financial interests.

To begin your search for that technology stock, point your browser toward Yahoo, the most popular and one of the best of the so-called search engines that organize and sift online information for you. At Yahoo Finance, one of many subcategories listed, you find a prompt for the Online Investor, a financial information site in its own right that is hyperlinked to Yahoo.

There, one day earlier this year, you would have hit paydirt: a "stock of the day" pick for Andrew Corp., a cable and wireless communications equipment maker whose stock (ANDW) was trading on Nasdaq near its 52-week low.

TOOLS OF THE TRADE

Is this, or any specific investment option, right for you? Using the Internet to help answer that question is where the online world really shines. Investors have access to a vast array of financial data and investment tools. A brief report on the Online Investor site notes that Andrew's stock is positioned to benefit from the long-term growth in wireless communications. But in early 1997 its revenue growth stumbled badly, sending investors to the exits.

Then, in 1998, the company was hammered by the economic slowdown in Southeast Asia. So on that day the stock was down 55% from its high and trading at a price/earnings ratio of about 16, compared with long-term growth prospects of 20% a year. (The Online Investor site features founder Ted Allrich's philosophy of searching for stocks priced below their long-term growth rates.) Allrich, author of the book *The On-Line Investor*, cautions there is still uncertainty with Andrew, "but this may be a stock worth watching for when the global telecom build-out gets back on track."

So far, so good, but you need more information. Check out recent media coverage on any of dozens of sites that carry news feeds from Reuters, AP, or other sources. CBS MarketWatch is another good news-oriented site. The PRNewswire site posts company announcements. These are often self-serving, but they also include details that may have been omitted from news accounts. And don't forget the most obvious source of information about a company—its own Website. Corporate Websites often carry company announcements as well as data on recent financial performance.

If you want financial information from a Website with the government's imprimatur, go to the SEC site, which posts all filings that public companies are required to make.

In addition to these sources, the Net is heavily populated with sites focusing primarily on investment information. For example, investorama.com is a site created by Doug Gerlach, author of another book about online investing. This "site of sites" contains links to thousands of Websites, including a directory of more than 4,000 corporate sites, Wall Street research reports, and an array of basic investing tools for laymen and sophisticated investors alike.

A word of caution about online information at these and any sites: Always check the "freshness" date of any information you are viewing. If the latest earnings figures on a company you can find are from two years ago, they aren't going to give you much of a basis on which to make an investment decision.

If you don't have a particular stock in mind but want to invest based on a set of parameters such as a five-year earnings growth rate exceeding 20% a year, then check out StockScreener, which sorts through more than 7,500 stocks for matches based on up to 20 such criteria.

At the Motley Fool Website, which is one of the best-known financial sites, founding brothers Tom and Dave Gardner dispense market information while promoting their philosophy that dedicated investors can pick winning stocks.

The Motley Fool, the Online Investor, and similar sites are also excellent sources of offbeat but often illuminating information from investors who post their musings—and rantings—on Website bulletin boards. Though you should be very cautious of anything you read in an online discussion, there is nothing like an investor scorned to generate a needed corrective to the rosy scenarios issued by companies and many Wall Street analysts. The bulletin boards crammed with comments from Andrew Corp. investors, for example, are no exception. As one investor complained on the Online Investor, "After the first quarter in January '98, it looked like we were back on track. But along came the earnings warning [about S.E. Asia] and the rest is history. You can imagine that I bought some more after the drop, so I am very stupid."

PAY TO PLAY

So far, you've used sites that are "free," if you ignore access fees and the cost of a modem. (You're not doing this on company time, are you?) There are those who insist the maxim "You get what you pay for" applies to the online world as well. It's no sur-

PICKING A STOCK ONLINE: TIPS AND TECHNIQUES

▲▼▲

▶ *Find It*

Financial information sites touting various investing philosophies and bulletin boards at sites like the Motley Fool and Silicon Investor are crawling with tips on the next "can't miss" stock. Take everything you read with a huge grain of salt—everyone has an ulterior motive. The better way to get started is at a stock-screening site, which will search for stocks based on the criteria you enter.

▶ *Research It*

Once you have a stock in mind, check it out. Hoover's has detailed corporate profiles, and the SEC posts every document companies are required to file. And don't forget a company's own Website—the best information is often there.

▶ *Buy It*

When you've found the stock you want, there are plenty of online brokers ready to make the trade. Commission price is a clear difference between some, but also consider the less obvious benefits, like execution time. A higher level of service may be worthwhile in the long run.

prise that these same folk tend to charge for access to their sites, or at least to proprietary portions of their sites.

The best of the subscription sites is also no surprise. The *Wall Street Journal* offers a comprehensive online version, including access to *Barron's* and *SmartMoney* magazine, at $49 a year ($29 for print subscribers). If you want more attitude in your stock picks, try TheStreet.com, an online offering from hedge fund manager and financial writer James Cramer. TheStreet charges $9.95 a month, although some information on the site is free. America Online also has a fairly extensive selection of financial information, and offers different pricing plans based on how much access you want. Hoover's, an authoritative source for corporate profiles, offers some free information, but the most detailed is reserved for those willing to pay a $12.95 monthly fee. (All these prices are for mid-1998.)

Still want to take the plunge? If you're ready to buy a stock, there are more than 60 online brokers queued up, ready to take your order. In 1997, the country's three million online customers accounted for an estimated 17% of all retail stock trading. Forrester Research estimates that the number of online accounts will balloon to 14.4 million by 2002.

That growth curve has caught the attention of Wall Street's leading full-service brokers. Both Donaldson Lufkin & Jenrette and Morgan Stanley Dean Witter have online trading subsidiaries. Even giant Merrill Lynch is getting into the online act, albeit one toe at a time. Merrill is beginning by offering online trading to its high-net-worth clients, expecting subsequently to roll out the online service to all customers. Merrill says, though, that it has no intention of competing on price with the cheapest online brokers.

KEEPING SCORE

To help investors through the maze of competing services, Gomez Advisors (scorecard.com) surveyed the performance of 69 online brokers during the second quarter of 1998. Some offered a menu of options rivaling full-service brokerages, while others courted the middle with $19.95 commissions. Another group sought bargain-hunters with bare-bones services and $8 trades.

Gomez ranked DLJDirect as the top online broker, based on several criteria, including order execution and price. Next were E*Trade, Waterhouse Securities, Lindner Funds, and WebStreet Securities. Before signing up with a broker, it's worth a trip to the site run by the National Association of Securities Dealers to see if the firm you're considering has a history of regulatory run-ins.

Don't put too many of your assets in one online basket. To see how a stock trade fits in with your broad asset allocation goals, use one of the many online portfolio management tools.

Fans of Quicken, the well-known financial management software from Intuit, will find much to like at its site jointly produced with CNNfn. Another option is the S&P Personal Wealth site, which debuted earlier this year. Mutual fund mavens will want to visit the Morningstar site.

Prefer to manage your portfolio full-time? Cyber-savvy investors who wonder how soon they can quit their day jobs need look no further than FinanCenter.com, which has more than 100 "calculators" to figure out all sorts of "what if?" exercises. A hands-down fave: "What will it take to become a millionaire?" Even for those who passed that milestone long ago, the Net provides an almost limitless array of financial tools. All it takes is an online connection—and a bull market.

CHAPTER FIVE

▲▼▲

RETIRING WELL:
A GUIDE TO PROSPERITY

HOW THE MILLIONAIRE NEXT DOOR GOT THAT WAY

BY ANDREW SERWER

▲▼▲

*Save. Don't spend. When you do
have to spend, be frugal. Then
someday you, too, could be a
millionaire. Really!*

▲▼▲

*M*ost people think real wealth comes from inheritance, or
from striking it rich on Wall Street or in Silicon Valley.
Bestseller The Millionaire Next Door *shows that most millionaires
don't fit that stereotype at all. Instead, they are hard-working,
hard-saving folks who literally live next door. Their secret, says co-
author Tom Stanley, is not so much earning a megasalary as it is
saving and not spending. For some lucky people, accumulating
wealth is second nature. Fortunately for the rest of us, Stanley says
it is behavior that can be learned.* FORTUNE's *Andrew Serwer
dropped by Tom Stanley's house in suburban Atlanta to chat with
him about his book and the millionaires next door.*

**So, Tom, it was F. Scott Fitzgerald who said the rich "are
different from you and me." Turns out that's true, but not
in the way most people think.**

That's right. They're different in ways that are hard to see. The rich
are like the guy I know who owns a pest-control company in
Miami. Or the guy who owns a heating and air-conditioning con-
tracting company. He's worth over $5 million. But he lives in a
$150,000 house and drives a pickup. He's different all right, in that
he has common tastes in terms of consumption, so you'd never
know he was rich. He's not throwing his money away on consumer goods that depreciate. Most rich people aren't like the doc-
tor who makes $300,000 a year and lives in a fancy neighborhood.
That person often has a lot of income, a lot of clothes, a lot of
house, a lot of car, but no real wealth—no money in the bank.

That's a key distinction you make: the difference between income and wealth. Explain.

There is a big difference, and most people don't recognize it. We are so focused on income in this country. But income is not wealth. Wealth is not income. You can't retire on income! Wealth is your assets less your liabilities.

You have that wonderful formula for determining how much wealth you should have.

Your expected wealth should be one-tenth your age times your annual household income. If you make $100,000 and you're 50, take one-tenth of 50, which is five, times $100,000, and you should be worth $500,000. I tell people to do the math on themselves.

If you have double, or more than double, the expected wealth threshold, you're a prodigious accumulator of wealth, or PAW. That's the category where you can retire and be very comfortable.

So in the previous example, you would need $1 million or more?

Yes. On the other hand, if you're 50 and make $100,000, and you have a net worth less than half the expected threshold, you're an under-accumulator of wealth, or UAW. So in this example, you would have $250,000 or less. These people are going to have a tough time retiring. UAWs are famous for stacking the balance sheet. They'll add in the value of their clothes, the value of their furniture, the value of their dog, the value of everything that has no value. What's interesting about PAWs, or millionaires, is that they consistently underestimate what they're worth.

What happens to the UAWs?

They have to keep working. Or they have what we call shock theater, where they live a lot worse off than they thought they would. It's not fun to see. On the other hand, if you're a PAW, you can live for years without ever earning a dollar. The typical millionaire can live somewhere between 12 and 16 years without earning a salary. If you have a big net worth and a relatively low income, you're going to have a wonderful time in retirement.

So what's the actual profile of the millionaire next door?
He's typically a male with a net worth of between $1 million and $5 million. He lives in a house valued at $278,000, which is not extravagant. He's self-employed or owns a business or is a partner in private business, maybe pest control, carpentry, or plumbing. High tech is overblown. The typical millionaire is frugal. He went to a public school. He inherited nothing. He's been married since his early or middle 20s. His wife is a housewife. They have three children. They drive a three-year-old car, usually American. The No. 1 car in the group is Ford, particularly the F150 pickup truck. The typical millionaire never spends more than $400 for a suit. He's more likely to be active in a trade association or affinity group related to improving his position than in a country club. He buys stocks. Rarely sells. It's an amazing group of people who mostly got rich in one generation.

What about entrepreneurs vs. corporate types?
Building wealth in America is directly a function of having equity in a business. It may be through owning stock in a public business, but more likely it's that you own your own business. Too often, executives at big companies think they're the company. In fact, they could be put away anytime. They rely too much on the pension plans, etc. Having said this, we do find many, many people who are employees of major companies becoming millionaires. But they took the initiative. They said to themselves, "Hey, I need to do these things: Save money, prepare, organize myself."

But being an entrepreneur goes against the grain.
Sure. In this country, corporate types have the status. Self-employed people have trouble getting health insurance. Wouldn't you rather go around and say, "I work for IBM," as opposed to saying, "Oh, I'm in the exterminating business, or a scrap metal dealer, or a port-a-john dealer?" But the most obscure businesses are the ones that very often produce wealthy people.

What are the biggest mistakes people make trying to become wealthy?
They spend too much. The problem is, Americans are the mar-

keting geniuses of the world. We have convinced people that if their incomes increase, they're superior beings. There's a ratchet effect. If you're a high school graduate, you should be driving a used Chevrolet; if you're a college graduate, a new Chevrolet; if you have an MBA, a BMW. As soon as we have an income change upward, we've been programmed to buy bigger houses and more expensive clothing.

So you're suggesting we don't buy things, which sounds depressingly frugal. Do you have to give up all the finer things in life to become rich?

No, not at all. I know a wonderful physician who's in his mid-50s. He's owned only two cars since he graduated from medical school. Both were Mercedes. Both were used. He said to me, "Tom, these are the finest cars in the world. They should last 200,000 miles, but I don't have to buy them new." The last time he went back to buy one, five years ago, they tried to sell him a new one. He said, "How much is the used one?"—which was three or four years old. It was $20,000 to $30,000 cheaper, so he asked himself if the pride of new ownership was worth $20,000. And he said, "Hell, no." He bought the used one. In fact, according to our surveys, 37% of millionaires buy used cars.

What real steps can people take to become wealthy?

Maximize your unrealized income. Let me explain. Realized income is reportable, taxable income. Unrealized income is when your wealth appreciates, but you don't take it in income. That's the key to becoming wealthy. For example, you might be buying stocks in companies that don't pay dividends. The problem with mutual funds is that every year they've got to declare a dividend, and you're going to pay tax on that. The wisest investors, and the majority of the millionaires we've interviewed, are people who own stocks directly and don't trade much. They're not taking capital gains. They're not taking dividends. They're building a portfolio. Other unrealized income might come from a business. You might have a factory or a company that's growing, and you're putting money back into it. You're not taking it as income, and the business becomes more and more valuable.

How big a salary do you need to become rich?

Most millionaires have realized income of under $100,000 a year. We've interviewed millionaires who make $60,000 a year. If the typical millionaire has a net worth in the $3 million to $4 million range, his total realized income—and that includes wages, salaries, commissions, capital gains, all reported taxable income—is something like 6% to 7% of his wealth.

What about taxes? How should people think about them?

Think about taxes in terms of your net worth, not your income. The typical household makes between $35,000 and $45,000 a year. It pays about 10% of that income in taxes. It just so happens that the typical household in America is also worth about $40,000. That means it's spending the equivalent of 10% of its wealth every year on taxes. Okay, now let's look at a millionaire who's worth $4 million. He made $200,000 last year, and he's in the 36% bracket, so he pays taxes of about $70,000. Now $70,000 as a percentage of $4 million ain't a lot of money; he's paying about 2% of his total wealth in taxes. A lot of people others might consider rich because they have big incomes spend 20% or 30% or 40% of their net worth every year on taxes. They are doing that because they don't have much net worth. They're what you call "big hat, no cattle." People should look at all their expenses—a new car, an education, a home—as a percentage of net worth rather than just income.

How much money should you give your kids?

First of all, there are different ways of giving money. One is education. Absolutely wonderful; 43% of millionaire grandparents pay for their grandchildren to go to private grammar schools and high schools. So education, fine. But you have to draw a line. A guy called me the other day. His son makes $30,000 a year. The son wants his father, who's worth $20 million, to buy him a $500,000 house. The father said to me, "Isn't a house a good idea?" Of course it's a good idea. That's not the problem. When you buy a house that costs $500,000, you've got to have a decorator. You've got to have it painted. You're going to live in a neighborhood where kids go to private schools.

But even worse than buying houses for your kids are indiscriminate cash gifts, or what we call economic outpatient care. That has a detrimental effect on the productivity of kids. People between the ages of 30 and 45 who have been given substantial cash gifts have significantly less income and drastically less net worth than kids who haven't gotten anything. What happens is, we end up subsidizing the weak. Let's say you have two kids. One is an entrepreneur. Kicks ass. Quits college. Spits in your face. Does really well. He gets nothing. You've got another kid who's an alcoholic. He's had two illegitimate children. He's had 14 car wrecks, he's been in drug rehab. He will need so much help that eventually he'll end up with the bulk of your estate.

This works against women, too. Say you've got a guy who's worth $10 million. He's got six children—three girls, three boys. He thinks the deck is stacked against the girls, so he gives them more, even the unproductive ones. This encourages them to do less. Forty-five percent of women in America who have incomes over $100,000 a year do not work for a living. I mean, this is astonishing. Why? Because they're getting economic outpatient care. Take it a step further: The daughter who is productive, who has the courage to start her own business, is not going to get a whole lot. But the sister who married poorly, who did poorly in school, and who's weak will get the bulk of the estate and squander it. This is why wealth changes hands over time.

So have you been able to turn yourself into a millionaire next door?

Yeah, I have, and it's really not a big deal. I think it's having basic values, not being extravagant, and having an accountant who's a wonderful financial planner. He encouraged me to start my pension plan 20 years ago. I thought he was crazy. But I struggled to put in $1,000 a month, and it's amazing how it's paid off.

HOW DOES YOUR NET WORTH STACK UP?

BY ANONYMOUS

▲▼▲

*You need to know this number, but
it can be hard to face squarely. A
FORTUNE staff writer bares all.*

▲▼▲

Four hundred fourteen thousand one hundred dollars. According to the formula in the bestselling *The Millionaire Next Door*, that's what I should be worth. I'm not optimistic. But when it comes to net worth, you have to face facts. It's an exercise in clarity—the first, unskippable step in devising a financial plan.

The math is easy: what you own minus what you owe. The difficult part is confronting the hard, cold results. I'm thinking of choices I made in my 20s and 30s that are costing me now, in my 40s: I'm happy, but am I rich? Assets, even hard ones, are shifty suckers, capable of monstrous deceptions. So are liabilities. Can't kid myself. Here goes:

▶ *House:*

Time was, just sitting in one long enough could make you rich. But nowadays, with inflation at rest, that's problematic. We closed on ours on St. Patrick's Day in 1995; paid $163,000. Immediately poured in $50,000 more. The plan is to fix the bathrooms and restore the facade to its 1842 Greek revival splendor, for which last month we refinanced and took out another $50,000. The appraiser's number was pretty thrilling: up 40% in 30 months. But that's not sustainable: Houses don't grow and then split in two. *Total: $265,000*

▶ *Car:*

Just one, thankfully, a 1997 Plymouth Voyager. Cost $19,022 new, 15 months ago. I checked the Kelly Blue Book on the Web, watched $5,217 vanish right before my eyes. New cars will do that. *Total: $13,805*

▶ **Bank accounts:**
Heading into the July 4 weekend, our checking account is minus
$192.53 and sinking. Not a problem, I say to my wife. That's what
overdraft protection is for. We're over, we're under—as long as the
next paycheck puts us back in the black, I don't think about it.
Besides, over in savings we're flush: $5,237.51, which should be
working harder for us, I know, but then we'd lose free checking.
Total: $5,045

▶ **Brokerage accounts:**
The first stock I ever bought was Agnico Eagle Mines, 80 shares
at $8\,^{15}/_{16}$, recommended by my wife's grandfather. Fourteen years
later my portfolio consists of those same 80 shares plus 150 more
I bought in February for no good reason at $6^{1}/_{8}$. Since then it's
down 50 cents. So my stake's worth, uh, $1,293.75, proving that
even a rising tide won't lift a boat with a damn hole in it.

What else? Let's see, $6,866.89 in a money market fund, wait-
ing for a good idea. And $48,849.46, the net proceeds from the
house refinancing, waiting for my contractor.
Total: $57,010

▶ **Retirement accounts:**
Like houses used to be: net-worth igniters. Tax deferred, self-
feeding, and inaccessible. But tax bills loom. And just because I
can't get at my money doesn't mean it's safe. My IRAs, Keoghs,
and 401(k)s—like your stock options, if you're so lucky—may
look great today, but tomorrow, who knows?

So what do I have? My ancient IRA, unfed for many years; my
wife's; a dormant 401(k); and my new Time Inc. 401(k). Those
come to $73,991.71. Now for the Keoghs. Ugh, this is hard. Keoghs
let you put away as much as 25% of your nonsalary income, tax
deferred; a blessing for anyone who runs a profitable business on
the side, which, for several highflying years in the mid-1990s, I did.

Okay, so it's April 1995, and I've got two new Keoghs. For the
first I choose a Fidelity fund. It has since grown smartly. For the
second I buy nitroglycerin, specially packaged for household use
and sold as the Fidelity Emerging Markets fund. As my business
grows, I keep buying. All over Asia, banks are failing, currencies

are going to hell, soldiers are battling mobs, and I'm voting yes with my pocketbook. No, I can't tell you why. The really painful part is knowing that I lost a piece of my soul along with my shirt. Why do I invest in states run by dictators? I put in $20,872.51. I've got $11,800.33 left. Serves me right.
Total: $111,446

▶ *Household possessions.*

I asked my mother-in-law, who deals in antiques, to put a price on everything we own—a key step, but one where many of us stumble. Forget retail. Think what your stuff would bring if you had to sell it all tomorrow.

Antiques? The cherry dining room table with chairs, $3,200; the mahogany Morris chair restored by my father-in-law, $600; and so on. My violin, $5,000. My wife's jewelry, $3,000 (including the Cartier rolling ring, symbol of our Year of Living Opulently, 1995). Add $2,000 for our clothes, $200 for Beanie Babies, and total it up: $39,520. But that's retail. An auctioneer might give us 50%.

On the things we bought new, she says, figure 25 cents on the dollar. Comes to $1,812.50. The CDs and vinyl? I'll say $250, net. My ticket to game two of the 1964 World Series at Connie Mack Stadium (never played)? Probably worthless; I checked. Our bichon? Priceless (but maybe we won't spay her after all).
Total: $21,823

TOTAL ASSETS: $474,129

Now for the liabilities.

▶ *Mortgage:*

"Borrower owes Lender the principal sum of One Hundred Eighty Thousand and 00/100 Dollars." By the time I'm done on July 1, 2028, I'll have spent half a million dollars. Enough said.
Total: $180,000

▶ *Home equity loan:*

I'm not saying this is my only fun, but sometimes, after the kids are in bed, I'll fire up Quicken and play with my accounts. I don't

WHAT ARE YOU WORTH REALLY?

▲▼▲

If you had to liquidate your assets today, how much would you have? Don't forget to subtract taxes and penalties.

House value(s) $_____
(minus mortgage and realty fees)

401(k) $_____
IRA $_____
Keogh $_____
TOTAL $_____ (minus taxes and penalties) $_____

Cars (value minus loans) $_____

Bank accounts $_____

Stock options (market value) $_____ (minus taxes) $_____

Investments (minus taxes) $_____

Pension (lump-sum value minus taxes and penalties) $_____

Odds and ends (antiques, art, jewelry, etc.) $_____

Subtotal $_____

Minus other debts $_____
(credit cards, equity line, outstanding bills)

I'M WORTH $_____

mind balancing the checkbook or even paying bills. At the end of the evening, I'm secure in the knowledge that my Affairs are in Order.

I used to bring my wife printouts showing how much money we were socking away. She was never impressed. Somehow she knew it wasn't real. She was right. Last year we got hit with a monster tax bill (I goofed), plus a sudden need for thousands to fund our Keoghs (or pay more tax). That's when the Blazer started making a funny noise. We cleaned out the money market fund, cashed in my life insurance, delayed filing—and still it wasn't nearly enough. Time for a home equity loan.

Then, last fall, my wife called me at the office, near tears. No, not an affair. It was about her credit cards. She hadn't paid them off after all. Hadn't quit using them, either. Now she wanted to come clean. I was incredibly understanding about the whole thing. "That's okay," I said. "We'll just add it to the home equity loan."

Total: $9,069

▶ *Credit cards:*

Now I guess I have no choice. Me, too, sweetheart. The Visa card. I don't know how it happened. You forgive me, don't you?

Total: $962

TOTAL LIABILITIES: $190,031

NET WORTH: $284,098

GETTING THE MOST OUT OF YOUR PENSION

▲▼▲

Mark your calendar: The day you qualify for early retirement, the value of your pension could go through the roof.

▲▼▲

If you gave more than a moment's thought to your pension last year, you either (a) care more about actuarial science than the average salaryman, or (b) have way too much time on your hands. We're talking here about the old-fashioned defined-benefit pension, the one that paid your father a check a month in retirement and that is promising to do the same for a new generation of employees today. Four out of five large corporations still offer them, and they mean it: Today's pension promises are backed by more than $1.9 trillion held in pension trust funds, according to the research firm Spectrem Group. That's almost twice as much as in all 401(k)s.

But that's not why you might want to focus a tad more on your pension. The reason is that if you are within shouting distance of qualifying for early retirement, this boring, misunderstood asset may offer the highest potential return of any investment you own—more than your house, more than your 401(k), more than your company's stock, more than your personal portfolio.

Once you reach the combination of age and years of service that your plan defines as the threshold for early retirement, the typical pension metamorphoses from a vague promise into what is essentially a richly leveraged option on your career longevity. The day you qualify for an early out, the potential lump-sum value of your benefit could literally double—creating what could be the single best-paid day of your career. From that moment until you reach the standard retirement age of 60 or 65, the value of your pension continues to grow at an accelerated pace, whether the stock market goes up, down, or sideways. "Pensions are like a crazy relative in the attic," says William Arnone, Ernst

& Young's national director for employment and financial education. "You're vaguely aware it's there, but you never think about what it's worth until you need it."

Don't start counting your pension checks yet, though. Odd as it may sound, your pension is probably also your riskiest asset. This has nothing to do with market fluctuations (in a pension, your employer bears those risks, not you) and everything to do with the typical plan's complicated, back-loaded design. Anything that interrupts your service with your current employer, from job hopping to early retirement (voluntary or involuntary), can have a devastating effect on your pension's growth path. So can any corporate action that affects your plan, such as a merger that folds your plan into an acquirer's benefit package or a conversion of your old pension into any other kind of retirement plan.

True, a pension doesn't require as much hands-on attention as, say, a 401(k). Relics of a more paternalistic era in employee relations, pensions are designed to reward long, loyal service; to earn one, you don't have to do much more than hold on to your job. But that doesn't mean you can afford to ignore your pension. It's quite possible, for example, to blow benefits that are almost within your grasp through some rash or uninformed move (like, say, storming in to your boss and quitting the day before you qualify for early retirement). "The best advice is to make the effort to understand your plan," says Andy Stratton, a principal at the benefits consulting firm Buck Consultants. "You may discover it's worth more than you thought." (Or could be soon.) Better yet, you'll learn what you can do to keep it on track.

In the most common form of the traditional pension, the size of your eventual benefit depends on your age at retirement, how much you earn, how long you work at your company, and the benefit formula built into the plan. A typical formula calculates the size of your benefit by multiplying a percentage (1% to 2%, say) of your final pay—or more precisely, of the average of your last three to five years' pay—by the number of years you worked for the firm. Regardless of when you actually leave work, you can't start collecting that benefit until you reach the plan's standard retirement age, typically 60 to 65, unless you qualify for early retirement. That's usually decided by some combination of

HOW DOES YOUR PENSION GROW?

▲▼▲

Hardly at all until you reach early-retirement age. If the hypothetical worker in the chart below were to leave the company at age 50, his pension would be worth less than a third as much as if he'd stayed to 55.

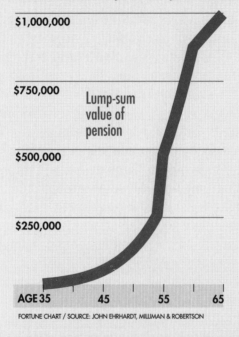

$1,000,000

$750,000   Lump-sum value of pension

$500,000

$250,000

AGE 35   45   55   65

FORTUNE CHART / SOURCE: JOHN EHRHARDT, MILLIMAN & ROBERTSON

age and years of service. You might be in line for early retirement at the tender age of 50 if you're a longtime employee.

What really kicks in the afterburners is the fact that most companies subsidize pensions for early retirees. In other words, to help you afford to leave before age 65, your employer probably credits you with a larger benefit than you'd deserve if actuarial assumptions were strictly applied. Actuaries call this transition point—the point at which your pension benefits take off—the "cliff." If you're almost at that point in your career with your company, it's worth sticking around for. Just showing up to work the morning you qualify for early retirement could boost the lump-sum value of your pension by 100% or more of a year's salary. A couple of things can get in the way of this pleasant scenario, however. First of all, you can blow the whole scheme by leaving your job in the middle of your pension's meteoric accumulation phase or (even worse) right before the phase begins. So get a copy of your pension's summary plan description from your plan's administrator, and find out what the early retirement rules are. (Or just ask the administrator to explain them.) Don't squander your pension out of ignorance.

This is not to say that you should hold on to a dead-end job solely to let your pension accrue. However, if you do decide it's time to move on, know what you're forgoing in pension benefits and make sure you're fairly paid for it. "If one of my clients is changing jobs, I'll figure out the present value of his pension, along with options and bonuses he otherwise could expect to get," says Paul Westbrook, a Ridgewood, N.J., retirement planner. "Then, in negotiations with his new employer he can say, 'Look at everything you're asking me to give up for you.'"

Another reason to get familiar with your plan is that it will help you recognize the effect that changes imposed by your employer can have on your pension's growth. Remember, the employer owns the pension. As long as the company doesn't disturb the benefits you've already earned, it is completely within its rights to "amend" the plan in ways that will lower benefits you might earn in the future. Scrooge-like amendments do happen. In 1991, for example, Thiokol (now Cordant Technologies) raised the normal retirement age in its pension formula from 65 to 67.

Your company may also try to switch you from the traditional final-pay pension model to what's called a cash-balance pension, a plan that blends features of traditional pensions and 401(k)s. In a cash-balance plan, the company makes annual contributions to an account in your name, so that you get periodic statements. Employers like the greater predictability that cash-balance plans offer, and employees, especially younger ones, like the fact that benefits grow faster in the early stages of a career than they do with traditional plans.

But if you're at or near early retirement in a traditional pension, your company does you no favor by converting to a cash-balance plan. The latter's steady growth simply can't match the traditional pension's soaring benefit growth at this stage. So if your plan converts to a cash-balance plan and you have a choice of retaining the old plan, figure out where you are in your traditional plan's growth curve and consider standing pat.

More frequently than they'd like to admit, companies can also shortchange pensioners purely by accident. Benefit formulas tend to be complicated to begin with and are subject to more than their share of absurdly tangled tax rules. Not surprisingly, companies do goof in calculating benefits. Allen Engerman, president of the National Center for Retirement Benefits (NCRB) in Northbrook, Ill., says roughly a third of the payouts that pensioners hire his firm to review are in error. (One caveat about that figure: NCRB is a for-profit firm that helps employees check the accuracy of retirement benefits they receive, in return for contingency fees of up to half the money the firm recovers for its clients; obviously it's not in the business of underestimating the incidence of pension errors.) Continental Airlines, GTE, MCI, and Tyson Foods, to name a few, have all had to make good on honest errors in recent years.

It may be particularly wise to check your employer's math if your pension plan undergoes any fundamental change, such as converting to a cash-balance pension (without giving you a choice of staying with your final pay plan) or any other type of retirement plan. You want to make sure you get full credit for the benefits you've already earned. "Anytime there's a plan merger, a plan termination, or a conversion from one kind of defined-benefit plan to another, a host of potential problems confront employees," says Jeffrey Lewis, an Oakland attorney specializing in pension cases.

Obviously, you won't be able to check for errors yourself. You'll need to bring in an experienced actuary (figure on $100 to $200 a hour) or a contingency firm like NCRB. (Its toll-free number is 800-666-1000.) But at least there is one error you won't make anymore: You won't underestimate the value of keeping an eye on your pension.

PLAYING RETIREMENT'S WILD CARDS

▲▼▲

*Later life can be full of surprises,
from escalating taxes and mind-
boggling health bills to great new
job opportunities. Here are some
winning ways to play your hand.*

▲▼▲

GET SMART ABOUT TAXES

▼

After countless hours coping with crowded commutes, budget grinds, and bosses with personality disorders, you're about to be set free. Ahead lie plenty of power lunches with grandkids, afternoons at the beach, and an ever-improving handicap on the links.

But be warned that there is a wild card out there that threatens such blissful liberation, and it's been dealt by Uncle Sam. A basic fact most people forget when they enter retirement is that the IRS is waiting to collect its dues. It's not just the normal tax take that you have to worry about, but the real possibility that your tax rate could actually rise once you retire.

This unhappy state of affairs results from no secret clause in the tax code, just the simple unwinding of years of tax-deferred saving. Do the math yourself: Take all those marvelous tax breaks that encouraged you to sock it away over the years—IRAs, 401(k)s, 403Bs, SEPs, the works—and throw them into reverse. Even if you don't need that money in retirement, the government insists that you start withdrawing it in large chunks beginning at age 70$\frac{1}{2}$. Then add on to those sums any pension you receive from your employer, as well as income from Social Security. When those taxable sources of income are tallied, you may well find yourself with a much bigger tax bill than when you were in midcareer.

The reason is not just the artificial swell in your income, but the fact that you will no longer have mounds of deductions to offset it. Consider: By the time you retire, your mortgage will most likely be paid off, so you'll lose the biggest single tax reducer of all. You will also be without standard exemptions for dependents, since the kids will probably have moved on. Sure, you'll still have property taxes, and in some places that's a handsome deduction, but that won't be enough to offset your tax-deferred savings. Result: a painful outflow of cash to the IRS.

Think it can't happen to you? Think again. Let's say you and your spouse don't touch your IRAs until age $70^{1}/_{2}$, when it becomes mandatory, and by then they've grown to more than $1 million (even if you didn't contribute much to your IRA, you may well wind up stashing your lump-sum pension payment in one). If you use the term-certain method of distribution with a joint life expectancy of 20.6 years, that first year you're going to get $48,543 in distributions from your IRA (and let's not forget Social Security), on which you owe income tax. By now your good old deductions have pretty much dried up as well. Say hello to a 28% tax bracket, or if your total income tops $100,000, even higher brackets—up to 40%.

Before you start packing for one of those Caribbean tax havens, there's at least one simple move you can make to keep your tax bill in check—stay leveraged. Maybe you don't need a mortgage on your home anymore, but that doesn't mean you shouldn't have one.

Beyond such bold strokes, you'll probably need the advice of a sophisticated planner or tax adviser. That was the conclusion of Shirley and George Waring of Long Island, who faced the IRA problem when they retired about ten years ago. A hard-working couple all their lives, the Warings had saved faithfully and invested wisely, accumulating a sizable sum in their IRAs. But as they neared the mandatory withdrawal age, they suddenly realized how vulnerable they were on the tax front: "We own our house, the family business, and all of the business' buildings. Other than some property taxes, we didn't have any big deductions," sighs Mrs. Waring. Faced with an abrupt rise in their tax bill, the Warings quickly enlisted help.

"Their tax bracket would have gone through the roof," concurs Seymour Goldberg, the Warings' tax attorney in Garden City,

N.Y. Fortunately, Goldberg had a partial solution—the Warings should use their IRA money to establish trusts for their two grandchildren. Such a move would change the distribution schedule on the IRA from one that was based on the Warings' ages to a schedule that took into account the life expectancies of the grandchildren as well. So if the original life expectancy was 20.6 years for the couple at 70½, it was now 26.2 years, according to a complex IRS formula. Going back to the $1 million IRA example, under this distribution method, $38,167 would be paid out the first year, significantly less than the $48,543 under the other method. Also, as long as the IRA money that's earmarked for the trust is less than $1 million upon the surviving Waring's death, the generation-skipping tax (55%) can be avoided.

Many other tax-reducing moves are simpler. A schoolteacher for more than 30 years, Teresa Latorre, 65, of Hamden, Conn., had invested conservatively in annuities that were ready to be rolled into IRAs or cashed out when she retired. Since retiring five years ago, Latorre has been taking out modest sums from her IRAs, which, along with a payout package from the last school at which she taught, kept her in the 28% tax bracket. "I didn't want to go above that bracket," Latorre says. But that happy circumstance was threatened as she approached 70½. Therefore, with the help of her niece, Mary Ellen Gordon, a financial planner at Aetna Financial Services in Hartford, Latorre converted about 20% of what she held in regular IRAs into the new Roth IRA, which doesn't have a mandatory withdrawal date. "She just didn't think she'd have to tap into the money at 70½," says Gordon. "Now that money can grow tax-free, so her heirs will get a much larger chunk of money than they would have."

Take note that if you convert your existing IRA to a Roth IRA, you're going to have to pay the income taxes on the earnings that have accumulated. But if the conversion occurs in 1998, those taxes can be spread equally over four years. That's great, but also be aware of a few caveats, because the Roth IRA is by no means for everyone. First, if your adjusted gross income is more than $100,000 a year, you can't do it. Period. Also, the money to pay the taxes should come from outside the IRA, or you'll lose much of the benefit of conversion.

THE TAX WILD CARD

▲▼▲

Uncle Sam can deal older couples a nasty tax card. Income from IRAs that has never been taxed, and the lack of big deductions, can result in bigger taxes than those for younger couples of equal income.

COUPLE IN THEIR 50s		COUPLE IN THEIR 70s	
INCOME		**INCOME**	
Wages	$100,000	Corporate pension	$30,000
		Mandatory IRA withdrawal	$55,000
		Social Security (both)	$12,750
TOTAL INCOME	**$100,000**	**TOTAL INCOME**	**$97,750**
DEDUCTIONS		**DEDUCTIONS**	
Personal exemptions	$10,800	Personal exemptions	$5,400
Property taxes	$7,000	Property taxes	$7,000
Interest on mortgage	$15,000		
State taxes	$4,412	State taxes	$4,138
TAXABLE INCOME	$62,788	TAXABLE INCOME	$81,212
TOTAL FEDERAL TAXES	$12,075	TOTAL FEDERAL TAXES	$17,234

FORTUNE CHART / SOURCE: PRICEWATERHOUSECOOPERS

But if the Roth IRA does fit your needs, it can mean a big difference in income later in life. Let's say an investor who's 57 and has an adjusted gross income of less than $100,000 decides to convert $100,000 from a regular IRA to a Roth. Assuming an 8% annual return, a 28% federal income tax rate, and a 6% state tax rate, the Roth IRA can mean the difference between having $277,000 after taxes in 20 years and having $249,000 after taxes. Which would you prefer?

One tax problem that is buffeting retirees with increasing frequency is something akin to a success tax, because it's a byproduct of the bull market. Say the bulk of your 401(k) is in your company's stock when you retire, increasingly the case these days. Worth merely nickels and dimes when you received it 30 years ago, it's now valued at hundreds of thousands, perhaps millions. If you roll the stock into an IRA when you retire, you're going to end up taking a big income-tax hit later. But if you take a lump-sum payout at retirement, there's an often ignored way to pay the lower capital-gains rate on the bulk of the stock, says Howard Averbach, a fee-only financial planner and attorney in Pittsburgh. "The employee can take possession of the corporation's stock from the retirement plan at retirement and pay ordinary income tax only on the value of the stock when it was contributed to the plan, not at the current value," explains Averbach. When the stock is eventually sold, the proceeds will be taxed at the lower capital-gains rate.

Once you've figured out how much you'll have going into retirement—and how much you'll probably need—it makes sense to start doing some estate planning. One of the biggest mistakes people make is arranging to give after they're gone, when estate taxes are levied, as opposed to while they're alive, when taxes can be deducted from their estate. "The maximum estate tax is 55%, which is very painful," says Diahann W. Lassus, a financial planner in New Providence, N.J. "But it's a sliding scale. The more money you have, the higher percentage of tax your beneficiaries will pay. The lower the dollars, the lower the tax liability on your estate." Bottom line: Give generously while you're alive.

If you're charitably inclined, a way to have your cake and eat it too might be to set up a charitable remainder trust. Into this you can put your IRA or any other asset that has appreciated greatly and on which you probably owe income or capital-gains tax, and earmark it for a charity of your choosing. But you can also spin off 5% or more annually to yourself and your spouse for your life-time. "If a person wants to leave $500,000 to Princeton and he's got stock in Microsoft that he bought for $10 and it's now worth $500,000, he can put it in a charitable trust and pay himself and his wife a taxable 9% a year," says William D. Zabel, a partner at the New York–based law firm Schulte Roth & Zabel. "They increase their income, avoid the large capital-gains tax they would have incurred had they sold the stock outright, get an immediate income-tax deduction figured on the value of what Princeton will get when they pass away, and Princeton gets the money." That looks good from all angles.

—JULIE CRESWELL

A HEALTH PLAN TO LOWER RISK

Researchers at the National Institutes of Health in Bethesda, Md., announced earlier this year that in about a decade they would finish mapping virtually every human gene. At that point, effective treatments may start to materialize for diseases ranging from genetic cancer to arthritis. Consequently, the quantum leaps in life expectancies that we've seen in the 20th century may continue into the 21st century.

Yet even such impressive strides in medicine cannot erase the one indelible fact of our later years: In retirement, your health is on the downward side of the slope, so it is likely to consume a higher share of your income than it does now. Health will also become an ever more important issue in where—and how—you choose to live.

Fortunately, there is plenty of help to enable you to meet those challenges, from Medigap insurance policies that bridge the difference between doctors' bills and Medicare payments, to ever-improving long-term-care policies, to new communities that are designed to adapt to changes in your health.

The important step you need to take now is to plan. Not only are health-care costs rising, but today's generation of retirees is paying a much larger share of the tab than their parents did. If you had entered a nursing home several decades ago, for example, the government through Medicare and Medicaid would have paid most of the cost. Now Medicare pays full benefits for only the first 20 days in a Medicare-approved facility and scales back to zero after 100 days, reimbursing only 4% of the nation's long-term-care expenses. "Soaring out-of-pocket medical costs among older Americans is one reason the savings rate has fallen so low in the 1990s," says Stephen Roach, chief economist at Morgan Stanley Dean Witter. "The trend shows no signs of slowing down."

To keep those trends from robbing your retirement, take charge of the possibilities. Self-empowerment was exactly why Rhoda Scheiner, a 68-year-old retired bookkeeper in Bayside, N.Y., decided in early July to purchase a long-term-care insurance policy. A variant of disability insurance for retirees, these policies provide substantial benefits in the event that purchasers require home care or must move into a nursing home. To trigger benefits from most policies, you must demonstrate that you are unable to perform at least two in a list of five or six activities of daily living, such as bathing, eating, and getting in and out of bed. In other words, as you rev down, these policies rev up.

Scheiner admits to being confused about whether to purchase the insurance, a Travelers policy with annual premiums costing her about $2,500, but she concluded she'd rather be safe than sorry. "I have children, and I wouldn't want to be a problem," she explains. "The greatest pleasure would be if I don't need it."

That's one reason that long-term-care insurance, which typically starts paying full benefits after two or three months of home or institutional care, has emerged as the fastest-growing type of insurance in the U.S. When these policies were introduced in the 1970s, most paid benefits only if the insured entered a nursing home. Over the past two decades, most insurers have liberalized benefits to cover home care.

Several important questions: First and most important, would an extended stay in a nursing home devastate your savings? If you're under 50, you're probably too young to have thought about it. But if you're older, it's worth asking. You should also look beyond your own family's genes and consider some statistics: A retiree has a 43% probability (52% for females and 33% for males) of entering a nursing home, according to *The New England Journal of Medicine*. Data on home-care usage are all over the map, but experts generally agree that retirees have a 55% to 65% chance of requiring such services.

You have two ways to play those odds: Purchase a long-term-care policy, or set aside sufficient funds to cover all late-life possibilities. Choose the latter, and you'll have to set aside considerably more than if you had just gone out and bought the policy, assuming that you want enough savings to cover one year in a nursing home. If you never require long-term care, of course, you win. But is that a risk you're comfortable taking?

For most new retirees, here-and-now health insurance is a more immediate concern than long-term care. Many government and private-sector employees can take some coverage with them, but those policies should be checked to see how they dovetail with Medicare. To cover the expenses that neither Medicare nor former employers' insurance picks up, there's Medigap, which comes in ten different policy types ranging from A (the most basic) to J (comprehensive). While Medigap benefits are standardized, insurance premiums can vary by as much as 100% within the same state. It's worth shopping around, though purchasing a reasonably priced policy from an established company often is wiser than going for the cheapest policy. For retirees with modest incomes, Medicare HMOs are another option.

Oldsters today are hiking and· playing tennis and golf into their 80s, and baby-boomers are likely to be even more active when they reach retirement. But those little knee sprains you got jogging in your 40s could become torn ligaments in your 80s, so it's important to retire near first-rate medical facilities, particularly if you live far from family members.

To meet the living needs of retirees, a variety of retirement communities are being designed for disparate lifestyles. One can enter an assisted-living facility as an independent person and move into an onsite nursing home eventually. One appeal of these setups is the ongoing diversity. "Couples with different needs can live down the hall from each other," explains Meredith Beit Patterson, an elder-care consultant in Concord, Mass. Marriott International and Holiday Corp. are among the biggest players in this field. Even more traditional retirement communities, like those built by Del Webb and U.S. Home and designed primarily for active living, offer a nod to the changing needs of retirees. For example, most are single-story homes with wide doors (to accommodate walkers) and convenient electrical outlets. A few even have onsite medical- and convalescent-care facilities.

Continuing-care retirement communities, which ensure all stages of late-life care, may charge high entry fees ranging from $60,000 to $300,000, but those fees are often treated like the bonds you might put up to join a club—up to 90% ultimately returns to your estate. Also, these communities may charge monthly fees of between $1,500 and $5,000 in return for services. As yet, there is no uniform policy defining what aspects of assisted living a long-term-care insurance policy will cover, so it's important to check the terms of coverage before buying a particular policy.   —Evan Simonoff

HIS PAYCHECK IS HIS PEP PILL

We keep, all of us, a mental calendar of our lives: We know when we're in our spring, we know when autumn approaches. But all of a sudden that calendar is out of whack. Summer lasts far longer than it used to; the fall is gentler. Plan your life by the old schedule, and you'll put up storm windows on your life long before the first snow.

—Bill McKibben, *Maybe One: A Personal and*
Environmental Argument for Single-Child Families

Bill McKibben is an essayist and a nature writer. He comes to the subject of retirement indirectly, by way of hoping to persuade more of us to be content with having fewer babies. The overburdened planet would be grateful, yes, but what about the overburdened Social Security system? Aren't we going to need those extra workers to support us in our old age? Maybe not, is McKibben's provocative point, not when so many of us are living longer and choosing to work beyond 62, or 65, or whatever people mean nowadays by the phrase "normal retirement age."

For most of the postwar era, the average retirement age was falling. But the latest data show something altogether new developing. "It's very clear that somewhere around 1985, the downward trend ceased and leveled off," says the Wharton School's Olivia Mitchell. Joseph Quinn of Boston College goes one step further: He believes that the average retirement age may already be creeping back up, reversing a decades-old trend.

The contributing factors are many. They include the outlawing of mandatory retirement; changes in Social Security that have reduced the actuarial penalty for choosing to work longer (and will soon eliminate it altogether); and the decline of traditional defined-benefit pension plans, most of which have built-in disincentives for staying on the job, in favor of 401(k) plans, which are age-neutral.

There may be a generational factor as well, just now coming into play as the leading wave of baby-boomers tumbles toward retirement. A lot of them are people for whom work counts as living. They chose their careers deliberately. For many of them there appears to be a new version of retirement, one in which they keep their career jobs longer than they have to and never really retire but ease into a transitional stage labor economists call a bridge job.

Using the latest data from the National Institute on Aging's far-reaching Health and Retirement Study, Professor Quinn found that about one-third of men and two-thirds of women who were not working at the time of the survey had last worked in some version of a bridge job. Among his conclusions: "The importance of gradual retirement is likely to increase in the future."

Think about what that means. It may be, first of all, that instead of the usual three sources of retirement income—pension, savings, and Social Security—you'll want to consider the possibility of having four, and structure your retirement savings accordingly. "Historically, stocks have outperformed bonds," says Barry Shapiro, a financial consultant in New York. "If you think you'll still be working anyway and won't need the income, you can position more of your portfolio toward growth."

Second, what kind of work do you have in mind? Do you want to stick with what you're doing, or try something new? Do you have enough contacts to branch out? Do you have the right skills? Is income the key variable, or job satisfaction, or family time? Is it really a new job you're looking for, or a freelance gig, or a chance to start your own business? In short, are you ready for this?

John McMorrow spent 31 years in human resources at AT&T, working his way up to vice president for education and training. While still in his 40s, McMorrow began assembling his bridge job. He wanted exposure to a broad range of companies; that got him thinking about consulting. He knew he didn't want to spend all his time selling; that nudged him toward joining a firm rather than going independent. And he and his wife were sure they didn't want to stay in New Jersey, so they began choosing vacation spots with an eye toward scouting new places to live. At 58, their children grown, the McMorrows took an early-retirement package and moved to Bozeman, Mont. Today John is CEO of Talent Alliance, a not-for-profit consortium funded by 13 companies (including AT&T). It has a program called Bridges that helps displaced workers and retirees learn new skills and pursue second careers. For potential bridge jobbers like himself, McMorrow offers these four issues to think about.

▶ *Balance:* "When we were younger," says McMorrow, who's 60 now, "we were trying to balance money, time, and health, and we often had to sacrifice time and health for money. As we become older, we can reassess that equation."

▶ *Networking:* Keep up with friends, acquaintances, and business contacts. McMorrow says about three-quarters of all job vacancies are filled informally, through networking.

▶ *Support:* "Family, friends, fitness, and faith. If you're going through transitions, you'd better be sound in those areas, because they're the support mechanisms."

▶ *Leverage:* Have fun, be creative, try something new. But consider leveraging skills you already possess. "Generally, engineers don't become bakers," he says.

McMorrow has an elder soul mate in Dave Cooley, 69, who stepped down three years ago as president of the Memphis Chamber of Commerce. For nearly half a century, almost everywhere he lived, Cooley was the Chamber Man; it's how folks knew him and how he knew himself. Cooley's career was a working life spent always at the center of things, "involved," he says, "in community issues and things that affect more than just me." But by 1995, the time had come to wrap things up. He could see that himself, without waiting to be told.

So Cooley went home to Hendersonville, N.C., the little mountain town where he was born, transformed after all these years into a retirement mecca. Income from Social Security checks totaled $184 million in Henderson County last year, second to the combined payroll of all the county's manufacturers. The Catholics are building a roomy new sanctuary, and the Methodists are adding on, the state is widening the roads, and developers are planting vast stands of townhouses on what used to be lonely Appalachian hilltops. The newest invaders are members of the tribe known locally as Halfbacks: Northerners who moved to Florida, missed the change of seasons, and went halfway back.

Cooley has acquaintances among the idle Halfbacks. And sometimes he joins his townie friends for coffee at the old Justus Pharmacy on Main Street, now known as Days Gone By. He has a library card, a membership at the Y, and an abiding interest in Abraham Lincoln. He drives around with a bag of golf clubs in the trunk of his BMW, just in case. But all that's just noise. The melody of Cooley's life, even now, is real work for real pay.

Cooley is first of all a consultant to Towery Publishing, a Memphis company that publishes directories for local chambers of commerce. He mans the Towery booth at trade shows, takes clients to dinner, and generally spreads the good word among his wide circle of professional contacts, cultivated over a lifetime. "And for that I get a modest fee," says Cooley. "Plus I get an opportunity to hook up with my old buddies at meetings on somebody else's nickel."

Cooley also does accreditation reviews for the U.S. Chamber of Commerce, which take him to cities and towns all over the country. ("I meet new people and hopefully help them do something a little bit better because I suggested it to them.") He and his daughter-in-law have a deal going with the American Osteopathic Association, which wants to build a viable chapter in North Carolina; Cooley knows something about how to do that, having spent several years in Washington, D.C., as head of the American Chamber of Commerce Executives. And most thrilling for him, he travels the globe for CIPE, the Center for International Private Enterprise, promoting the American way in developing countries.

For all that, Cooley insists he's not busting his hump. He may work 40 hours one week, ten the next, and zero the week after that. "When I get up each morning," he says in his singsong Carolina lilt, "I know I don't have to do anything if I really don't want to do it." Most of the money that touches his hands doesn't stick; it's just for expenses. Until he's 70, he can't earn more than $13,500 a year anyway, not without cutting into Social Security. But for Cooley, even that little bit of extra income is key. It's been the difference, so far, between tapping his retirement nest egg for living expenses and just letting it grow.

Cooley's business partner—the other half of Coo-Coo Enterprises—is his kid brother, Art, 63, who owns and manages the local AM radio station, WHKP ("where the heavens kiss the peaks"). On a hot day in July, Dave and a visitor stopped by Art's office for a chat.

"The people who are retired have to have somewhere to go," Art was saying. "So Mama prepares this big list of honey-do projects, and they do a few of them and get tired, and they go out to the mall and walk around and sit down on them benches and watch people go by."

"Get 'em an ice-cream cone in the middle of the day!" Dave said.

"Yeah. And you have people all over town doing this. Not only in the mall, but they go downtown—nice downtown area— sit on benches. But they're looking for something to while away their time."

"Uh-huh."

"Because time is heavy on one's hands in retirement years." The Cooley brothers lingered for a few minutes more. Then Dave stood up and glanced at his watch. He had things to do, places to be.

—DAVID WHITFORD

CHAPTER SIX

▲▼▲

HOT STUFF IN THE
DIGITAL WORLD

FOUR FORCES THAT WILL SHAPE THE INTERNET

BY ANDREW KUPFER

▲▼▲

*The Net's supposed to melt
hierarchies, leap borders, and
create free information and
communication. It won't do all
that. But in the next five years, the
reality will be more interesting than
the dream.*

▲▼▲

One of the virtues of a virtual place is that it can be whatever you want it to be. For much of its history, that was the charm of the Internet—a cross between a swimming hole and a cosmological worm hole, a secret place where nerds, geeks, and others in the know could gather, and then, collapsing time and distance, travel anywhere in the world, often to the electronic inner sanctums of institutions that would have turned them away had they shown up in person and knocked on the door.

Everyone was equal on the Net. It operated outside the tariffs and rules that governed the rest of telecommunications, even as the Net became the Web and commercial interests began to encroach on it, and Web addresses appeared on magazine covers and movie ads and business cards. The Net took hold of the popular imagination as a way both to connect with others and to hide behind a screen of anonymity. Outsiders became insiders, and they did it almost free.

The Net is now morphing from ad hoc grassroots semi-anarchy to mainstream big-money commerce. With data communications exploding and about to dwarf the volume of ordinary phone calls, the Internet's language—Internet protocol, or IP—is becoming a lingua franca for torrents of digital information: computer files, video, and voice. Huge industries are remaking themselves as this transformation gains momentum—the $700-billion-a-year telecommunications industry, which the Net threatens with irrelevance, and the $1 trillion computer industry, which sees the Net as its best hope for growth.

The furious pace of change means that many things people have been expecting from the Net are about to happen within the next five years. Thanks to the example of companies such as smooth-as-silk Amazon.com, electronic commerce is accelerating toward widespread acceptance. Businesses are beginning to see the Internet as essential to their operations: Networking giant Cisco Systems, to cite a dramatic example, no longer does business with suppliers that can't fill orders via the Web. And new technologies are already helping the Net insinuate itself into everyday life. Grainy and herky-jerky though the video images may be, a Website operated by the city of Las Vegas posts live feeds from highway surveillance cameras to help drivers to plan their morning commute.

The bulk of traffic growth on the Net will come from transactions between computers—unmediated by any human. Devices such as boxes atop the television set, palm computers, pagers, cell phones, and perhaps even wearable computers will depend on data automatically transmitted via the Net.

This buzzing undercurrent of data is already baffling institutions accustomed to managing the flow of information, knowledge, and money. Antitrust regulators on two continents are groping to figure out whether the far-flung facilities of WorldCom and the potent software of Microsoft give them market-crushing power. In the next five years, governments will have to decide who has jurisdiction over borderless cyberspace, who can tax whom for transactions there, who is responsible when something goes wrong. Corporations will have to decide whether and how to use the Net in manufacturing, distributing, advertising, and recruiting—whether to make it part of the warp and woof of American business, to set off, as Microsoft chief technology officer Nathan Myhrvold predicts, "the era of the recomputerization of America."

What emerges from conversations with dozens of the Net's nervous guardians—network builders, corporate executives, regulators—is consensus on four powerful trends shaping how the Net will grow and what it will do to us.

WALLED GARDENS

Billion-dollar telecom investments and dazzling technology breakthroughs are coming so fast that, at first blush, networks' capacity for data seems sure to outpace demand. In the first quarter of 1998, $20 billion in high-yield debt was issued to finance upstart telecom ventures, like Level3, that are building high-speed networks in the U.S. Spurred by the challenge, entrenched telcos like Sprint are announcing multibillion-dollar initiatives designed to pump more data. New laser technology and software enable a single strand of optical fiber to carry light signals on 40 wavelengths simultaneously. Such a strand could, theoretically, carry all the long-distance phone calls in the U.S. Cisco engineers say the time is near when a strand will carry 300 colors, and then 1,000.

Even so, network bandwidth will always be a scarce commodity. A familiar vicious circle applies: New highways built to relieve urban congestion encourage more driving and in turn become choked; so it goes with the Internet. As Lucent optical networking chief Gerry Butters says of the Net, "Every time the size of the pipeline is increased, the growth in traffic blows the forecast, not in a matter of years but in weeks or months." For the past few years, traffic has grown by a factor of ten each year, in part owing to new users. At the end of 1997 about 41 million American adults used the Web, according to Cyber Dialogue, a New York research firm. That figure is up from 14 million only two years earlier. By 2002, the projection is for at least 92 million users.

There's no reliable way to predict how many of those 92 million will have high-speed connections from their homes to the Net, similar to the hookups many people now enjoy in their offices. The consensus, though, is that a large percentage will. These empowered home users will devour massive amounts of data, including the live video and audio that now take forever to download at home. The result will be enormous pressure on what's called the Internet backbone: the fat optical pipes into which Internet service providers feed traffic for transport around the world, and the computers and routers and switches that serve as junctions between the pipes.

Heavy traffic today can cause delays: Web pages take forever to load, and data packets get routed via circuitous pathways. Mostly it doesn't matter; no one cares if an E-mail takes three seconds or three minutes to reach its destination. In the future, though, the backbone will carry phone calls and video and crucial business communications, all of which must reach their destination smoothly, and right away.

So Internet companies are looking for ways to banish nonessential data from the long-haul backbone and move high-priority traffic more efficiently. One way to do that is to price the Internet differently. Today, users pay a flat rate for delivery of any data anywhere in the world. In the future, predicts Microsoft consumer-platforms chief Craig Mundie, "all Internet services will have tiered rates." Providers will create hierarchies of users: Payers of premium prices will fly first class with guaranteed, high-speed service anywhere in the world; the rest will fly coach, with a promise of best effort from their provider.

Owned by a consortium of cable-TV companies including TCI, Comcast, and Cox, @Home Network is addressing this problem by creating the cyber equivalent of a walled garden. Subscribers to @Home will get Internet access via special cable modems, which cost about $40 a month to lease. The payoff: blazingly fast connection to the Net. At least that's the sizzle. But it's not exactly what CEO Thomas Jermoluk provides. "I'm not selling you the Internet," he says. "I'm selling you the service." The service turns out to be high-speed transit to certain Websites that pay to be warehoused in @Home's computers. Getting data from anywhere else on the Web will be no quicker than it is today. If a high-speed link should someday exist between @Home's servers and far-flung servers caching other Websites, subscribers might have to pay extra to take that fast road beyond @Home's garden.

Sprint's recent announcement of ION, a completely overhauled network that will carry data, video, and voice over a standard phone line, sounds more democratic. But it may suffer the same limitation that @Home has chosen to impose: high speeds for short runs. If Sprint's plan works, traffic between its customers and its network would travel at lightning speeds; but if the signal must go, say, to another caller not on the Sprint network, or to a Website linked to a rival backbone, the speed might be much slower

Even Internet companies with high-speed links around the world will use sleight of hand to divert some traffic. WorldCom, for instance, boasts of the data network it is building around the U.S., beneath the Atlantic, and onward through Europe's major cities. Yet networking chief John Sidgmore says, "Deploy flat-rate broadband service from Denver to Frankfurt? Forget it. It's just too expensive to haul bits long distances." Long-haul travel would be reserved for when WorldCom customers need it—say, for a videoconference between locations that are far apart.

Like others, including @Home's Jermoluk, Sidgmore plans to save space for such high-priority, point-to-point traffic by keeping much more Internet traffic local. Today most Websites reside on a single server, and any user wishing to visit must travel there electronically, wherever "there" is. The greater the average distance between surfers and Websites, the more fiber and lasers and switches Internet companies must install and maintain. Sidgmore, like other service providers, plans to push Websites closer to users by replicating them among many different computers around the world. Without knowing it, surfers will take shorter trips—and faster ones too.

Despite these efforts, Websites will still be swamped from time to time by floods of traffic. But new software will allow the businesses that operate the sites to discriminate among classes of users, to create walled gardens of their own. Programs that link a firm's Website with its databases, for example, will use customer information to sort incoming traffic, so that important customers do not lose access in periods of heavy demand.

A NEW MASS MEDIUM

It's a paradox that even as hidden software will keep some Internet customers on the sidewalk behind a velvet rope, the Net appears to be the first new mass medium since TV. Not only are tens of millions of people logging on via PCs, but in addition, tens of millions more will reach the Net in other ways.

In the home, a host of consumer-electronics devices will be wired to the Net, starting with the TV itself. Microsoft's WebTV is a stand-alone box that plugs into the phone line and delivers Web pages to the set, while WorldGate Communications, in Bensalem, Pa., will do the same using software in cable-TV set-top boxes. Digital cameras will download data to a film processor via the Net, and prints will arrive a day or two later in the mail. Baby monitors hooked to the Web will let parents see their children's bedrooms via remote camera.

When they leave their homes and offices, people will take the Net along. Some may stay in constant radio contact with the Web via digital pagers, cell phones, and laptops, perhaps even wearable computers that use new flexible transistors invented by Bell Labs. Users will gather E-mail, directions, maps, and news updates on these devices.

But the application that will really establish the Net as a mass medium is "streaming video," the sending of moving images over the Net in real time. Surfers love PC software that decodes audio and video streams from the Net. RealNetworks, in Seattle, is uploading 100,000 copies of its free "players" each day. Whereas video delivered via the Web is grainy and jerky today, as bandwidths around the Net increase it will become smoother, like TV.

Ordinary Joes may well be the creators of much of this Net video. The Website www.jennycam.com already offers many links to regularly updated images sent from digital cameras around the country: In Whitefish, Mont., for example, a camera offers live pictures in and around the Great Northern Brewing Co.; from Osage Beach, Mont., you can see who's on the Lake of the Ozarks. As streaming video becomes more widespread, a fan might bring a digital camcorder to a high-school football game and post the video on the Net that night for interested alums.

Such potential has not gone unnoticed by the world's media moguls. Fox, CNN, Sony, Warner Music, and Disney all deploy RealNetworks technology in one form or another. Fox, CNN, and Disney's ABC, for example, let Web users tap in to video clips of network news. The commercial possibilities are vast. Content developed for broadcast will soon be resold on demand via the Net. Shows on WebTV already have Net-borne enhancements—clickable images that let viewers communicate with the studio and with advertisers.

As streaming video proliferates, it will confront advertisers with the same sorts of tough decisions they had to make when TV eclipsed radio. Microsoft's Myhrvold says, "Lots of advertisers never made the transition when consumer products squeezed through the knothole of TV." Companies will have to decide whether to shift billions of dollars in ad budgets to the Internet. Those that do shift will need new kinds of ads that take advantage of the extra medium: ads that offer viewers options ("Would you like to see a clip about this car's crashworthiness or its speed?") or that are automatically tailored to the spending habits of the viewer.

THE CLICKABLE CORPORATION

When you click "yes" on Dell's Website, something happens in its plant. The PC maker relays online orders directly to assemblers. That seamless link between user and corporation, hard to imagine five years ago, will gradually become the norm.

The Net also allows companies to anticipate customers' wants with uncanny precision—a hallmark of the Web's slickest book-seller, Amazon.com. CEO Jeff Bezos, a pleasantly rumpled man with a Klaxon laugh, recalls how in 1997, when $2.8-billion-a-year Barnes & Noble launched a rival Web service, an analyst started calling his company Amazon.toast. Since then, Amazon has added some one million customers to its rolls (2.25 million have bought books so far) and increased sales from a $65-million-a-year rate to $350 million.

Bezos has stayed a jump ahead of his huge rival by concentrating on customer-friendly technology. One seductive feature of the Website is a section for book reviews by customers, who sometimes engage in lively debate. Such customer input serves an added purpose. Using so-called collaborative filtering, Amazon's computers track the likes and dislikes of people with similar buying patterns, so when a customer calls up a title onscreen, the Website helpfully lists other books that have appealed to like-minded readers.

Software embedded in the Web and triggered by the click of a mouse will help turbocharge business-to-business commerce as well. Some programs will help businesses cope with one of the Internet's biggest pitfalls: its anonymity. A company might use the Net to find the lowest price for a year's supply of paper clips, but the buyer would have no way to be sure that the best bid didn't come from a fly-by-night clip joint. Nor could a legitimate office supplier be certain that the buyer would pay the bill. Companies like Concentric Network and IPHighway offer technology for parties in online deals to verify each other's identity.

Web commerce won't be just about buying and selling goods. Companies will use so-called virtual private networks to link employees and even suppliers and customers. A VPN piggybacks on the Internet to create the functional equivalent of a proprietary data network at a fraction of the cost. Employees can log on to a VPN from remote locations. Suppliers and customers who have the right passwords can too.

Aventail of Seattle operates a VPN for a large New York investment bank. Customers in the financial services industry use the bank to process transactions and get information. Until recently, the bank needed complex and expensive database software to perform routine tasks like clearing checks and trading stocks; clients would put in their requests by fax. Now clients tap into the bank's VPN via the Internet and download software that lets them handle transactions in less time than it used to take merely to put in a bid.

The casbah of cyberspace is changing the social contract with employees and profoundly affecting the notion of what a corporation is. Companies are already using the Net to decentralize; Boeing, for instance, uses video on its intranet for corporate communications, distance learning, and computer training. By untethering work from geography, the Web will let companies farm out functions like human resources and accounting to specialists anywhere in the world.

Indeed, for certain jobs, the competitive edge may lie with people who live as far from the employer as possible, creating a market for what might be called "antipodal commerce." The controller of a California firm with a number-crunching task can send it off to his accountants in Bombay at the end of the day knowing it will be finished when he returns the next morning. Besides getting work done fast, such arrangements can help workers in places that have been isolated from the global economy.

The Net's flexibility may upset some business verities—for instance, that good little companies are always more agile than good big ones, or that large companies win by controlling distribution channels. Instead, expect to see more small companies arise to challenge giants, and to see big companies pursue micro-markets that only local ones could profitably serve before.

WIRED CIV

The social consequences of a ubiquitous Internet will take decades to unfold, but in the next five years the Net is sure to cause lots of consternation. With its ability to negate distance, cross borders, and spread information, it means trouble for entrenched hierarchies, and nowhere will that be more apparent than in politics. Cisco CEO John Chambers predicts that streaming video will play the same role in presidential politics that TV has since 1960. He says: "In the elections of 2000 or 2004, voters will go straight to the Net and click on candidates' speeches—and at a fraction of the cost for the politicians."

While changes like that one can help make politics more democratic, the Net can be too much of a good thing. Symptoms of information overload are already endemic. One recent survey of people who surf found that they read and sleep less than they used to and spend less time with their families. Web-connected jobs can be more stressful, too. Robb Eglsaer, director of Internet sales for a Porsche Audi dealership in Cupertino, Calif., finds that customers who contact him via the Net expect a swift reply whenever they happen to write. He says: "I used to have an eight-hour job. Now I work 13 or 14 hours a day."

Not everyone will be plugged in at home, though, and those who can't surf at all may be at a disadvantage, especially if they want certain sorts of products. The Net is fast becoming some companies' preferred way to communicate with customers. MCI's Vinton Cerf recently bought a Macintosh G3 computer, which he likes very much; but it came with a note explaining that some of its software wouldn't work well with the machine's latest operating system, and instructing the buyer to download a compatible version via the Web. "That's chutzpah," says Cerf. "The Web has evolved from an interesting tool into an entity you expect customers to rely on."

The collision between values and technology stands out most sharply in efforts to control online pornography. The landmark Communications Act of 1996 forbade sending certain sorts of X-rated stuff over the Net; the courts quickly struck down that provision on constitutional grounds. Trying to censor online porn with technology won't help much either. Parents can install software filters on their PCs to block access to offending Websites—those they happen to know about. @Home network chief Milo Medin says, "The amount of material on the Net is growing exponentially. No one group could find all the bad stuff." The only way to be perfectly safe is to let children visit only sites that have been vetted, which means parents would end up restricting their kids' access to good information.

Privacy will be hard to defend as well. The same technology that tells your online broker how good a customer you are can also tell him where you were when you logged on—information that can be sold to interested parties, like marketers. This sort of trade is hardly new; catalogs don't arrive by accident, after all. Nor does everyone think trafficking in tidbits of information gleaned online is evil. Speaking at a recent conference on telecom and the Internet, John McQuillan of McQuillan Consulting in Concord, Mass., said, "Carrying information, noticing patterns, and selling this knowledge to others isn't bad. It's electronic commerce. That's a good thing, if it's properly managed."

The ease and speed that the Net will give to gathering and conveying information, though, is a change of epoch-making proportions. Indeed, international disagreements on privacy may end up throwing a wrench into some transatlantic Net business plans. After World War II, Europe imposed stringent limits on the distribution of information about consumers and employees. Starting in October 1998, the European Union will prohibit transfer of information on any of its citizens—medical information, say, or airline food preferences, and possibly even credit card numbers—to countries that don't meet EU standards of privacy protection. Whether the U.S. will pass the test has not yet been determined; the State Department is negotiating.

Such uncertainty will typify the coming five years, as people established in hierarchies and rooted behind borders learn to make money and communicate in a realm where ideas and information move freely and can be in all places at once. Their struggle is really the same tension between freedom and control that has run through much of the 20th century. It is reflected in the early picture of the Net, freeform and open, melting into the new one—buttoned-down and tightly managed—probably much better in many ways but with a little less soul.

"The history of the Net has been played out between two poles: central control and everything that tries to evade it," says the English writer Sadie Plant, who has written a book about women and the Internet called *Zeros and Ones*. "Like a lot of contemporary cities, the Net will have some very carefully monitored areas that will be its shiny models. Whether the back streets survive becomes the issue."

The Internet has always seemed a different kind of medium from, say, the phone system. Though state and corporate interests have built it and own its parts, the Net feels as though it belongs to the people who use it, even when they do so on the PC in the office. Whether they hold on to that feeling in the 21st century is another matter

HOME-OFFICE HARDWARE

▲▼▲

*With the help of a few pieces of vital
equipment, you can set up a
high-powered office in the comfort
of your own home.*

▲▼▲

Setting up an office at home once involved buying furniture, plugging in a telephone, buying a calculator and typewriter, and making sure you had plenty of filing cabinets. You'll still need the furniture, telephone, and filing cabinets, but your other equipment needs are a bit more complex.

First, there's your home computer. These days it's nearly impossible to run an office without a computer and a printer. And of course, you'll also need a modem for sending and receiving E-mail and visiting Internet sites. If you're already working at home, you probably have a second line, but if you're going to use the modem for more than a few minutes a day, it might be a good idea to install a third line. You'll want to send and receive faxes; while you can do so with your computer and modem, you may find investing in a fax machine is more productive.

And what about all that paper that still comes your way? Don't you want to get the graphics and text into your computer? If so, you should plan on purchasing a scanner. Add in a good office copier and a decent chair so you don't strain your back and neck, and you could be out a lot of money. There are, though, some good economical options that can make even the smallest home office a very productive place to work.

SOHO MARKET

▼

Manufacturers have brought out a wide range of products specifically created for what they like to call the SOHO (small office/home office) market, including sleek machines that marry function and form, multifunction devices (MFDs), and products that offer Internet access and networking equipment.

Of course, the digital heart of this market, like its larger corporate siblings, is the computer itself. You will address several issues when selecting a home office computer: whether to choose a Macintosh or a PC that runs Windows, and whether to buy a notebook or a desktop machine.

Both Macs and PCs are fine for basic office tasks. You will also need to decide whether to go for a traditional, fully loaded computer or for one of the new low-priced models that run $1,000 or less. The best advice will come from your friends and associates—the ones you'll turn to when you're desperate for help. Remember, though, that if you already have a computer at home or at work, your life will be easier if you go with what you're used to.

Your choice of desktop or notebook computer will depend mostly on whether you will be using your machine out of the office. You don't actually have to travel very much to justify a notebook. You can take it to a client's office, to the library, or even to the backyard or another room in the house. And with a laptop you do get three computers in one: a home computer, an office computer, and one for the road. If space is tight where you work, you'll benefit by having less stuff on—or under—your desk. And you can hook up a larger monitor to a laptop when you're in the office. But notebook computers cost considerably more than equivalent desktop systems, and they're generally harder and more expensive to upgrade. Also, the more features you want, the heavier and pricier the machine.

STARTER KIT

A starter kit can help you get going relatively inexpensively, if you are just setting up a home office or want to add a second or third machine. Generally, though, the technology is a couple of steps behind that of today's leading-edge equipment, with older processors, smaller disk drives, fewer options for expansion, and other compromises. Another important trend for the home office is the multifunction device, which combines five or six key functions—printing, scanning, faxing, and others—in one machine. Brother, Canon, Hewlett-Packard, Sharp, and Xerox are among the manufacturers with affordably priced MFDs that are almost a self-contained office in a box. Each provides color printing, scanning, and faxing in a single unit. Brother's 6-in-1 Multi-Function Center, for example, is also a 50-minute-capacity digital answering machine and can capture video from a camcorder, VCR, or digital camera.

The advantages are clear: You'll save money and space buying one machine instead of five or six, and there's only one manual to read, one software package to install, and one technical support number. The drawbacks are obvious too. If you need to send your all-purpose digital home office away for repairs, you have a problem. It's one thing to live without a printer, a scanner, a copier, or a fax machine, but to give up all four at once could crimp your productivity. Go with a vendor that offers an exchange program if your product needs service.

PRINTING BREAK

If you prefer to choose separate components instead of a multifunction device, your must-have hardware list for the home and small office will include a printer and probably a scanner. You have two basic choices in printers: laser or inkjet. For fast, high-volume printing, a laser is your better bet. Color inkjets deliver superb color as well as monochrome text that is nearly as sharp as that of some laser printers. They've gotten faster, too, so you no longer need to schedule printing jobs during lunch or coffee breaks.

Once a specialized tool for graphic artists and designers, scanners transform photographs, drawings, and text from printed material into the digital language of computers. They can be a very useful addition to a home office. You have a choice between simple sheet-fed scanners or flatbed scanners, which look a bit like copying machines. For filing receipts and other simple chores, you can use an inexpensive sheet-fed scanner, but to scan color photographs, you'll be better off with a good flatbed unit.

RIVAL SCHEMES

In the near future most home offices will depend on a handful of separate ordinary phone lines for calls, faxes, and modem traffic, because high-speed access to the Internet, cable modems, and other options are not yet commonly available at affordable prices. Whether your home office is in the backwoods of Maine or on a hill in Marin County, you'll probably be relying on a few simple communications tools.

Desktop computers commonly include a data/fax modem. Fortunately, speeds are increasing. Unfortunately, the industry is having one of its periodic wrangles over technology standards.

The latest generation are so-called 56K modems. In theory, they receive data at 56 kilobits per second (Kbps), though they max out at somewhat less than that. Still, they are much faster for downloading graphics-laden Web pages than the previous generation of 33.6Kbps technology. They can only send data upstream at the slower pace, however.

There are two rival schemes for the 56K generation of modems: the x2 standard from U.S. Robotics (now owned by 3Com) and the 56Kflex technology developed by Rockwell International and Lucent Technologies. Make sure that your online service or Internet service provider supports the modem you've chosen.

Many of today's modems are actually multifunction communication devices, enabling you to use your computer to send and receive faxes and make phone calls. Some can turn your computer into a digital answering machine, while others add even more features, such as caller ID. Although these high-tech goodies are tempting, they don't always offer the same convenience or ease of use as stand-alone devices.

The advantage of regular fax machines or stand-alone digital answering machines is that they stand by 24 hours a day, use little electricity, and rarely break down. What's more, they do not interfere with any other machines. If you rely on your computer to be your all-purpose communications machine, you may miss an incoming fax or call when you're surfing the Internet. Even if

THE HOME-OFFICE CHECKLIST

▲▼▲

▶ *Computer*
Notebooks are more versatile but also more expensive than equivalent desktop systems. If price is a major concern, check out the sub-$1,000 desktops now available.

▶ *Printer*
Lasers are better for fast, high-volume printing, but inkjets do a better job with color.

▶ *Scanner*
No longer a specialized graphics tool, a scanner is becoming essential for the home office.

▶ *Fax*
A fax modem is convenient, but a stand-alone model is more reliable.

▶ *Modem*
The latest technology is 56Kbps, but make sure your ISP supports the standard you choose.

▶ *Networking*
As your home office grows, you'll need to connect computers to one another—and to the Internet.

you're not online, an incoming call or fax could interrupt what you're doing. And when your computer is turned off, none of these services are available.

Another option is an external fax device that connects to your PC and works even when it is turned off. There are plenty of simple, inexpensive ones that do this, including the $129 FaxPal II from InfoImaging Technologies, which saves your faxes when the PC is turned off.

PC TELEPHONE

▼

When you need to have two or more computers share information, or have several computers get simultaneous access to the Internet, you will find there are some simple, affordable ways to link computers and some clever new equipment to help you access the Net.

The simplest networking equipment creates the digital equivalent of two cans and a string—with PCs at either end passing data to each other. Some affordable desktop computers already come with networking capability built in, such as Apple's 4400 line for small businesses. Otherwise, equipment is available for less than $100 from companies such as 3Com.

As the number of computers in your business or family grows, you may wind up creating the equivalent of a small local area network, a miniature version of the technology widely used in offices. That way, the computers can exchange information and share resources such as printers. A simple box—called a hub—will take care of most of what you need. You plug each computer into the hub and let it take over the connections. You can get started with a low-end product like Farallon's Streamline Starlet 5. An even easier solution, supported by Microsoft, is a product due in 1998 called HomeRun, from Tut Systems; this system will use home telephone wiring and simple plug-in PC adapters to link PCs in a home or office.

There's also some innovative networking technology designed for small offices that makes it much easier to get on the Net. Ramp Networks, a young company in Santa Clara, Calif., has an Internet access device that uses ordinary phone lines and modems but gets much higher speeds, a big plus for downloading graphics-laden Web pages. Its WebRamp M3t Internet access device will combine—"multiplex"—up to three modems, taking advantage of the cumulative speed of all three. You'll need a separate phone line for each modem, but in most parts of the country, that's still cheaper than ISDN service from the phone company (typically $50 per month) or other high-speed Internet options. You can also call your home-based network from a remote notebook PC to gain access to any file or printer on the network.

INTERNET IN A BOX

▼

Several manufacturers have brought out communications hubs for the small office/home office market that provide more elaborate Internet networking gear in a box. The InterJet (starting at $1,995) from Whistle Communications, for example, has everything you need to connect PCs and Macs to the Internet and to each other. The compact appliance, about nine inches high, has its own built-in LCD display, can handle internal and external company E-mail, functions as a Web and intranet server with firewall security features and automatic configuration, and can provide everyone in a small company a direct connection to the Internet.

If you need still more firepower, it's probably time to call in the experts. Once you have more than a few computers and perhaps a small network to worry about, paying for help is worth it. The challenge for any home office or small company is to coordinate this technology and keep it working smoothly without a corporate technical staff.

▲▼▲

DO-IT-YOURSELF SOFTWARE

▲▼▲

*The latest generation of multimedia
software provides the tools and the
tutoring to help you do just about
anything, from learning a
language to writing a will.*

▲▼▲

As any Saturday-morning visit to Home Depot makes clear,
the American do-it-yourself tradition is alive and well. That's
true in the software business too. When affordable PCs equipped
with speakers, CD-ROM drives, and graphics processors
appeared a few years ago, they brought a flood of multimedia
software aimed at the home and family market. A PC user could
design a kitchen, improve typing skills, and cook like a three-star
chef—all with the hassle-free assistance of a virtual tutor. The age
of self-help software had arrived.

Since then, brutal competition for retail shelf space and a
shakeout in the multimedia software industry have weeded out
the shovelware in favor of a tighter selection of more useful and
compelling products. The best entries don't merely translate how-
to books into a point-and-click format. Rather, they combine
graphics, text, sound, and interactivity in unprecedented ways
that make learning and doing a bit more fun. Some of them teach
skills, like foreign languages or speed reading. Others help users
perform jobs hitherto reserved for experts, such as designing a
house or a landscape plan. Still others provide templates and
expert guidance for creating special documents like a family tree
or a will. Nearly all these self-empowering programs ship on one
or more CD-ROMs, so the sheer quantity of their content is
impressive. Some of them augment their out-of-the-box resources
by linking to dedicated sites on the World Wide Web.

Foreign-language instruction is an ideal application for multimedia software, because many working professionals have no
time for total-immersion courses, and many others find the ones
they attend unsatisfying. One of the more attractive language

packages on the market is the Learn to Speak series, produced by the Learning Co. The programs are effective for beginning- to intermediate-level students of French, German, Spanish, and Japanese. Priced at $79.95, all Learn to Speak titles are available in Windows 3.1, Windows 95, and Macintosh versions. One cool feature—an interactive speech-recognition engine that grades your pronunciation—works only on Windows machines.

Learn to Speak French, *par example*, opens with enticing images of Parisian landmarks and impressionist paintings, accompanied by music that makes you want to stroll along the Seine. A menu leads to sections organized by various day-to-day conversational needs— greeting strangers, asking for directions, hailing a taxi—each with vocabulary, dialogue, and quizzes attuned to your fluency level. Recording and playing back your voice juxtaposed with those of native speakers helps improve your pronunciation and accent.

These programs, as the series title implies, aim to teach you to speak a new language—not necessarily to read great literature in the original or master the finer points of grammar. With diligence, though, you should be able to handle the basics of your chosen language in everyday situations.

UP TO SPEED AND BUILDING MATERIALS

One of the earliest self-teaching programs was Speed Reader from educational-software publisher Davidson & Associates (now a wholly owned subsidiary of CUC International). The current edition of this classic, Ultimate Speed Reader, is available for Mac, Windows 3.1, or Windows 95 systems for around $30. Although its suggested techniques are better applied to the newspaper than to Proust, Speed Reader is a perennial bestseller with obvious relevance in the Information Age.

Ultimate Speed Reader teaches users to move their eyes more efficiently down the page and take full advantage of peripheral vision. The CD-ROM software includes more than 200 reading passages on various subjects; you can also import your own text from outside sources. Many of the timed exercises have an arcade-game-like quality that makes the drills pleasantly diverting. A recent update gives you techniques for plowing through loads of E-mail in record time. Davidson's extensive collection of self-help titles for adults also includes programs for brushing up on math, English grammar and vocabulary, touch-typing, chess, and résumé preparation.

Since 1992, Books That Work has established a reputation for bringing thoughtful, well-executed interactive content and programming to the field of home improvement. Its first product, 3D Deck, is now in its third edition and costs $29.95 (available on CD for Windows 95 only). The program combines a powerful computer-aided-design engine with a database of building materials to help users design their own decks. Once you've designed your multilevel masterpiece, you can view it in realistic 3-D graphics, watch an animated construction sequence, and then print out detailed plans and your shopping list of materials.

Books That Work also developed similar programs on home repair, electrical wiring, landscaping, and home design. After Books That Work was acquired by Sierra On-Line (which was then gobbled up by CUC), the new company created CompleteHome, a bundled product that integrates Books That Work's Home Improvement Encyclopedia, 3D Deck, and an Electrical Wiring guide. Priced at $49.95 (CD-ROM for Windows 95 only), the software package is a good value. While 3D Deck is aimed at true build-it-yourselfers, CompleteHome is primarily a planning tool; it generates floor plans and an attractive three-dimensional rendering of your proposed home, rather than professional blueprints. You can assemble rooms onscreen and fill them with realistic furnishings and appliances. The database includes 250 complete house plans and renderings you can customize. Then, take a virtual walk onscreen through the 3-D rendering of your dream house.

ANCESTOR WORKSHOP

Explore your roots with Brøderbund Software's Family Tree Maker. Built on a customized database, this genealogy program gives you templates for filling in names and dates, a feature for importing photos into a multimedia scrapbook, and an assortment of fonts and forms for printing heirloom-quality results.

Family Tree Maker Standard Edition III ($54.99 for Windows only; other editions available for the Mac) comes with four CD-ROMs crammed with data. Two disks hold birth, death, marriage, and census references for 130 million Americans, dating back to the 17th century; the other two include a database of Social Security death records for 55 million people who died between 1937 and 1996. Family Tree Maker's companion Website, accessible through hot links in the software, offers a wealth of additional online resources for genealogical research.

If you are more concerned about your descendants than your forebears, consider buying WillMaker ($29.97 for Windows or the Mac), produced by Nolo Press in Berkeley, Calif. Now in its sixth version, WillMaker is so easy and fast to use that the manual is not even necessary. WillMaker begins its refreshingly painless routine with a few introductory questions; then it follows a customized track that conforms to your specific needs. The program prompts you to name primary and backup guardians for minor children, to appoint an executor, and to create a letter to the executor outlining his or her duties. Once you've answered all the questions, WillMaker weaves your answers into a will that's legally valid in any state.

For people with larger estates who want to avoid the costs and delays of probate, another Nolo program called Living Trust Maker applies the same method to generating a standard living trust. As in WillMaker, the program shows you where you are in the process and offers both legal and program-related help at each step along the way. Once you've completed and signed the document, Nolo's electronic lawyer tells you how to transfer ownership of your property to your living trust. It even tells you when you should call in a real attorney.

Another Nolo antidote for procrastination is Personal RecordKeeper 4.0, which helps you create electronic records of insured property, credit card numbers, investments, deeds, and tax records. With the program you can generate reports on home inventory or net worth, and it can import or export data from financial programs such as Quicken.

GETTING STARTED ON THE INTERNET

▲▼▲

Everything you need for getting hooked up on the Internet, from choosing software to navigating through the maze of cyberspace.

▲▼▲

Whether you're a novice or you rely on the Net every day, the online world is changing so rapidly that it's difficult to keep up with new sites, new services, new equipment, and the latest buzzwords. Until recently, if you wanted to get on the Internet you had to run a gantlet of challenges, from choosing among Internet service providers (ISPs) to mastering each of the kinds of software necessary to gain access to the various resources on the Net. Many people who wanted to go online outside the halls of academe—where the Internet served to link researchers across the country—chose the more user-friendly world of commercial online services such as America Online (AOL), which greatly reduced the need to worry about the details of computer communications.

All that changed a few years ago with the advent of the World Wide Web, which made it so easy to use the Internet that it suddenly became a global resource and communications network for millions of people. The runaway success of Netscape Communications' Web browser helped spark a transformation of the software business, creating a vast market for easy-to-use software and services that enable consumers to take advantage of the Net. Now the Net is beginning to have an impact on many segments of the economy, from telecommunications to retailing, finance, news, and entertainment.

The travails the early adopters faced are over too. These days, you have numerous choices for getting onto the Internet. If you buy a new computer, the software you'll need to use will almost certainly be part of the free package bundled with the machine. (Microsoft's Internet Explorer 4.0 is widely available that way, while Gateway 2000 ships an InfoHighway CD-ROM with its machines, and Apple's Internet Connection Kit extends that brand's emphasis on easy access to the Internet.) Choose an Internet service provider, and the software will come to you as part of that package. Buy a shrink-wrapped browser in a store, and you'll find automated procedures written into the software to help you hook up with major ISPs.

As with almost everything else in the computer world, however, you'll want to make sure that your system is properly equipped, so you can use the Net efficiently.

BASIC EQUIPMENT AND WEB SURFING

Here are the basics: You'll need a computer that runs an Intel 80486 microprocessor or better. If you use a Macintosh, it should have a 68030 microprocessor or faster. (You'll be much better off with a Pentium-based PC, or in the Mac world with a Power Mac.) You will also want plenty of internal memory to deal with the graphics-heavy demands of the World Wide Web; 16MB is okay, but building up to 32MB will ensure better performance.

You will need a modem too. Those running at speeds of 14.4Kbps are inexpensive but so slow that the wait for Web pages to load onto your computer can be agonizing. Go for the faster 28.8Kbps models or, better yet, 56Kbps models, if your online provider supports them. Some run faster still; whatever you spend will pay off in time saved.

If you become a heavy user of the Internet, you might consider having the local telephone company sign you up for the rather expensive, higher-speed connection known as an ISDN line, which can also be used to carry your telephone traffic. To take full advantage of the Net, you need a software program known as a browser, which enables you to easily mine the riches of the Web. One of the two leading browsers is Netscape's Navigator. The most recent Netscape Communicator suite, which includes manual and installation support, is available in retail stores. Netscape is also packaged with many new computers and available through online service subscriptions like America Online or internet service providers like EarthLink.

GOING ONLINE CHECKLIST

▶ *Computer*

You'll be much happier with at least a Pentium or a PowerPC chip in your computer and 16MB of memory.

▶ *Modem*

The faster the better. A 28.8Kbps model—or 56Kbps if your ISP supports it—will make the wait for graphics-laden Web pages less interminable. If you are a heavy user, see if your phone company offers an ISDN line for even faster connection.

▶ *Connection*

Online services like AOL offer E-mail, custom content, and an easy-to-use interface on their own networks as well as access to the Internet. Internet service providers (ISPs) connect you directly to the Internet and let you do the exploring yourself. Some have added limited content or user-friendly services like Snap Online. Whatever you choose, you can get unlimited access for about $20 a month.

▶ *Browser*

Netscape's Navigator and Microsoft's Internet Explorer are still battling it out. One of them will probably come free with with your ISP or bundled with your computer, but you may also want to download the other free and check it out. Each provides full access to the Web's multimedia capabilities.

The other leading browser is rival Microsoft's Internet Explorer. The latest version, Internet Explorer 4.0, is included in all new computers that come with Windows 95 operating system software; it is also part of the package of software that comes with many online service subscriptions. It can even be downloaded free from the company' Website.

Both Netscape and Internet Explorer provide access to the full panoply of information that can be found online, so you can't go wrong with either one—the difference comes down to personal preference. As you can acquire versions of both programs free, it's worth taking each one for a test drive.

GETTING CONNECTED

This is the one part of the online world that has become much more complicated over time. Everybody, it seems, now wants to connect you to the Internet—choosing a telephone long-distance service is easy by comparison. In fact, telephone companies such as AT&T and Bell Atlantic also offer Internet service. So do many companies devoted solely to Internet access, such as Earthlink and Netcom. The competition is fierce, with providers striving to find new ways to draw in customers. MCI, a major provider, has even put its Internet startup kits in Blockbuster video stores, with tie-in deals offering the usual $19.95 monthly fee plus free video rentals to new customers.

The market is full of providers—large cities sport hundreds, ranging from national companies (a list can be found at www.boardwatch.com.) to small mom-and-pop operations. Which to choose? The majority of Internet service providers have settled on a monthly price of about $20 for unlimited Internet access. Some also offer space on their computers for users to maintain Websites of their own free, and some offer hourly rates for people who don't expect to burn up the phone wires.

People who travel for business often go with the largest nationwide providers, which are always only a toll-free phone call away. If your computing is going to be largely local, however, you might also consider working with a local company. It's worth asking any prospective ISP, especially the local ones, about the ratio of phone lines to subscribers—a fair indication of how many of your calls will end in the frustration of a busy signal. If the service offers a ratio worse than 1:13, you might want to look elsewhere.

And if you're just starting out, consider the commercial online services, such as America Online. Each of these has invested millions of dollars in order to make its features easy to use. And each has had years to build up proprietary libraries of software and communities of users that add much to the online experience. The medical discussion groups available on America Online, for example, are invaluable sources of expertise and support. AOL also makes E-mail wonderfully intuitive—especially the traditionally tricky notion of sending and receiving digitized photographs.

For beginners and those who don't want to own a full-fledged computer, there are some new options available. A service called WebTV (from Microsoft) hooks up directly to your television, using a set-top box similar to cable TV boxes. The service provides access to the Internet at acceptable transfer speeds and displays Web pages on your TV screen. Sony, Philips, and other consumer electronics companies are selling the equipment you'll need to tune in WebTV.

Once online, most Internet users rely on a few services to help them navigate through cyberspace. A burgeoning class of search engines and other guides to the Internet vastly simplify the task. Each has its own features, and it's worth checking a few to figure out which you like best. Yahoo is perhaps the best known of the general service and search sites. Built like a gigantic outline that categorizes the Internet by subject, the Yahoo site also includes up-to-the-minute news feeds, financial information, and local information for a number of cities. In effect, Yahoo is building a diverse media company based on the Web. Yahoo organizes the news into finely honed groupings. If you want news about biotech, the most recent stories will be available in one place.

As a search service, Yahoo is at its best when you want information on a class of sites. Say you plan to take a cruise: "Drill down" through Yahoo's outline, selecting increasingly narrower subject categories. You could start with the Business and Economy sector, select the subcategory Companies, then choose Travel, and finally Cruises. Websites for more than 30 cruise lines appear, some offering specials.

You can also find specific information by using keyword searches at Yahoo and many other search engines like AltaVista, Excite, Lycos, or HotBot. For example, if you're looking for information about the children's author Daniel Pinkwater, go to a search engine and enter his name. A list of Websites mentioning him will appear almost immediately.

WRETCHED EXCESS

Many searches, however, are much more difficult, because search engines pull up too much information—too many "hits" that don't contain the information you want. If you will be doing frequent searches, learn to fine-tune. Looking for information on fancy eyewear? Ask for pages about "glasses" but exclude the word "wine" from your search so that you don't have to wade through pages of information on table settings.

Most of the time, however, you'll probably be revisiting familiar sites rather than searching for new ones. Sites for news, financial information, entertainment—everyone quickly builds a long list of such favorite resources.

To help you keep up with the continually expanding resources, some institutions offer Web pages with useful lists and links that are regularly updated. Two popular sites, assembled by librarians at the University of California at Berkeley, are the Recommended Search Tools Page and the Librarians' Index to the Internet.

At this point, however, the Web is much more than a global storehouse of information. The Net is brimming with cheap or free software, and it also provides a welter of commercial ventures and other services. For example, CNET, a site for tech enthusiasts, has a software library that offers thousands of programs for everything from word processing and financial planning to anti-virus software and tools for developing programs of your own. Some of the software offerings available over the Net are demonstration versions that work only for a limited time; others are slimmed-down versions of programs that the vendors hope you'll replace by purchasing the full program. Still others are so-called shareware, software that costs nothing to download but comes with the hope that the user will someday send a check to the developers.

There's a startling panorama of resources, services, and commercial products available on the Internet these days; everything from sports information and gardening sites to investment advice and online trading. Once you get started, there's no turning back.

IT'S YOUR CALL

▲▼▲

*Choosing the right cell phone
matters, but choosing the best
service matters too.*

▲▼▲

Hollywood producers have wielded cell phones for a decade, to chat with stars in Malibu while doing lunch with agents at Spago. Then mobile professionals and nearly everyone who drove a German car began using these phones. Now, with one speed-dial button programmed for the babysitter and another for a personal tow-truck valet, cell phones are regarded as standard safety equipment in any vehicle.

Some 55 million people, or well over a third of all households in the U.S., subscribe to wireless phone services—a fivefold increase since 1992. As the numbers of users has ballooned, wireless telephones have been getting sleeker and more full-featured. But as the market has grown, so has chaos in the industry.

For consumers, the good news is that thanks to deregulation and the government's auction of additional airwaves for wireless services, the average monthly cellular bill has dropped from $81 in 1990 to $42 today, and prices are still coming down. The bad news is that you need a master's degree in wireless telecommunications to be a well-informed shopper.

Where you once were able to choose a cellular phone and then pick the service, you usually now must do the reverse. Where once there was a small selection of phones that would work with any wireless service, you now have to pick a phone compatible with the service you've chosen. There are analog phones, digital phones, PCS (personal communications service) phones, dual-band and tri-mode phones, and more. If you haven't shopped for one lately, get ready for a barrage of terms like CDMA, TDMA, AMPS, and D-AMPS.

You can blame this confusion on the increased competition for your wireless dollar and on the emergence of digital technologies. Digital may be old hat in the computer arena, but it's relatively new in wireless communications, because digital's transmitting efficiency was not needed until recently.

Now that analog systems are brimming over with voice traffic, the time for digital solutions has come. Digital technology, which converts sound waves into dense streams of ones and zeros and back again, is more efficient and less prone to fraud, particularly the midair theft or "cloning" of phone numbers. It also offers better sound quality.

But the biggest appeal of digital may be added services and longer reach. Many newer digital phones can serve as alphanumeric pagers. Some support emerging data services too, such as those that provide news or stock quotes via the Internet, displaying the information on larger LCD screens. A few can even act as two-way radios for direct, less costly connections. And many digital carriers are adding voice mail, caller ID, call waiting, three-way calling, and other standard telephone services to the mix.

The longer reach will come mainly in the form of new national digital cellular and PCS networks. Nextel and AT&T Wireless are each building countrywide cellular systems, for example, while Sprint PCS and PCS PrimeCo, among others, are piecing together national PCS networks. These new digital networks will simplify using your wireless phone outside your home area, and typically eliminate the widely varying "roaming" charges—those per-day or per-minute premiums you pay for using your cell phone when you travel to other cities or states. With this new plan, you may pay home-area rates for local calls wherever you are, plus a flat rate for long-distance charges.

Given this alphabet soup of digital and analog offerings, which wireless phone makes the most sense? The best advice is to sort through the service options available in your area.

ANALOG CELLULAR SERVICE

In the rush toward an all-digital age, it may be tempting to rule out traditional analog cellular service. But analog cellular still has the widest range of phones available—and the most extensive geographical coverage. It's virtually everywhere in the U.S., and it's made up of myriad local and regional networks that all use the same transmission method, known in the cellular industry as AMPS (for advanced mobile phone service). Those two factors mean that you can use your analog phone almost anywhere you go, no matter what your primary cellular carrier is. And you'll have plenty of phones to choose from, starting with basic, low-cost (sometimes free) models to pricier fashion statements such as Motorola's StarTAC analog products.

Yet the ubiquity of analog cellular service comes at a price. Under federal regulation, the nation was carved into various markets with no more than two analog carriers permitted in each. When you travel outside your local market, cellular carriers in those other markets handle your calls for a fee—which will show up on your monthly bill as a roaming charge.

The clarity of analog calls sometimes leaves much to be desired, too, and your calls, which are unencrypted, are easier to intercept, which makes them susceptible to cloners and uninvited listeners. Some carriers require that their analog customers dial a personal ID code before every call, though many newer analog phones have a password feature, called authentication, that performs the secret handshake for you.

Increasingly, analog service may not be the best financial deal in town, either. A growing number of cellular carriers want you to go digital to relieve capacity and security problems, and they are offering better prices for their digital service plans than for analog plans.

DIGITAL CELLULAR SERVICE

Sometimes called D-AMPS (for digital advanced mobile phone service), digital cellular amends many of analog's shortcomings. Calls are generally clearer and more consistently completed, and with the stronger encryption methods, there's little worry about prying ears—plus, there are no ID codes or authentication steps to worry about.

Better still, practically all digital cellular phones are actually dual-mode phones that can use the analog system outside your

CELL PHONE GLOSSARY

AMPS *(advanced mobile phone service)* The technical specifications that define standard analog cellular systems.

Analog cellular The original, most basic form of cellular telecommunication.

CDMA *(code division multiple access)* A way of packing several channels of digital information (including voice conversations and data) over the same wireless transmission link using a sophisticated coding system.

DAMPS or D-AMPS *(digital advanced mobile phone service)* The technical specifications that define digital cellular systems, which use the same portion of the radio spectrum as analog cellular service.

Digital cellular Wireless digital services carried over the traditional (800MHz band) radio frequencies allotted to cellular-phone communications.

Dual-mode, dual-band, and tri-mode phones Hybrid phones that accommodate several different services. Dual-mode phones can operate in digital or analog modes. Dual-band models use either PCS or cellular frequencies. Tri-mode phones support analog cellular, digital cellular, and PCS.

PCS *(personal communications service)* Digital wireless voice and data services that use a newly allotted portion of the radio spectrum (the 1900MHz band). Includes digital voice calls, alphanumeric paging, text messaging, and other services.

TDMA *(time division multiple access)* A way of packing two or more channels of digital information (voice or data) on the same link by allocating a different time interval for the transmission of each channel. That is, the multiple channels take turns using the link. A synchronizing signal or other identifier is usually required.

home-area digital network. Another benefit: Carriers often reduce or eliminate roaming fees. Low-cost ($20 to $30 a month) service plans for digital cellular are common, and many of the latest, coolest phone designs are for digital models.

You also get a seldom-noticed bonus with these phones: Talk (calling) time and standby (receiving) time are generally much longer—often by 50% or more—with digital service than analog.

Digital opens the door for all kinds of other data services as well. Motorola's MicroTAC SC-725, for instance, supports caller ID, text messaging, and voice mail alerts.

But digital cellular is not available yet in many areas. Many carriers are signing up customers for their "digital cellular" service plans before their digital networks have been completed. When you travel outside the digital network service area, you can still use these dual-mode phones, but they'll be operating strictly in analog mode—without the voice-quality, security, and talk-time advantages that you signed on to get.

The government did not mandate a single standard for digital cellular transmission as it did with analog services. So some carriers are using a transmission standard called CDMA (code division multiple access), while others use a rival scheme known as TDMA (time division multiple access). And there are variants, such as the Motorola iDEN system used in Nextel's network. (And Europe and Asia have other standards.) As a result, you cannot necessarily use your new phone in another carrier's digital network and reap the benefits of digital technology. Your dual-mode phone may fall back to analog instead.

PCS

When the federal government auctioned off additional spectrum for wireless services several years ago, it set aside a special frequency band for personal communications service, or PCS. (PCS occupies the 1900MHz band, whereas traditional analog and digital cellular calls are in the 800MHz band.) PCS uses digital technology and offers many of the same advantages as digital cellular—such as transmission quality and anti-fraud protection. In addition, PCS carriers are aggressively marketing messaging and data services.

With prices ranging from $150 to $500, PCS phones generally cost more than typical cell phones. But they can offer more, too. For example, Qualcomm's Dual-Mode Q Phone, which switches automatically between analog and digital modes, can double as an alphanumeric pager. It also supports Internet data services such as news and E-mail delivery.

Although the phones themselves tend to be higher priced, PCS plans can bring savings for heavy wireless users because many include hundreds of local minutes for one flat rate. The biggest current disadvantage of PCS is its often limited range. Only one PCS carrier, Sprint PCS, has assembled a national network; by mid-1998 it was in about 150 metropolitan markets and expanding.

Other PCS carriers cover much more limited areas. And when you're outside that network's service area, you may be out of luck. Newer dual-band PCS phones let you use the analog cellular system as a fallback, just as digital cell phones do. But not all PCS carriers offer the analog option—or offer it in all parts of the country. So it pays to study PCS coverage maps carefully—even within a given metropolitan area—before signing on with a provider.

Unfortunately, the wireless world won't get simpler anytime soon. There's no single global standard emerging as there is in the personal computer business. The vast expansion of the wireless market is leading to a greater range of choices and services— but it has also made the task of navigating those options more difficult than ever.

JARGON WATCH

*A short guide to help you decode
digital technology lingo.*

▲▼▲

The world of digital technology is famous for its rapid pace of innovation, and the language that describes it changes just as quickly. If you're new to shopping for a notebook computer, comparing cellular phones, or exploring the World Wide Web, there will be terms you haven't seen before, so we've put together a list of jargon words for you and defined them below.

A

Active matrix screen A computer display, found in notebook computers, that uses a liquid crystal display. Each dot, or pixel, on the screen is represented by a separate transistor, resulting in a sharper, brighter image.

Address A label that enables machines on a computer network or the Internet to identify each other uniquely. An E-mail address usually takes the form of an individual name, a group name, and a domain name, separated by the @ sign and periods, such as fortune-letters@pathfinder.com.

Agent A program that performs tasks independently, such as sorting E-mail messages or searching the Web, according to preset preferences.

Application Computer software that enables users to perform specific tasks, such as word processing or desktop publishing.

Aspect ratio Ratio of width to height of a computer display or TV screen.

B

Backup An extra copy of a file or application created in case the original is damaged or destroyed.

Bandwidth The transmission capacity of a computer connection. Bandwidth is usually measured in bits per second.

Bit The smallest unit of information a computer can hold; an abbreviation of binary digit.

Bps Bits per second. Describes the transmission speed of a modem or other communications device.

Browser Software, such as Netscape Navigator or Microsoft's Internet Explorer, that enables a computer user to search for, display, and download the multimedia information that appears on the World Wide Web.

Byte The basic unit of memory. Represents the amount of memory (eight bits) needed to specify one letter, number, or symbol.

C

Cable modem A special modem that uses the cable TV network as a gateway for sending and receiving information.

Cache A portion of RAM set aside as a temporary storage area, or buffer, to speed communications between the microprocessor and the hard drive or other components.

CD-ROM *(compact disk-read only memory)* A disk, similar to a music CD, that stores large quantities of information, such as an encyclopedia or a software application.

CDMA *(code division multiple access)* A specification for dividing up digital cellular phone frequencies by assigning each user a unique code.

Chat A form of interactive communication that enables computer users in separate locations to have real-time conversations. Usually takes place at Websites called chat rooms.

Client/Server Computing systems in which the workload is split between desktop PCs (the client) and one or more larger computers (the server) that are connected via a network.

Cookie A string of numbers a Website uses to identify visitors. The cookie can contain information about online-service subscriptions and memberships and other data.

CPU *(central processing unit)* Refers to the microprocessor around which a personal computer is built (such as the Pentium Pro or the PowerPC chip).

Cyberspace A term used to describe the world set up by global networks, especially the Internet. Originally coined by author William Gibson in his novel *Neuromancer*.

D

Database A set of data that is structured and organized for quick access to specific information.

Desktop A metaphor for the onscreen computing environment. It includes the screen background and the windows, icons, documents, and tools that appear on it.

Dial-up Connection to the Internet through an Internet service provider's (ISP's) host computer over standard telephone lines; the most common type of Internet account for home users.

Disk drive The device that reads data from and writes data onto a magnetic (or optical) disk. Today every personal computer has a hard disk drive and typically also includes a drive for a floppy disk.

Download To transfer data or software code from a disk, computer, or network to your own computer.

DPI *(dots per inch)* Refers to the number of pixels or dots of ink in one square inch. It is a measurement of the resolution or sharpness of text and graphics that a printer can print or a monitor can display.

DSL *(digital subscriber loop)* A high-speed modem technology, operating at 768 kilobytes per second or faster, which may be available for home and business use in 1998.

Dual-scan display A variant of a passive-matrix display in which the top and bottom halves of the screen are refreshed simultaneously, yielding better display quality.

DVD A disk, similar to a CD, that can hold a two-hour movie. Originally an acronym for "digital video disk."

DVD-ROM A high-capacity, read-only disk with 4.7 gigabytes of storage capacity.

E

E-mail Electronic mail. A method of sending messages, usually text but also graphics and document attachments, via a computer network.

Encryption A technology for making data being transmitted across a network unreadable to anyone except the recipient.

Ethernet A widely used, local area network technology for connecting computers, printers, servers, and other devices in the same building or campus.

Extranet A network built on Internet protocols and operated over the Internet for private business-to-business communication.

F

Firewall Software that protects a private network from intrusion via the public Internet.

Flash memory A solid-state memory product that can take the place of a hard disk drive or other storage device.

Floppy disk A portable 3.5-inch disk used to store information magnetically.

G

GIF (graphics interchange format) A digital format for displaying and compressing/decompressing images.

Gigabyte (abbreviated GB) A unit of memory equal to 1,000 megabytes.

Groupware Programs that permit simultaneous work on a file by more than one networked user. Users can see changes made by any other person as they occur.

H

Hard disk The main form of data storage for computers.

Hardware The keyboard, monitor, circuitry, and other non-software components that make up a computer.

Home page The primary site on the Web for an organization or individual. Usually contains links to other related pages.

HTML (hypertext markup language) The software language used to create and link pages on the World Wide Web.

HTTP (hypertext transfer protocol) The standard protocol used for sharing information on the Internet. It is the basis for the World Wide Web.

Hyperlink A highlighted area on a Website that calls up another Web page when clicked. Hyperlinks are created using HTML.

I

Inkjet printer A printer that works by spraying ink through a nozzle onto the paper.

Internet A worldwide collection of interconnected networks that enables users to share information electronically and that provides digital access to a wide variety of services.

Intranet A private network, set up within a corporation or an organization, that operates over the Internet and may be used to link geographically remote sites.

ISDN (integrated services digital network) An internationally standardized digital telephone technology. Provides very high data-transfer rates, often used for fast connections to the Internet and for videoconferencing.

ISP (Internet service provider) A company that provides access to the Internet, usually via the public telephone network.

J

Java A scripting language for writing computer applications that can be run on any operating system. Developed by Sun Microsystems.

JPEG (joint photographic experts group) One of two digital formats for displaying and compressing/decompressing photographs and other still images. The other is the graphics interchange format, or GIF.

K

Keyword A word used to focus an online search.

Kilobyte (abbreviated K or KB) A unit of memory equal to 1,024 bytes (or about 1,000 bytes, hence kilobyte).

L

LAN (local area network) A group of personal computers linked together in a building or campus to share programs, data, E-mail, peripherals, and other resources.

Laser printer A printer that uses laser-beam scanning to produce very-high-resolution output.

LCD (liquid crystal display) A portable-computer-screen technology that uses a liquid crystal compound sealed between two polarized filter sheets.

LED (light-emitting diode) A semiconductor diode used in digital displays, as on a clock radio. In computers, most LED displays have been replaced by LCDs; the small colored lights found on computer equipment are LEDs.

M

Megabyte *(abbreviated MB)* A unit of memory equal to one million bytes.

Megahertz *(abbreviated MHz)* The unit of measure that describes the rate at which computers operate. A rough guide to computer performance but not the only benchmark for comparing dissimilar computers.

Memory A data storage area for information and applications. RAM and ROM are types of computer memory.

MIME *(multipart Internet mail extension)* A standard for transmitting nontext media with E-mail over the Internet.

MMX A built-in enhancement on some Intel microprocessors that enables them to deliver better performance in multimedia and communications applications.

Modem A device that enables computers to communicate over telephone lines.

MPEG *(moving-picture experts group)* A digital format for compressing/decompressing moving-picture files. MPEG-2 is the latest version of this format.

N

NC *(network computer)* A desktop terminal with limited local storage capability that is designed primarily to execute programs delivered over a network.

Net PC A desktop computer designed for easier centralized management over a network than a traditional PC.

Network A group of computers linked to share resources. Common types are LANs, WANs, and intranets.

Newsgroup A forum on the Internet where users can debate topics by posting and replying to messages. Unlike chat, newsgroup discussions do not take place in real time.

O

Online service A commercial service that gives computer users access to a variety of online offerings, such as reference sources, shopping, and games, as well as access to the Internet.

Operating system *(abbreviated OS)* The master software that controls a computer's fundamental operations. PCs generally run a version of Windows; Macintoshes run a version of Mac OS.

P

Packet switching A data transmission technology that breaks down a stream of data into smaller units, called packets, and routes them separately over a network.

Parallel interface An interface, or port, between a computer and a peripheral in which the computer sends multiple bits of information to the peripheral, such as a printer, simultaneously.

Passive matrix display A type of liquid crystal display for portable computers in which the pixels are activated by intersecting horizontal and vertical wires. (See active matrix screen.)

PC *(personal computer)* PC formerly referred to the microcomputer brought out by IBM in the early 1980s. But now it is more widely used as a generic term for any microprocessor-based computer controlled by one person at a time.

PC card Also known as PCMCIA card. A standard hardware expansion circuit card, used mainly in notebook and hand-held computers.

Pentium A family of microprocessors manufactured by Intel. Advanced models include the Pentium Pro and Pentium II.

Peripheral An accessory such as a printer, monitor, or disk drive that can be attached to a computer.

Pixel A graphics term for the smallest picture element that can be displayed on a screen.

Plug-and-play Used to describe peripherals and other devices that only need to be plugged in to a computer to function.

Port A plug on the back of a computer used to connect peripherals or network connectors.

PowerPC A family of microprocessors used in Macintosh and other computers. Developed by Motorola, IBM, and Apple.

Protocol A set of standards that define communications between computers.

R

RAM *(random access memory)* A form of computer memory

used by applications. Information stored in RAM can be altered by the user and is lost when the computer is shut off.

ROM *(read only memory)* The memory that contains the basic instructions for the computer's microprocessor. Users cannot change this information, and it remains intact when the computer is shut off.

S

Scanner A peripheral used to produce digitized images of documents and photographs, which can be stored as files and edited on a computer.

SCSI (small computer system interface) A high-speed port used to connect computers with printers and other peripherals.

Search engine A server-based application used to search large databases for selected words or phrases. Common search engines use keywords to search for information on the World Wide Web.

Serial interface An interface, or port, between a computer and a printer in which the computer sends single bits of information to the device, one after the other.

Server See Client/Server.

SSL *(secure socket layer)* Encryption protocol that enables information to be sent over networks securely.

SVGA *(super video graphics array)* Graphics specifications for video output on PCs that surpass the older VGA standards.

System software See Operating system.

T

TCP/IP transmission *(control protocol/Internet protocol)* A system of network standards that enables computers with different architectures and operating systems to communicate over the Internet.

TDMA *(time division multiple access)* A technology for dividing up airtime frequencies for digital cellular phone service by interweaving simultaneous phone calls from many users.

U

Unix A computer operating system developed by AT&T that is commonly used on workstations. It is designed to be used by many people simultaneously and enables them to use several programs at once.

UPS *(uninterruptible power supply)* A backup unit that provides continuous electrical power when the normal power supply is interrupted.

URL *(uniform resource locator)* The standard format for the address of any computer or resource on the World Wide Web. It contains information about the server to be contacted and the method and path of access, e.g. http://www.patriots.com.

USB *(universal serial bus)* An external bus standard that supports data transfer rates of 12 megabytes per second.

V

VGA *(video graphics array)* The eight-bit graphics standards for video output on PCs, which feature 640 x 480 resolution and 256 colors.

Videoconference A communications system that enables people in separate locations to meet using live video pictures and sound.

Virus A destructive software program that "infects" a computer through a disk or downloaded program.

W

WAN *(wide area network)* A network that covers a large geographic area, such as a state or country.

Web See World Wide Web.

Window A rectangular area on the screen, showing a section of a program or document.

Windows The operating system written by Microsoft. Windows 95 is intended for individual PCs, while Windows NT is designed to provide networking services.

Wizard Part of a software program that guides the user through a complex process like signing up with an ISP or posting a Web page to the server.

World Wide Web *(abbreviated WWW)* The vast collection of documents on the Internet that are linked by hypertext, offering easy access to an immense range of information available as text, graphics, sound, as well as other multimedia resources.

THE 1998
FORTUNE 500 DIRECTORY

▲▼▲

Profit growth at America's biggest companies slipped into the slow lane in 1997 as earnings gains decelerated dramatically from the supercharged pace of the mid-1990s. Total income for the FORTUNE 500 rose 7.8% in 1997, a far cry from the stunning 23.3% jump in 1996. Surprisingly, the slowdown in net income growth came even as shares of the typical FORTUNE 500 corporation gained momentum on Wall Street. The median stock market return of companies on the list was over 30%, well ahead of the 21% return registered in 1996.

Despite this seemingly ominous combination of slowing earnings growth and rising stock prices, business leaders and Wall Streeters alike insisted that 1997 was, to quote Ol' Blue Eyes, "a very good year." Explained Salomon Smith Barney strategist John Manley: "You can't hit a home run every time you go to the plate, and we shouldn't look at 1997's squeeze double as anything bad."

But 1997 is still likely to be remembered as the year when companies could no longer count on cost reductions, reengineering, and other restructuring efforts as sure paths to far higher profits. What's more, by early 1998 it looked as if the "low-hanging fruit"—Wall Street argot for easy cost cuts—had already been picked. Of course, that wasn't the only reason huge profit spikes were harder to come by in 1997. Rising labor costs, weakness in Asian economies during the second half of the year, a strong dollar, and little room for price hikes all conspired to keep profit margins from expanding beyond their already rich levels.

NELSON D. SCHWARTZ

RANK 1997	COMPANY	REVENUES $ millions	PROFITS $ millions	Rank	ASSETS $ millions	Rank
1	**GENERAL MOTORS** Detroit	178,174.0	6,698.0	5	228,888.0	13
2	**FORD MOTOR** Dearborn, Mich.	153,627.0	6,920.0	4	279,097.0	8
3	**EXXON IRVING,** Texas	122,379.0ᴱ	8,460.0	1	96,064.0	30
4	**WAL-MART STORES** Bentonville, Ark.[1]	119,299.0	3,526.0	14	45,525.0	64
5	**GENERAL ELECTRIC** Fairfield, Conn.	90,840.0	8,203.0	2	304,012.0	5
6	**INTL. BUSINESS MACHINES** Armonk, N.Y.	78,508.0	6,093.0	7	81,499.0	36
7	**CHRYSLER** Auburn Hills, Mich.	61,147.0	2,805.0	29	60,418.0	50
8	**MOBIL** Fairfax, Va.	59,978.0ᴱ	3,272.0	19	43,559.0	67
9	**PHILIP MORRIS** New York	56,114.0ᴱ	6,310.0	6	55,947.0	56
10	**AT&T** New York	53,261.0	4,638.0	8	58,635.0	52
11	**BOEING** Seattle[3]	45,800.0	(178.0)	480	38,024.0	76
12	**TEXACO** White Plains, N.Y.	45,187.0ᴱ	2,664.0	32	29,600.0	92
13	**STATE FARM INSURANCE COS.** Bloomington, Ill.	43,957.0	3,833.3	11	103,626.2	27
14	**HEWLETT-PACKARD** Palo Alto[4]	42,895.0	3,119.0	24	31,749.0	88
15	**E.I. DU PONT DE NEMOURS** Wilmington, Del.	41,304.0ᴱ	2,405.0	35	42,942.0	68
16	**SEARS ROEBUCK** Hoffman Estates, Ill.	41,296.0	1,188.0	68	38,700.0	75
17	**TRAVELERS GROUP** New York[5]	37,609.0	3,104.0	26	386,555.0	2
18	**PRUDENTIAL INS. CO. OF AMERICA** Newark, N.J.[6]	37,073.0	610.0	144	259,482.0	12
19	**CHEVRON** San Francisco	36,376.0ᴱ	3,256.0	21	35,473.0	82
20	**PROCTER & GAMBLE** Cincinnati[8]	35,764.0	3,415.0	16	27,544.0	101
21	**CITICORP** New York	34,697.0	3,591.0	13	310,897.0	4
22	**AMOCO** Chicago	32,836.0ᴱ	2,720.0	31	32,489.0	86
23	**KMART** Troy, Mich.[1]	32,183.0	249.0	291	13,558.0	174
24	**MERRILL LYNCH** New York	31,731.0	1,906.0	44	292,819.0	7
25	**J.C. PENNEY** Plano, Texas[1]	30,546.0	566.0	151	23,493.0	116

STOCKHOLDERS' EQUITY		MARKET VALUE 3/18/98		EARNINGS PER SHARE				TOTAL RETURN TO INVESTORS			
				1997 $	% change from 1996	1987–97 annual growth rate %	Rank	1997 %	Rank	1987–97 annual rate %	Rank
$ millions	Rank	$ millions	Rank								
17,506.0	18	54,243.8	40	8.62	43.2	5.5	206	19.5	301	12.2	291
30,734.0	5	73,923.0	21	5.62	54.4	2.2	251	57.0	88	15.3	233
43,660.0	1	158,783.6	4	3.37	12.7	7.0	185	28.3	246	17.4	186
18,502.0	17	113,730.8	8	1.56	17.3	18.8	45	74.8	47	20.5	129
34,438.0	3	260,147.2	1	2.46	13.9	11.9	111	51.1	117	24.3	73
19,816.0	13	98,321.9	14	6.01	20.0	3.3	233	39.6	180	9.5	328
11,362.0	41	28,368.8	75	4.09	(13.7)	3.3	232	11.7	338	17.0	195
19,461.0	15	58,409.6	36	4.01	10.8	10.1	129	21.7	282	18.9	158
14,920.0	25	102,931.6	12	2.58	1.6	14.9	77	25.0	269	25.3	65
22,647.0	7	105,878.7	11	2.84	(22.4)	4.2	221	46.2	140	16.2	216
12,953.0	32	50,868.1	43	(0.18)	(109.7)	—		(7.1)	408	22.0	102
12,766.0	35	31,576.6	65	4.87	32.3	—		14.3	328	18.5	161
37,635.4	2	N.A.		N.A.	—	—		—		—	
16,155.0	22	65,060.0	29	2.95	19.9	16.8	64	25.3	265	16.8	201
11,270.0	43	77,018.9	19	2.08	(34.6)	5.4	209	30.3	235	19.3	153
5,862.0	98	22,573.8	89	2.99	(4.2)	(3.7)	302	0.2	389	17.3	192
20,893.0	11	69,419.7	24	2.54	8.9	41.3	9	79.8	32	32.7	19
19,718.0	14	N.A.		N.A.	—	—		—		—	
17,472.0	19	54,852.2	39	4.95	24.4	12.9	97	22.1	281	19.5	148
12,046.0	38	113,634.8	9	2.43	13.3	26.4	25	50.4	118	25.2	66
21,196.0	10	66,105.3	27	7.33	(1.3)	—		24.8	270	25.2	67
16,319.0	21	41,328.7	50	5.52	(2.6)	7.6	176	8.9	351	13.9	266
5,434.0	110	8,204.9	216	0.51	—	(11.3)	321	10.8	342	1.0	372
8,329.0	62	29,152.2	71	4.83	17.5	18.4	50	81.4	29	32.7	20
7,357.0	77	18,605.4	108	2.10	(6.7)	0.2	273	28.8	242	15.3	234

RANK 1997	COMPANY	REVENUES $ millions	PROFITS $ millions	Rank	ASSETS $ millions	Rank
26	**AMERICAN INTERNATIONAL GROUP** New York	**30,519.5**	**3,332.3**	17	**163,970.7**	17
27	**CHASE MANHATTAN CORP.** New York	**30,381.0**	**3,708.0**	12	**365,521.0**	3
28	**BELL ATLANTIC** New York[9]	**30,193.9**	**2,454.9**	34	**53,964.1**	59
29	**MOTOROLA** Schaumburg, Ill.	**29,794.0**	**1,180.0**	69	**27,278.0**	102
30	**TIAA-CREF** New York[10]	**29,348.4**	**1,226.6**	65	**214,295.6**	14
31	**PEPSICO** Purchase, N.Y.	**29,292.0[1]**	**2,142.0**	38	**20,101.0**	132
32	**LOCKHEED MARTIN** Bethesda, Md.	**28,069.0**	**1,300.0**	64	**28,361.0**	97
33	**FANNIE MAE** Washington, D.C.	**27,776.9**	**3,055.8**	28	**391,672.7**	1
34	**DAYTON HUDSON** Minneapolis[1]	**27,757.0**	**751.0**	118	**14,191.0**	167
35	**MORGAN STANLEY DEAN WITTER** New York[11,12]	**27,132.0**	**2,586.0**	33	**302,287.0**	6
36	**KROGER** Cincinnati	**26,567.3**	**411.7**	198	**6,301.3**	273
37	**LUCENT TECHNOLOGIES** Murray Hill, N.J.[13]	**26,360.0**	**541.0**	159	**23,811.0**	115
38	**INTEL** Santa Clara, Calif.	**25,070.0**	**6,945.0**	3	**28,880.0**	95
39	**ALLSTATE** Northbrook, Ill.	**24,949.0**	**3,105.0**	25	**80,918.0**	37
40	**SBC COMMUNICATIONS** San Antonio[14]	**24,856.0**	**1,474.0**	54	**42,132.0**	70
41	**UNITED TECHNOLOGIES** Hartford	**24,713.0**	**1,072.0**	77	**16,719.0**	149
42	**COMPAQ COMPUTER** Houston[15]	**24,584.0**	**1,855.0**	47	**14,631.0**	164
43	**METROPOLITAN LIFE INSURANCE** New York[6]	**24,374.0**	**1,203.0**	66	**201,907.0**	15
44	**HOME DEPOT** Atlanta[1]	**24,155.7**	**1,160.0**	72	**11,188.9**	202
45	**CONAGRA** Omaha[16]	**24,002.1**	**615.0**	142	**11,277.1**	199
46	**MERCK** Whitehouse Station, N.J.	**23,636.9**	**4,614.1**	9	**25,811.9**	105
47	**BANKAMERICA CORP.** San Francisco	**23,585.0**	**3,210.0**	22	**260,159.0**	11
48	**GTE** Stamford, Conn.	**23,260.0**	**2,793.6**	30	**42,141.7**	69
49	**JOHNSON & JOHNSON** New Brunswick, N.J.	**22,629.0**	**3,303.0**	18	**21,453.0**	125
50	**SAFEWAY** Pleasanton, Calif.[17]	**22,483.8**	**557.4***	155	**8,493.9**	227

STOCKHOLDERS' EQUITY		MARKET VALUE 3/18/98		EARNINGS PER SHARE				TOTAL RETURN TO INVESTORS			
				1997 $	% change from 1996	1987–97 annual growth rate %	Rank	1997 %	Rank	1987–97 annual rate %	Rank
$ millions	Rank	$ millions	Rank								
24,001.1	6	87,964.4	15	4.73	15.9	12.1	108	51.1	116	23.1	89
21,742.0	8	58,150.6	37	8.03	60.0	—		25.4	263	24.6	71
12,789.1	34	77,650.0	18	3.13	(28.2)	0.0	275	46.5	138	16.4	213
13,272.0	31	32,601.3	63	1.94	2.1	12.5	101	(6.0)	406	17.6	178
5,776.6	99	N.A.		N.A.		—		—		—	
6,936.0	83	63,351.5	31	1.36	88.9	13.7	89	36.1	196	23.6	79
5,176.0	121	22,465.4	90	(3.12)	(151.2)	—		9.0	349	20.7	127
13,793.0	28	67,592.9	26	2.83	14.1	22.0	33	54.5	99	39.2	9
4,375.0	150	18,606.7	107	3.18	63.1	14.8	80	74.0	50	24.6	70
13,956.0	27	46,842.4	46	4.25	52.3	—		81.3	30	—	
(784.8)	499	11,473.7	174	1.57	16.3	0.5	269	58.1	84	25.9	56
3,387.0	180	78,366.7	17	0.84	—	—		73.5	53	—	
19,295.0	16	125,741.0	6	3.87	33.4	36.5	12	7.4	356	35.9	12
15,610.0	23	40,657.1	52	7.11	53.6	—		58.0	85	—	
9,892.0	49	75,223.7	20	0.80	(53.5)	(0.8)	284	45.6	144	20.7	125
4,073.0	160	20,988.6	99	4.21	21.0	6.4	194	11.7	339	19.3	152
9,429.0	54	36,052.1	57	1.19	28.0	25.8	26	89.9	20	31.4	26
14,007.0	26	N.A.		N.A.		—		—		—	
7,097.9	81	50,019.3	44	1.55	19.8	30.1	18	76.9	42	41.8	5
2,471.7	236	15,365.5	131	2.68	239.2	12.5	100	35.6	198	22.0	103
12,613.5	36	156,964.7	5	3.74	19.9	17.6	56	35.6	199	22.6	95
19,837.0	12	57,839.8	38	4.32	18.2	—		49.0	130	39.4	8
8,037.6	68	54,186.9	41	2.90	0.7	5.8	204	20.0	296	17.4	185
12,359.0	37	100,630.6	13	2.41	13.7	14.8	78	34.3	211	24.0	75
2,149.0	263	16,993.9	119	1.12	15.5	—		48.0	132	—	

RANK 1997	COMPANY	REVENUES $ millions	PROFITS $ millions	Rank	ASSETS $ millions	Rank
51	**WALT DISNEY** Burbank, Calif.[13]	**22,473.0**	**1,966.0**	43	**37,776.0**	78
52	**UNITED PARCEL SERVICE** Atlanta	**22,458.0**	**909.0**	94	**15,912.0**	154
53	**COSTCO** Issaquah, Wash.[18]	**21,874.4**	**312.2**	247	**5,476.3**	296
54	**NATIONSBANK CORP.** Charlotte, N.C.[19]	**21,734.0**	**3,077.0**	27	**264,562.0**	9
55	**USX** Pittsburgh	**21,057.0**E	**988.0**	82	**17,284.0**	147
56	**BELLSOUTH** Atlanta	**20,561.0**	**3,261.0**	20	**36,301.0**	79
57	**ENRON** Houston[20]	**20,273.0**	**105.0**	388	**23,422.0**	117
58	**INTERNATIONAL PAPER** Purchase, N.Y.	**20,096.0**	**(151.0)**	478	**26,754.0**	104
59	**CIGNA** Philadelphia[21]	**20,038.0**	**1,086.0**	76	**108,199.0**	26
60	**DOW CHEMICAL** Midland, Mich.	**20,018.0**	**1,808.0**	48	**24,040.0**	112
61	**SARA LEE** Chicago[8]	**19,734.0**	**1,009.0**	81	**12,953.0**	181
62	**MCI COMMUNICATIONS** Washington, D.C.	**19,653.0**	**2.0**	453	**25,305.0**	108
63	**LOEWS** New York	**19,647.8**E	**793.6**	112	**69,577.1**	44
64	**ATLANTIC RICHFIELD** Los Angeles	**19,272.0**E	**1,771.0**	50	**25,322.0**	107
65	**AMERICAN STORES** Salt Lake City[1]	**19,138.9**	**280.6**	271	**8,536.0**	226
66	**CATERPILLAR** Peoria, Ill.	**18,925.0**	**1,665.0**	51	**20,756.0**	130
67	**NEW YORK LIFE INSURANCE** New York	**18,899.3**	**650.7**	137	**84,067.1**	35
68	**COCA-COLA** Atlanta	**18,868.0**	**4,129.0**	10	**16,940.0**	148
69	**COLUMBIA/HCA HEALTHCARE** Nashville[22]	**18,819.0**	**(305.0)**	485	**22,002.0**	123
70	**AMR** Fort Worth	**18,570.0**	**985.0**	83	**20,915.0**	128
71	**AETNA** Hartford	**18,540.2**	**901.1**	96	**96,000.6**	31
72	**XEROX** Stamford, Conn.	**18,166.0**	**1,452.0**	56	**27,732.0**	100
73	**AMERICAN EXPRESS** New York	**17,760.0**	**1,991.0**	42	**120,003.0**	23
74	**J.P. MORGAN & CO.** New York	**17,701.0**	**1,465.0**	55	**262,159.0**	10
75	**UAL** Elk Grove Township, Ill.	**17,378.0**	**949.0**	90	**15,803.0**	156

STOCKHOLDERS' EQUITY		MARKET VALUE 3/18/98		EARNINGS PER SHARE				TOTAL RETURN TO INVESTORS			
				1997 $	% change from 1996	1987–97 annual growth rate %	Rank	1997 %	Rank	1987–97 annual rate %	Rank
$ millions	Rank	$ millions	Rank								
17,285.0	20	72,754.1	23	2.86	45.9	13.5	91	42.8	162	21.6	108
6,087.0	92	N.A.		1.63	(19.7)	3.5	228	—		—	
2,468.1	237	11,789.7	170	1.47	18.5	(0.2)	280	77.6	39	3.5	364
21,337.0	9	68,437.1	25	4.17	6.4	15.2	74	27.3	252	25.8	57
5,400.0	112	13,915.6	143	N.A.	—	—		—		—	
15,165.0	24	61,132.0	33	3.28	14.3	6.6	190	43.5	157	17.3	190
5,618.0	104	14,589.7	139	0.32	(85.2)	—		(1.4)	393	19.7	143
8,710.0	60	15,110.0	133	(0.50)	(148.1)	—		8.8	352	10.2	317
7,932.0	73	14,737.6	137	14.64	5.2	5.4	208	28.8	241	20.4	132
7,626.0	74	21,208.1	97	7.70	1.3	6.0	198	34.4	210	9.8	320
4,280.0	154	28,242.3	76	2.03	10.9	13.2	96	54.2	102	23.5	84
11,164.0	45	35,129.1	59	0.00	(99.9)	(35.3)	334	31.1	227	25.0	68
9,655.1	50	12,190.0	162	6.90	(42.1)	4.5	220	13.7	330	13.4	276
8,680.0	61	24,448.2	83	5.41	6.3	4.9	213	25.6	262	14.0	262
2,309.1	254	6,952.8	252	1.01	2.5	6.8	188	2.1	382	14.5	250
4,679.0	134	21,367.6	96	4.37	24.9	17.4	57	31.3	225	14.0	261
4,621.7	140	N.A.		N.A.	—	—		—		—	
7,311.0	78	184,861.7	3	1.64	18.8	18.4	49	27.9	249	32.6	21
7,250.0	79	20,046.9	103	(0.46)	(120.7)	—		(27.1)	443	—	
6,216.0	90	12,946.3	150	10.78	(3.7)	12.6	99	45.8	143	13.8	269
11,195.4	44	12,419.9	158	5.60	18.6	(3.4)	300	(11.0)	420	9.7	324
5,690.0	102	31,829.0	64	4.04	21.7	8.5	154	43.1	160	19.3	150
9,574.0	53	45,270.0	47	4.15	16.6	13.2	95	59.9	77	19.5	149
11,404.0	40	23,450.3	87	7.17	(6.0)	33.8	14	19.5	300	16.6	205
2,337.0	251	5,283.5	294	8.95	76.9	19.5	40	48.0	131	21.8	105

RANK 1997	COMPANY	REVENUES $ millions	PROFITS $ millions	Rank	ASSETS $ millions	Rank
76	**RJR NABISCO HOLDINGS** New York	**17,057.0**[E]	**381.0**	214	**30,678.0**	89
77	**LEHMAN BROTHERS HOLDINGS** New York[11]	**16,883.0**	**647.0**	138	**151,705.0**	19
78	**BRISTOL-MYERS SQUIBB** New York	**16,701.2**	**3,204.7**	23	**14,977.0**	161
79	**INGRAM MICRO** Santa Ana, Calif.	**16,581.5**	**193.6**	317	**4,932.2**	320
80	**SUPERVALU** Eden Prairie, Minn.[23]	**16,551.9**	**175.0**	332	**4,283.3**	346
81	**DUKE ENERGY** Charlotte, N.C.[24]	**16,308.9**	**974.4**	84	**24,028.8**	113
82	**AMERITECH** Chicago	**15,998.0**	**2,296.0**	36	**25,339.0**	106
83	**FEDERATED DEPARTMENT STORES** Cincinnati[1]	**15,668.3**	**536.0**	161	**13,738.2**	171
84	**PHILLIPS PETROLEUM** Bartlesville, Okla.	**15,424.0**[E]	**959.0**	88	**13,860.0**	170
85	**PG&E CORP.** San Francisco[25]	**15,399.9**	**716.0**	122	**30,557.0**	90
86	**FLEMING** Oklahoma City	**15,372.7**	**25.4**	441	**3,924.0**	361
87	**US WEST** Englewood, Colo.	**15,352.0**	**697.0**	129	**39,860.0**	73
88	**ELECTRONIC DATA SYSTEMS** Plano, Texas	**15,235.6**	**730.6**	120	**11,174.1**	203
89	**MINNESOTA MINING & MFG.** St. Paul	**15,070.0**	**2,121.0**	39	**13,238.0**	176
90	**SPRINT** Westwood, Kan.	**14,873.9**	**952.5**	89	**18,184.8**	140
91	**EASTMAN KODAK** Rochester, N.Y.	**14,713.0**	**5.0**	450	**13,145.0**	178
92	**ALBERTSON'S** Boise[1]	**14,689.5**	**516.8**	167	**5,218.6**	310
93	**ALLIEDSIGNAL** Morristown, N.J.	**14,472.0**	**1,170.0**	71	**13,707.0**	172
94	**SYSCO** Houston[8]	**14,454.6**	**302.5**	251	**3,436.6**	379
95	**FEDERAL HOME LOAN MORTGAGE** McLean, Va.	**14,399.0**	**1,395.0**	59	**194,597.0**	16
96	**FIRST UNION CORP.** Charlotte, N.C.[26]	**14,329.0**	**1,896.0**	46	**157,274.0**	18
97	**FLUOR** Irvine, Calif.[4]	**14,298.5**	**146.2**	356	**4,697.8**	332
98	**AMERICAN HOME PRODUCTS** Madison, N.J.	**14,196.0**	**2,043.1**	41	**20,825.1**	129
99	**ARCHER DANIELS MIDLAND** Decatur, Ill.[8]	**13,853.3**	**377.3**	217	**11,354.4**	197
100	**RAYTHEON** Lexington, Mass.	**13,673.5**	**526.8**	164	**28,100.0**	99

STOCKHOLDERS' EQUITY		MARKET VALUE 3/18/98		EARNINGS PER SHARE					TOTAL RETURN TO INVESTORS			
					% change from 1996	1987–97 annual growth rate			1997		1987–97 annual rate	
$ millions	Rank	$ millions	Rank	1997 $		%	Rank		%	Rank	%	Rank
9,631.0	52	11,041.6	179	1.03	(40.8)	—			17.1	312	—	
4,523.0	143	8,686.6	207	4.72	45.7	—			63.5	72	—	
7,219.1	80	106,332.8	10	3.14	12.1	9.8	134		77.3	40	20.9	122
1,038.2	383	5,406.1	290	1.32	50.0	—			26.6	254	—	
1,307.4	358	2,905.5	374	2.60	6.6	8.0	167		51.8	112	11.9	296
8,028.7	70	21,453.1	95	2.50	(25.8)	1.3	261		25.2	267	15.8	225
8,308.0	63	51,636.4	42	2.08	8.3	7.0	186		37.6	187	19.8	139
5,256.3	117	10,717.4	184	2.41	94.4	—			26.2	257	—	
4,814.0	132	12,912.3	151	3.61	(26.5)	50.6	4		13.2	332	17.6	180
8,897.0	57	13,339.2	146	1.75	0.0	1.4	260		51.9	111	14.1	259
1,089.7	377	763.6	451	0.67	(5.6)	(9.7)	319		(21.8)	433	(3.8)	374
11,324.0	42	47,790.0	45	N.A.	—	—			—		—	
5,309.4	114	24,549.3	82	1.48	68.2	—			3.1	376	—	
5,926.0	95	37,943.0	55	5.06	39.8	9.7	138		1.1	385	13.3	277
9,025.2	56	30,234.4	69	2.18	(21.3)	—			50.0	123	22.8	93
3,161.0	193	20,050.3	102	0.01	(99.7)	(44.5)	335		(22.8)	435	8.5	339
2,419.5	240	13,327.2	147	2.08	6.7	16.0	68		34.9	205	24.1	74
4,386.0	149	23,485.3	86	2.02	14.8	7.6	177		17.4	311	22.3	97
1,400.5	345	8,685.0	208	1.71	12.5	17.2	60		42.0	170	22.4	96
7,521.0	76	33,447.1	60	1.88	13.9	—			53.4	106	—	
12,032.0	39	35,836.9	58	2.99	15.9	8.9	148		42.1	166	22.8	92
1,741.1	301	4,307.8	327	1.73	(45.4)	18.0	54		(39.6)	454	11.5	302
8,175.3	65	58,859.1	35	3.11	6.5	8.1	166		33.5	216	20.0	136
6,050.1	94	12,330.3	159	0.66	(45.4)	4.6	216		4.5	372	14.7	245
10,400.0	47	20,251.8	100	2.18	(31.2)	3.6	226		6.7	362	14.6	248

		REVENUES	PROFITS		ASSETS	
RANK 1997	COMPANY	$ millions	$ millions	Rank	$ millions	Rank
101	DELTA AIR LINES Atlanta[8]	13,590.0	854.0	102	12,741.0	185
102	ASHLAND Russell, Ky.[13]	13,567.0[E]	279.0	272	7,777.0	243
103	VIACOM New York	13,504.5	793.6	113	28,288.7	98
104	ALCOA Pittsburgh	13,481.7	805.1	108	13,070.6	180
105	MCKESSON San Francisco[27]	13,478.8	133.9	366	5,172.8	311
106	NORTHWESTERN MUTUAL LIFE INS. Milwaukee	13,429.9	689.1	130	71,080.6	43
107	NGC Houston	13,378.4	(102.5)	472	4,800.0	329
108	WALGREEN Deerfield, Ill.[18]	13,363.0	436.0	186	4,207.0	352
109	HARTFORD FINANCIAL SERVICES Hartford[28]	13,305.0	1,332.0	61	131,743.0	21
110	TIME WARNER New York	13,294.0	246.0*	295	34,163.0	84
111	TOSCO Stamford, Conn.	13,281.6[E]	212.7	306	5,945.3	279
112	IBP Dakota City, Neb.	13,258.8	117.0	380	2,838.9	405
113	BANC ONE CORP. Columbus, Ohio[29]	13,219.1	1,305.7	62	115,901.3	24
114	WINN-DIXIE STORES Jacksonville[8]	13,218.7	204.4	314	2,921.4	401
115	GOODYEAR TIRE & RUBBER Akron	13,155.1	558.7	153	9,917.4	211
116	GEORGIA-PACIFIC Atlanta	13,094.0	69.0	411	12,950.0	182
117	CVS Woonsocket, R.I.[30]	13,086.5	37.7*	436	5,357.0[31]	304
118	DIGITAL EQUIPMENT Maynard, Mass.[8]	13,046.8	140.9	360	9,692.9	213
119	DEERE Moline, Ill.[4]	12,791.4	960.1	87	16,319.8	153
120	MAY DEPARTMENT STORES St. Louis[1]	12,685.0	775.0	114	9,930.0	210
121	NATIONWIDE INS. ENTERPRISE Columbus, Ohio[6]	12,644.4	805.6	107	87,829.9	33
122	SOUTHERN Atlanta	12,611.0	972.0	85	35,271.0	83
123	KIMBERLY-CLARK Irving, Texas	12,546.6	901.5	95	11,266.0	200
124	PFIZER New York	12,504.0	2,213.0	37	15,336.0	158
125	DELL COMPUTER Round Rock, Texas[1]	12,327.0	944.0	91	4,268.0	348

STOCKHOLDERS' EQUITY		MARKET VALUE 3/18/98		EARNINGS PER SHARE				TOTAL RETURN TO INVESTORS			
					% change	1987–97 annual growth rate				1987–97 annual rate	
$ millions	Rank	$ millions	Rank	1997 $	from 1996	%	Rank	1997 %	Rank	%	Rank
3,007.0	202	8,951.6	204	11.30	695.8	6.7	189	68.3	59	13.7	270
2,024.0	273	4,244.5	331	3.80	27.9	5.9	199	25.2	266	9.6	327
13,383.6	30	18,014.0	113	2.07	(35.9)	—		18.8	304	—	
4,419.4	147	12,210.7	161	4.62	58.8	15.2	75	11.8	337	14.4	252
1,260.8	362	5,662.7	281	3.01	3.8	—		96.7	14	—	
4,100.6	159	N.A.		N.A.	—	—		—		—	
1,000.0	387	2,267.3	398	(0.61)	(173.5)	—		(24.5)	436	—	
2,373.0	245	17,858.3	115	0.88	17.3	15.4	70	57.4	87	25.3	64
6,085.0	93	12,498.1	156	11.16	—	—		41.6	174	—	
9,356.0	55	42,537.1	49	(0.13)	—	—		66.5	68	13.1	280
1,944.1	282	5,684.2	280	1.37	18.1	2.7	245	44.5	149	31.6	25
1,237.1	364	2,234.0	400	1.25	(39.6)	—		(13.3)	422	—	
10,376.0	48	39,868.9	53	2.19	(23.5)	9.4	143	30.4	232	20.4	131
1,337.5	354	8,760.6	205	1.36	(19.5)	7.2	184	42.1	167	18.3	166
3,395.5	179	11,157.0	178	3.53	443.1	(5.7)	307	26.2	258	10.6	312
3,474.0	175	8,406.4	213	0.73	(57.3)	(16.1)	326	20.8	289	12.6	288
2,236.0[31]	257	12,474.2	157	0.14	(75.4)	(25.4)	331	56.1	92	13.9	265
3,545.0	170	7,100.9	245	0.68	—	(22.3)	330	2.4	378	(12.1)	381
4,147.3	156	14,808.4	136	3.78	20.4	—		46.2	139	20.8	124
3,809.0	165	14,568.0	140	3.10	9.2	7.9	171	15.3	321	18.3	167
8,795.4	59	N.A.		N.A.	—	—		—		—	
9,647.0	51	18,452.2	109	1.42	(15.5)	4.0	223	21.3	284	16.6	207
4,125.3	157	27,919.3	77	1.61	(35.1)	5.6	205	5.5	368	18.6	159
7,933.0	72	114,195.5	7	1.70	13.7	12.8	98	81.9	27	32.3	23
1,293.0	360	41,294.2	51	2.56	93.9	—		216.2	2	—	

RANK 1997	COMPANY	REVENUES $ millions	PROFITS $ millions	Rank	ASSETS $ millions	Rank
126	EMERSON ELECTRIC St. Louis[13]	12,298.6	1,121.9	74	11,463.3	196
127	BANKERS TRUST NEW YORK CORP. New York[32]	12,176.0	866.0	101	140,102.0	20
128	MARRIOTT INTERNATIONAL Bethesda, Md.	12,034.0	335.0	238	6,322.0	271
129	ABBOTT LABORATORIES Abbott Park, Ill.	11,883.5	2,094.5	40	12,061.1	191
130	UNITED HEALTHCARE Minnetonka, Minn.	11,794.0	460.0	178	7,623.0	246
131	ROCKWELL INTERNATIONAL Costa Mesa, Calif.[13]	11,759.0¶	644.0	139	7,971.0	236
132	LIBERTY MUTUAL INSURANCE GROUP Boston	11,670.0	521.0	166	44,891.0	66
133	BERGEN BRUNSWIG Orange, Calif.[13]	11,660.5	81.7	405	2,707.1	412
134	FDX Memphis[16,33]	11,519.8	361.2	222	7,625.5	245
135	MCDONALD'S Oak Brook, Ill.	11,408.8	1,642.5	52	18,200.0	139
136	JOHNSON CONTROLS Milwaukee[13]	11,387.4¶	288.5	265	6,048.6	278
137	MICROSOFT Redmond, Wash.[8]	11,358.0	3,454.0	15	14,387.0	165
138	COCA-COLA ENTERPRISES Atlanta	11,278.0	171.0	335	17,487.0	145
139	PUBLIX SUPER MARKETS Lakeland, Fla.	11,224.4	354.6	225	3,295.0	387
140	WEYERHAEUSER Federal Way, Wash.	11,210.0	342.0	234	13,075.0	179
141	ANHEUSER-BUSCH St. Louis	11,066.2[E]	1,179.2	70	11,727.1	193
142	OCCIDENTAL PETROLEUM Los Angeles	11,061.0[E¶]	(390.0)	487	15,282.0	160
143	TOYS "R" US Rochelle Park, N.J.[1]	11,037.8	490.1	173	7,963.1	237
144	UNION PACIFIC Dallas	11,014.0	432.0	187	28,764.0	96
145	CARDINAL HEALTH Dublin, Ohio[8]	10,968.0	181.1	328	3,108.5	392
146	TRW Cleveland[34]	10,831.3	(48.5)	467	6,410.0	269
147	CSX Richmond[35]	10,621.0	799.0	109	19,957.0	133
148	TEXAS INSTRUMENTS Dallas	10,562.0	1,805.0	49	10,849.0	205
149	TEXTRON Providence	10,544.0	558.0	154	18,610.0	136
150	BERKSHIRE HATHAWAY Omaha	10,430.0	1,901.6	45	56,110.9	55

STOCKHOLDERS' EQUITY		MARKET VALUE 3/18/98		EARNINGS PER SHARE				TOTAL RETURN TO INVESTORS			
				1997 $	% change from 1996	1987–97 annual growth rate %	Rank	1997 %	Rank	1987–97 annual rate %	Rank
$ millions	Rank	$ millions	Rank								
5,420.7	111	28,542.1	73	2.52	10.8	9.7	137	18.9	303	15.8	226
5,708.0	101	11,907.5	167	7.66	13.3	81.3	2	36.1	194	19.5	147
1,463.0	338	10,252.7	189	2.46	9.3	—		26.0	259	—	
4,998.7	125	59,026.3	34	2.68	12.6	14.4	82	31.2	226	21.0	121
4,534.0	142	12,588.0	155	2.26	15.3	—		10.5	343	49.3	2
4,811.0	133	12,251.3	160	3.01	(9.9)	2.9	241	(0.4)	391	16.1	218
6,771.7	87	N.A.		N.A.		—		—		—	
644.9	438	2,100.2	406	1.61	10.0	14.3	83	85.5	24	21.5	110
2,962.5	203	8,481.6	212	3.12	15.8	—		37.2	188	11.8	297
8,800.0	58	36,145.2	56	2.29	6.0	11.3	120	6.0	366	16.8	199
1,687.9	309	4,630.8	318	3.29	22.1	11.6	115	17.6	310	17.7	177
10,777.0	46	199,046.4	2	2.63	53.4	43.3	7	56.4	91	45.6	3
1,782.0	296	13,529.4	144	0.43	51.8	7.4	179	120.7	10	22.7	94
2,019.3	274	N.A.		1.62	35.0	16.5	65	—		—	
4,649.0	137	10,984.2	181	1.71	(26.6)	(2.1)	293	6.8	359	10.7	311
4,041.8	161	22,736.8	88	2.36	4.0	8.8	151	12.6	333	12.8	284
4,286.0	152	9,636.8	196	(1.43)	(182.7)	—		30.5	231	8.6	338
4,427.9	145	8,093.9	219	1.70	10.4	9.4	142	5.2	369	8.4	340
8,225.0	64	12,906.7	152	1.74	(58.0)	(3.8)	303	7.1	357	16.4	212
1,332.2	355	9,245.2	202	1.66	43.9	19.7	39	29.2	240	40.2	6
1,624.0	317	6,717.2	258	(0.40)	(111.0)	—		10.3	344	12.0	292
5,766.0	100	12,593.4	154	3.62	(8.6)	23.5	29	30.4	234	17.4	188
5,914.0	96	21,665.9	93	4.54	2,570.6	17.6	55	42.2	165	14.2	257
3,228.0	187	12,003.2	164	3.29	123.8	8.5	156	34.9	206	22.2	99
31,455.2	4	79,739.8	16	1,542.00	(25.3)	22.4	32	34.9	207	31.6	24

RANK 1997	COMPANY	REVENUES $ millions	PROFITS $ millions	Rank	ASSETS $ millions	Rank
151	**REPUBLIC INDUSTRIES** Fort Lauderdale	**10,305.6**	**439.7[1]**	185	**10,527.3**	207
152	**NORTHWEST AIRLINES** St. Paul	**10,225.8**	**596.5**	145	**9,336.2**	218
153	**LOWE'S** North Wilkesboro, N.C.[1]	**10,136.9**	**357.5**	223	**5,219.3**	309
154	**FIRST CHICAGO NBD CORP.** Chicago	**10,098.0**	**1,525.0**	53	**114,096.0**	25
155	**GILLETTE** Boston	**10,062.1**	**1,427.2**	58	**10,864.0**	204
156	**BESTFOODS** Englewood Cliffs, N.J.[36]	**9,818.4[1]**	**344.1**	231	**6,100.0**	275
157	**NORWEST CORP.** Minneapolis	**9,659.7**	**1,351.0**	60	**88,540.2**	32
158	**COASTAL** Houston	**9,653.1**	**301.5**	253	**11,625.2**	195
159	**CBS** New York[37]	**9,632.0[1]**	**549.0**	156	**16,715.0**	150
160	**WELLS FARGO & CO.** San Francisco	**9,608.0**	**1,155.0**	73	**97,456.0**	28
161	**ENTERGY** New Orleans	**9,561.7**	**247.7**	293	**27,000.7**	103
162	**MASSACHUSETTS MUTUAL LIFE INS.** Springfield, Mass.	**9,551.2**	**351.8**	227	**63,088.0**	48
163	**MONSANTO** St. Louis	**9,457.0[1]**	**470.0**	177	**10,774.0**	206
164	**H.J. HEINZ** Pittsburgh[38]	**9,357.0**	**301.9**	252	**8,437.8**	228
165	**WASTE MANAGEMENT** Oak Brook, Ill.	**9,273.4**	**(1,176.1)**	496	**13,589.1**	173
166	**EDISON INTERNATIONAL** Rosemead, Calif.	**9,235.1**	**700.0**	128	**25,101.0**	109
167	**LIMITED** Columbus, Ohio[1]	**9,188.8**	**217.4**	305	**4,268.2**	347
168	**NIKE** Beaverton, Ore.[16]	**9,186.5**	**795.8**	110	**5,361.2**	302
169	**NORTHROP GRUMMAN** Los Angeles	**9,153.0**	**407.0**	202	**9,677.0**	214
170	**FARMLAND INDUSTRIES** Kansas City, Mo.[18,39]	**9,147.5**	**N.A.**		**2,645.3**	416
171	**COLGATE-PALMOLIVE** New York	**9,056.7**	**740.4**	119	**7,538.7**	248
172	**PACIFICARE HEALTH SYSTEMS** Santa Ana, Calif.[40]	**8,982.7**	**(21.7)**	462	**4,868.0**	323
173	**SUN** Philadelphia	**8,968.0[E]**	**263.0**	280	**4,667.0**	335
174	**SEAGATE TECHNOLOGY** Scotts Valley, Calif.[8]	**8,940.0**	**658.0**	136	**6,722.9**	261
175	**AMERICAN GENERAL** Houston[41]	**8,927.0**	**542.0**	158	**80,620.0**	38

STOCKHOLDERS' EQUITY		MARKET VALUE 3/18/98		EARNINGS PER SHARE				TOTAL RETURN TO INVESTORS			
					% change from	1987–97 annual growth rate		1997		1987–97 annual rate	
$ millions	Rank	$ millions	Rank	1997 $	1996	%	Rank	%	Rank	%	Rank
3,484.4	172	11,953.5	166	1.02	—	—		(25.3)	438	—	
(311.0)	494	5,988.6	272	5.21	0.2	—		22.4	278	—	
2,600.6	227	11,954.4	165	2.05	19.9	18.2	52	34.6	208	29.6	36
7,960.0	71	25,877.8	80	4.90	13.2	12.3	105	59.5	80	23.5	82
4,841.0	131	65,539.9	28	2.49	50.0	17.4	58	30.4	233	32.4	22
1,042.0	381	15,857.3	127	2.29	(40.5)	0.5	268	42.0	169	21.3	116
7,022.2	82	32,668.1	62	1.75	13.6	—		81.9	26	33.0	17
3,282.4	183	6,915.6	253	2.65	(26.6)	6.6	191	27.7	250	15.0	242
8,080.0	67	22,310.5	91	0.84	600.0	(10.5)	320	49.4	127	4.7	359
12,889.0	33	28,791.2	72	12.64	4.9	37.6	10	28.2	247	27.2	45
6,693.5	88	6,845.1	255	1.03	(43.7)	(5.1)	306	16.0	319	19.9	137
2,873.4	208	N.A.		N.A.	—	—		—		—	
4,104.0	158	30,745.8	67	0.77	20.3	3.2	235	19.2	302	22.2	98
2,440.4	238	21,131.7	98	0.81	(53.7)	(0.2)	277	46.2	141	17.8	174
1,345.7	352	14,419.0	141	(2.52)	—	—		(13.7)	424	5.5	356
5,527.0	107	11,249.4	177	1.73	6.1	0.2	274	42.8	163	12.9	282
2,045.0	271	8,106.6	218	0.79	(48.7)	2.4	249	41.8	172	13.2	279
3,155.8	196	13,261.9	148	2.68	42.2	36.9	11	(34.4)	449	33.6	16
2,623.0	223	7,172.0	244	5.98	44.1	11.5	116	41.3	175	21.1	120
822.0	421	N.A.		N.A.	—	—		—		—	
2,178.6	262	25,386.2	81	2.27	15.8	27.8	20	62.2	73	25.5	59
2,062.2	269	2,963.0	372	(0.75)	(133.0)	—		(38.2)	452	42.7	4
1,462.0	339	3,036.8	366	2.70	—	(1.7)	289	77.7	38	9.8	321
3,475.7	174	5,496.5	288	2.73	165.0	6.9	187	(51.3)	458	10.0	319
7,583.0	75	14,957.2	135	2.19	(16.7)	1.2	264	36.2	193	18.1	169

RANK 1997	COMPANY	REVENUES $ millions	PROFITS $ millions	Rank	ASSETS $ millions	Rank
176	**UTILICORP UNITED** Kansas City, Mo.	**8,926.3**	**122.1**	375	**5,113.5**	312
177	**HALLIBURTON** Dallas	**8,818.6**	**454.4**	179	**5,603.0**	288
178	**ITT INDUSTRIES** White Plains, N.Y.	**8,776.5**	**108.1**	386	**6,220.5**	274
179	**DANA** Toledo	**8,770.3**	**369.1**	220	**7,118.7**	254
180	**TENET HEALTHCARE** Santa Barbara[16,42]	**8,691.0**	**(254.0)**	483	**11,705.0**	194
181	**PRINCIPAL FINANCIAL** Des Moines[6]	**8,666.0**	**454.0**	180	**67,054.0**	46
182	**WHIRLPOOL** Benton Harbor, Mich.	**8,617.0**	**(15.0)**	460	**8,270.0**	233
183	**ULTRAMAR DIAMOND SHAMROCK** San Antonio	**8,606.5**E	**154.8**	348	**5,594.7**	290
184	**SUN MICROSYSTEMS** Palo Alto[8]	**8,598.3**	**762.4**	117	**4,697.3**	333
185	**ELI LILLY** Indianapolis	**8,517.6**	**(385.1)**	486	**12,577.4**	187
186	**US AIRWAYS GROUP** Arlington, Va.	**8,513.8**	**1,024.7**	80	**8,372.4**	230
187	**CROWN CORK & SEAL** Philadelphia	**8,494.6**	**294.0**	261	**12,305.7**	190
188	**BURLINGTON NORTHERN SANTA FE** Fort Worth	**8,412.0**E	**885.0**	97	**21,336.0**	126
189	**GENERAL RE** Stamford, Conn.	**8,246.6**	**967.7**	86	**41,459.0**	71
190	**AMERADA HESS** New York	**8,233.7**E	**7.5**	447	**7,934.6**	238
191	**JOHN HANCOCK MUTUAL LIFE INS.** Boston	**8,207.0**	**414.0**	195	**62,124.8**	49
192	**WARNER-LAMBERT** Morris Plains, N.J.	**8,179.8**	**869.5**	100	**8,030.5**	235
193	**FLEET FINANCIAL GROUP** Boston	**8,095.0**	**1,303.0**	63	**85,535.0**	34
194	**HONEYWELL** Minneapolis	**8,027.5**	**471.0**	176	**6,411.4**	268
195	**CAMPBELL SOUP** Camden, N.J.[43]	**7,964.0**	**713.0**	124	**6,459.0**	265
196	**TEXAS UTILITIES** Dallas[44]	**7,945.6**	**660.5**	134	**24,874.1**	111
197	**HUMANA** Louisville[45]	**7,880.0**	**173.0**	334	**5,418.0**	299
198	**AMERISOURCE HEALTH** Malvern, Pa.[13]	**7,815.9**	**45.5**	432	**1,745.0**	463
199	**BEST BUY** Eden Prairie, Minn.[23]	**7,770.7**	**1.7**	454	**1,734.3**	464
200	**ARROW ELECTRONICS** Melville, N.Y.	**7,763.9**	**163.7**	340	**3,537.9**	374

STOCKHOLDERS' EQUITY		MARKET VALUE 3/18/98		EARNINGS PER SHARE				TOTAL RETURN TO INVESTORS			
					% change from 1996	1987–97 annual growth rate		1997		1987–97 annual rate	
$ millions	Rank	$ millions	Rank	1997 $		%	Rank	%	Rank	%	Rank
1,163.6	373	2,006.5	414	2.26	3.2	3.3	234	52.5	109	17.7	176
2,584.7	228	11,787.1	171	1.75	47.1	22.8	31	74.3	49	19.0	156
822.3	420	4,493.4	325	0.89	(51.9)	(18.4)	328	31.1	228	18.1	168
1,701.2	307	5,958.3	274	3.49	16.7	7.8	173	49.4	129	15.0	241
3,224.0	188	11,290.9	176	(0.84)	(150.3)	—	—	51.4	114	16.0	223
5,284.0	116	N.A.		N.A.	—	—	—	—		—	
1,771.0	299	5,119.5	300	(0.20)	(109.6)	—	—	20.3	295	11.7	300
1,686.6	310	3,049.2	365	1.88	—	—	—	4.2	373	—	
2,741.9	217	16,614.1	121	1.96	62.0	30.3	17	55.2	97	25.3	63
4,645.6	138	72,808.6	22	(0.35)	(125.7)	—	—	93.5	17	25.3	62
725.3	427	6,769.7	257	9.87	320.0	6.5	193	167.4	5	6.5	353
3,529.2	171	6,712.3	259	2.10	(1.9)	8.2	163	(6.1)	407	16.1	220
6,812.0	86	16,171.0	124	5.64	(1.7)	1.4	259	9.1	348	21.4	115
8,161.0	66	17,262.8	118	11.76	9.1	8.8	150	35.6	197	16.2	217
3,215.7	189	5,298.5	293	0.08	(98.9)	(29.7)	332	(4.2)	401	9.7	323
3,157.8	194	N.A.		N.A.	—	—	—	—		—	
2,835.5	211	43,891.0	48	3.11	9.1	11.6	114	68.0	62	25.4	60
8,034.0	69	21,624.0	94	4.74	19.1	10.0	131	55.3	96	17.6	179
2,389.2	242	10,592.9	187	3.65	17.4	9.8	135	5.8	367	21.1	119
1,420.0	343	27,470.1	78	1.51	(53.1)	12.2	107	47.2	135	26.4	54
6,843.1	85	9,840.2	192	2.85	(14.9)	(4.6)	305	7.9	354	13.0	281
1,501.0	332	4,234.8	332	1.05	1,400.0	(1.6)	288	9.2	347	19.1	154
14.3	491	1,406.6	436	1.87	21.4	—	—	20.7	292	—	
438.3	464	2,996.4	370	0.04	(96.4)	(18.9)	329	247.1	1	29.6	35
1,360.8	349	2,980.8	371	1.64	(17.2)	—	—	21.3	285	25.4	61

RANK 1997	COMPANY	REVENUES $ millions	PROFITS $ millions	Rank	ASSETS $ millions	Rank
201	**DOMINION RESOURCES** Richmond	**7,677.6**	**399.2**	208	**20,192.7**	131
202	**CIRCUIT CITY GROUP** Richmond[23]	**7,663.8**	**136.4**	362	**3,081.2**	393
203	**TELE-COMMUNICATIONS** Englewood, Colo.	**7,570.0**	**(626.0)**	490	**32,323.0**	87
204	**EATON** Cleveland	**7,563.0**	**410.0***	199	**5,465.0**	297
205	**WASHINGTON MUTUAL** Seattle[46]	**7,524.4**	**481.8**	174	**96,981.1**	29
206	**DRESSER INDUSTRIES** Dallas[4]	**7,457.9**	**318.0**	243	**5,098.8**	313
207	**UNITED SERVICES AUTOMOBILE ASSN.** San Antonio	**7,454.2**	**1,189.1**	67	**25,007.0**	110
208	**TJX** Framingham, Mass.[1]	**7,389.1**	**304.8**	249	**2,609.6**	418
209	**PPG INDUSTRIES** Pittsburgh	**7,379.0**	**714.0**	123	**6,868.0**	259
210	**WORLDCOM** Jackson, Miss.	**7,351.4**	**383.7**	212	**22,389.6**	121
211	**LEAR** Southfield, Mich.	**7,342.9**	**207.2**	312	**4,459.1**	339
212	**BINDLEY WESTERN** Indianapolis	**7,311.8**	**23.7**	444	**1,274.2**	479
213	**FORT JAMES** Richmond[47]	**7,259.0**	**(27.0)***	463	**7,733.2**	244
214	**MANPOWER** Milwaukee	**7,258.5**	**163.9**	339	**2,047.0**	441
215	**AFLAC** Columbus, Ga.	**7,250.7**	**585.0**	148	**29,454.0**	94
216	**FOUNDATION HEALTH SYS.** Woodland Hills, Calif.[48]	**7,235.0**	**(187.1)**	481	**4,076.4**	358
217	**TENNECO** Greenwich, Conn.	**7,220.0**	**315.0**	246	**8,332.0**	232
218	**CONTINENTAL AIRLINES** Houston	**7,213.0**	**385.0**	211	**5,830.0**	281
219	**CONSOLIDATED EDISON** New York[49]	**7,121.3**	**712.8**	125	**14,722.5**	163
220	**UNISOURCE** Berwyn, Pa.[13]	**7,108.4**	**58.7**	419	**2,558.8**	422
221	**INGERSOLL-RAND** Woodcliff Lake, N.J.	**7,103.3**	**380.5**	215	**8,415.6**	229
222	**UNICOM** Chicago	**7,083.0**	**(852.9)***	492	**22,699.8**	119
223	**APPLE COMPUTER** Cupertino, Calif.[13]	**7,081.0**	**(1,045.0)**	495	**4,233.0**	351
224	**TECH DATA** Clearwater, Fla.[1]	**7,056.6**	**89.5**	401	**2,185.4**	435
225	**FORTUNE BRANDS** Old Greenwich, Conn.[50]	**7,000.8**[E,1]	**98.5**	390	**6,942.5**	257

STOCKHOLDERS' EQUITY		MARKET VALUE 3/18/98		EARNINGS PER SHARE				TOTAL RETURN TO INVESTORS			
					% change from	1987–97 annual growth rate		1997		1987–97 annual rate	
$ millions	Rank	$ millions	Rank	1997 $	1996	%	Rank	%	Rank	%	Rank
5,040.5	123	7,570.7	235	2.15	(18.9)	(3.4)	299	18.2	307	11.7	299
1,614.9	320	4,922.7	308	1.38	(24.2)	13.3	93	18.5	306	23.2	88
4,427.0	146	27,371.3	79	N.A.	—	—		—		—	
2,071.0	268	7,579.9	234	5.24	17.5	8.2	164	30.6	229	16.4	214
5,309.1	115	18,721.4	106	1.86	129.6	4.6	217	50.0	121	29.3	38
1,732.2	303	7,584.7	233	1.81	25.7	18.7	47	37.9	185	16.1	219
6,916.5	84	N.A.		N.A.	—	—		—		—	
1,164.1	372	7,373.5	239	1.74	(15.9)	3.6	225	46.1	142	26.5	52
2,509.0	234	11,747.7	172	3.94	0.3	9.5	141	4.1	375	16.6	204
13,509.9	29	39,550.6	54	0.40	—	—		16.1	318	—	
1,207.0	367	3,838.7	345	3.04	27.7	—		39.2	181	—	
354.3	468	541.5	455	1.59	16.9	19.0	44	59.9	78	16.0	222
584.3	447	9,444.7	200	0.28	(80.4)	(18.0)	327	16.9	314	8.0	342
617.6	443	3,233.9	361	1.97	1.5	—		8.9	350	—	
3,430.5	177	8,759.1	206	4.16	52.4	19.9	38	20.7	293	22.9	91
896.0	406	3,494.6	356	(1.52)	(200.0)	—		(10.1)	418	—	
2,528.0	232	7,294.6	241	1.84	(21.4)	—		(10.1)	417	6.1	354
916.0	402	3,610.6	354	4.99	19.7	—		70.4	57	—	
6,163.5	91	10,950.3	182	2.95	0.7	2.9	240	49.9	124	14.6	249
984.4	391	884.4	449	0.87	—	—		(26.4)	441	—	
2,341.4	250	7,981.0	222	2.31	4.4	12.3	104	38.6	182	15.6	227
4,918.7	127	7,306.6	240	(3.94)	(227.5)	—		21.1	287	8.9	335
1,200.0	369	3,448.5	357	(8.29)	—	—		(37.1)	451	(10.2)	380
702.6	428	2,020.5	413	1.92	42.2	24.3	27	42.0	171	30.9	27
4,017.1	162	7,003.1	251	0.56	(79.7)	(13.2)	323	21.1	286	15.1	240

RANK 1997	COMPANY	REVENUES $ millions	PROFITS $ millions	Rank	ASSETS $ millions	Rank
226	GUARDIAN LIFE INS. CO. OF AMERICA New York	6,983.8	299.3	256	22,088.9	122
227	RITE AID Camp Hill, Pa.[23,51]	6,970.2	115.4	381	6,417.0	267
228	U.S. BANCORP Minneapolis[52]	6,908.8	838.5	103	71,295.0	42
229	REYNOLDS METALS Richmond	6,900.0	136.0	363	7,226.0	252
230	HOUSTON INDUSTRIES Houston[54]	6,873.4	420.9	191	18,414.6	138
231	PNC BANK CORP. Pittsburgh	6,859.2	1,052.5	78	75,120.0	40
232	ANTHEM INSURANCE Indianapolis[6]	6,831.7	(159.0)	479	4,589.0	337
233	KELLOGG Battle Creek, Mich.	6,830.1	546.0	157	4,877.6	322
234	DILLARD'S Little Rock[1]	6,817.0	258.0	284	5,592.0	291
235	PACIFICORP Portland, Ore.	6,800.4	663.7	133	13,880.2	168
236	SCHERING-PLOUGH Madison, N.J.	6,778.0	1,444.0	57	6,507.0	264
237	PACCAR Bellevue, Wash.	6,763.7	344.6	230	5,599.4	289
238	BANKBOSTON CORP. Boston	6,727.2	879.2	98	69,268.0	45
239	OFFICE DEPOT Delray Beach, Fla.	6,717.5	159.7	346	2,981.1	399
240	PHARMACIA & UPJOHN Bridgewater, N.J.	6,710.0	323.0	242	10,383.0	209
241	CHUBB Warren, N.J.	6,664.0	769.5	116	19,615.6	134
242	ITT New York	6,658.0	291.0	262	9,187.0[31]	219
243	PAINE WEBBER GROUP New York	6,657.0	415.4	194	57,146.0	54
244	UNISYS Blue Bell, Pa.	6,636.0	(853.6)	493	5,591.3	292
245	WOOLWORTH New York[1]	6,624.0	(10.0)	457	3,182.0	391
246	TYCO INTERNATIONAL Exeter, N.H.[8]	6,597.6	419.0	192	5,888.3	280
247	NCR Dayton	6,589.0	7.0	448	5,293.0	306
248	KEYCORP Cleveland	6,568.0	919.0	93	73,699.0	41
249	GAP San Francisco[1]	6,507.8	533.9	162	3,337.5	384
250	UNION CARBIDE Danbury, Conn.	6,502.0	659.0	135	6,964.0	256

STOCKHOLDERS' EQUITY		MARKET VALUE 3/18/98		EARNINGS PER SHARE				TOTAL RETURN TO INVESTORS			
					% change	1987–97 annual growth rate		1997		1987–97 annual rate	
$ millions	Rank	$ millions	Rank	1997 $	from 1996	%	Rank	%	Rank	%	Rank
1,403.0	344	N.A.		N.A.	—	—		—		—	
2,488.7	235	8,669.3	209	1.25	(34.2)	2.8	242	50.3	119	15.4	231
5,890.0	97	30,244.8	68	3.34	(29.2)	53 16.4	66	67.4	66	23.4	85
2,739.0	218	4,647.0	317	1.84	124.4	(8.2)	315	8.7	353	5.0	358
4,896.5	128	7,655.3	231	1.66	0.0	(1.2)	286	26.5	255	14.5	251
5,384.0	113	17,988.2	114	3.28	13.9	8.3	159	56.8	90	17.4	184
1,524.7	328	N.A.		N.A.	—	—		—		—	
997.5	389	18,250.5	110	1.32	5.6	5.1	210	54.4	100	17.0	196
2,808.0	214	3,825.0	346	2.31	10.5	9.4	144	14.7	324	16.0	221
4,387.3	148	7,292.8	242	2.16	33.3	1.8	254	40.2	178	12.3	289
2,821.0	213	62,663.2	32	1.95	19.6	19.0	43	94.9	16	29.7	34
1,497.8	333	5,037.0	302	4.41	70.6	12.5	102	59.7	79	20.9	123
4,610.0	141	15,891.1	126	5.65	43.8	49.7	5	49.8	125	19.6	145
1,328.9	356	4,512.6	323	0.97	21.3	—		33.9	213	—	
5,541.0	105	21,842.8	92	0.61	(43.0)	(5.9)	309	(4.6)	402	9.2	332
5,657.1	103	13,370.9	145	4.39	52.4	8.2	160	43.3	158	21.4	113
3,369.0[31]	182	N.A.		2.45	16.1	—		90.5	19	—	
1,930.0	284	5,814.6	276	2.56	14.3	14.8	79	87.4	23	26.4	53
1,205.9	368	4,943.2	306	(5.30)	—	—		105.6	12	(7.2)	379
1,271.0	361	3,566.9	355	(0.07)	(105.6)	—		(7.4)	412	4.6	360
3,051.6	198	31,471.2	66	2.61	28.6	21.1	34	71.1	56	23.9	76
1,353.0	350	3,386.3	359	0.07	—	—		(17.3)	429	—	
5,181.0	120	16,531.1	122	4.13	23.7	8.2	162	44.2	150	20.6	128
1,584.0	324	18,181.3	112	1.30	22.6	23.1	30	77.8	37	37.3	11
2,348.0	249	6,436.3	265	4.41	13.1	9.6	139	6.8	360	21.2	118

RANK 1997	COMPANY	REVENUES $ millions	PROFITS $ millions	Rank	ASSETS $ millions	Rank
251	**TRANSAMERICA** San Francisco	**6,485.9**[1]	**793.8**	111	**51,172.9**	60
252	**RALSTON PURINA** St. Louis[13]	**6,470.6**[1]	**423.7**	190	**4,741.8**	331
253	**CISCO SYSTEMS** San Jose[43]	**6,440.2**	**1,048.7**	79	**5,452.0**	298
254	**LINCOLN NATIONAL** Fort Wayne	**6,437.0**[1]	**934.0**	92	**77,174.7**	39
255	**R.R. DONNELLEY & SONS** Chicago	**6,396.2**	**130.6**	371	**4,134.2**	353
256	**NAVISTAR INTERNATIONAL** Chicago[4]	**6,371.0**	**150.0**	353	**5,516.0**	294
257	**PUBLIC SERVICE ENTERPRISE GROUP** Newark, N.J.	**6,370.0**	**560.0**	152	**17,943.0**	143
258	**FPL GROUP** Juno Beach, Fla.	**6,369.0**	**617.5**	141	**12,449.0**	188
259	**TYSON FOODS** Springdale, Ark.[13,55]	**6,355.7**	**185.8**	323	**4,411.0**	342
260	**MEDPARTNERS** Birmingham, Ala.	**6,331.2**	**(820.6)**	491	**2,914.1**	402
261	**ARAMARK** Philadelphia[13]	**6,310.4**	**146.1**	357	**2,753.6**	411
262	**GATEWAY 2000** North Sioux City, S.D.	**6,293.7**	**109.8**	384	**2,039.3**	443
263	**ST. PAUL COS.** St. Paul	**6,219.3**	**705.5**	127	**21,500.7**	124
264	**AMERICAN ELECTRIC POWER** Columbus, Ohio	**6,161.4**	**511.0***	169	**16,615.3**	151
265	**BAXTER INTERNATIONAL** Deerfield, Ill.	**6,138.0**	**300.0**	255	**8,692.0**	225
266	**BEAR STEARNS** New York[8]	**6,077.3**	**613.3**	143	**121,433.5**	22
267	**UNOCAL** El Segundo, Calif.	**6,064.0**	**581.0**	149	**7,530.0**	249
268	**CASE** Racine, Wis.	**6,024.0**	**403.0**	205	**6,981.0**	255
269	**MARSH & MCLENNAN** New York	**6,008.6**	**399.4**	207	**7,914.2**	239
270	**AMERICAN STANDARD** Piscataway, N.J.	**6,008.0**	**96.2**	395	**3,670.0**	369
271	**GENUINE PARTS** Atlanta	**6,005.2**	**342.4**	233	**2,754.4**	410
272	**WELLPOINT HEALTH NETWORKS** Woodland Hills, Calif.	**5,826.4**	**227.4**	302	**4,533.4**	338
273	**BROWNING-FERRIS INDUSTRIES** Houston[13]	**5,783.0**	**265.2**	279	**6,678.3**	262
274	**SCI SYSTEMS** Huntsville, Ala.[8]	**5,762.7**	**112.7**	382	**1,869.9**	456
275	**AON** Chicago	**5,750.6**	**298.8**	257	**18,691.2**	135

STOCKHOLDERS' EQUITY		MARKET VALUE 3/18/98		EARNINGS PER SHARE				TOTAL RETURN TO INVESTORS			
				1997 $	% change from 1996	1987–97 annual growth rate %	Rank	1997 %	Rank	1987–97 annual rate %	Rank
$ millions	Rank	$ millions	Rank								
4,881.3	129	7,851.2	227	11.79	83.1	8.0	168	37.8	186	18.5	164
917.1	401	10,662.4	186	4.02	18.6	—		28.4	245	—	
4,289.6	151	64,568.0	30	1.52	10.9	—		31.4	223	—	
4,982.9	126	8,528.9	211	8.98	84.4	13.2	94	53.6	105	19.8	140
1,591.5	323	5,777.5	278	0.90	—	(4.3)	304	21.4	283	10.9	308
1,020.0	386	2,477.2	391	1.65	236.7	18.6	48	171.9	3	(5.2)	376
5,211.0	118	7,944.6	225	2.41	(4.4)	(0.6)	283	26.4	256	11.1	306
4,844.7	130	11,496.4	173	3.57	7.2	1.4	258	33.8	214	14.3	255
1,621.5	319	4,251.1	330	0.85	112.5	9.2	145	(9.8)	416	17.2	193
92.9	487	2,237.8	399	(4.42)	—	—		7.8	355	—	
370.0	467	N.A.		3.28	42.0	—		—		—	
930.0	398	6,242.2	269	0.70	(56.4)	—		22.3	280	—	
4,626.7	139	7,849.5	228	7.66	55.1	7.5	178	43.6	156	17.7	175
4,677.2	135	9,523.2	199	2.70	(14.0)	0.4	270	32.6	217	15.3	235
2,619.0	224	16,488.9	123	2.31	11.6	7.3	182	26.0	260	13.2	278
3,276.4	185	7,881.5	226	4.20	28.6	15.2	73	82.0	25	29.0	41
2,314.0	253	9,625.3	197	2.31	3,200.0	11.5	117	(2.9)	397	13.5	275
2,197.0	261	5,068.5	301	5.11	25.6	—		11.3	340	—	
3,198.8	191	15,793.8	128	2.39	(23.4)	1.6	256	47.5	133	15.6	229
(605.0)	498	3,427.1	358	1.26	—	—		0.2	388	—	
1,859.5	289	6,498.0	263	1.90	4.8	8.6	153	17.9	308	11.5	303
1,223.2	365	4,679.5	315	3.27	7.6	—		22.9	274	—	
2,660.8	220	6,412.3	266	1.30	—	1.2	263	44.1	152	5.2	357
594.7	446	2,214.4	401	1.85	37.5	17.0	61	95.2	15	20.7	126
2,822.1	212	10,899.0	183	1.68	(11.6)	4.8	214	44.5	148	23.6	80

RANK 1997	COMPANY	REVENUES $ millions	PROFITS $ millions	Rank	ASSETS $ millions	Rank
276	**AMP** Harrisburg, Pa.	**5,745.2**	**473.1**	175	**4,848.1**	325
277	**CHAMPION INTERNATIONAL** Stamford, Conn.	**5,735.5**	**(548.5)**	489	**9,110.6**	220
278	**CONSOLIDATED NATURAL GAS** Pittsburgh	**5,710.0**	**304.4**	250	**6,313.7**	272
279	**BANK OF NEW YORK CO.** New York	**5,697.0**	**1,104.0**	75	**59,961.0**	51
280	**ORACLE** Redwood City, Calif.[16]	**5,684.3**	**821.5**	104	**4,624.3**	336
281	**EL PASO NATURAL GAS** Houston	**5,638.0**	**186.5**	321	**9,532.0**	216
282	**CUMMINS ENGINE** Columbus, Ind.	**5,625.0**	**212.0**	307	**3,765.0**	367
283	**COMPUTER SCIENCES** El Segundo, Calif.[27]	**5,616.0**	**192.4**	318	**3,580.9**	373
284	**GENERAL MILLS** Minneapolis[16]	**5,609.3**	**445.4**	183	**3,902.4**	362
285	**FOOD 4 LESS** Compton, Calif.[56]	**5,599.1**	**(141.8)***	477	**3,076.8**	395
286	**CONSECO** Carmel, Ind.	**5,568.4**	**567.3**	150	**35,903.5**	81
287	**HOUSEHOLD INTERNATIONAL** Prospect Heights, Ill.	**5,503.1**	**686.6**	131	**30,302.6**	91
288	**BOISE CASCADE** Boise	**5,493.1**	**(30.4)**	464	**4,969.9**	317
289	**FRED MEYER** Portland, Ore.[1,57,58]	**5,481.1**	**12.1***	446	**4,430.8**	341
290	**AVNET** Great Neck, N.Y.[8]	**5,390.6**	**182.8**	326	**2,594.1**	420
291	**TANDY** Fort Worth	**5,372.2**	**186.9**	320	**2,317.5**	431
292	**RYDER SYSTEM** Miami	**5,351.0**	**174.7**	333	**5,509.1**	295
293	**QUANTUM** Milpitas, Calif.[27]	**5,319.5**	**148.5**	354	**2,158.3**	438
294	**HILTON HOTELS** Beverly Hills	**5,316.0**	**250.0**	290	**7,826.0**	241
295	**CENDANT** Parsippany, N.J.[59,60]	**5,314.7**	**872.2**	99	**14,851.2**	162
296	**COOPER INDUSTRIES** Houston	**5,288.8**	**394.6**	209	**6,052.5**	277
297	**WACHOVIA CORP.** Winston-Salem, N.C.	**5,269.6**	**592.8**	146	**65,397.1**	47
298	**CENTRAL & SOUTH WEST** Dallas	**5,268.0**	**153.0**	349	**13,451.0**	175
299	**FIRST DATA** Hackensack, N.J.	**5,234.5**	**356.7**	224	**15,315.2**	159
300	**FMC** Chicago	**5,231.5¶**	**162.4**	343	**4,113.1**	355

| STOCKHOLDERS' EQUITY | | MARKET VALUE 3/18/98 | | EARNINGS PER SHARE | | | | | TOTAL RETURN TO INVESTORS | | | |
| | | | | | % change from 1996 | 1987–97 annual growth rate | | 1997 | | | 1987–97 annual rate | |
$ millions	Rank	$ millions	Rank	1997 $		%	Rank	%	Rank		%	Rank
2,951.5	204	9,263.4	201	2.15	64.1	6.4	195	12.1	336		8.8	337
3,210.0	190	5,255.5	296	(5.72)	(486.5)	—		5.2	370		4.3	361
2,358.3	247	5,157.6	299	3.15	0.6	3.5	227	13.4	331		9.8	322
5,002.0	124	23,735.4	84	2.71	9.7	13.8	88	75.2	46		30.1	31
2,369.7	246	29,559.1	70	1.22	35.6	46.0	6	(19.8)	432		35.4	15
1,959.0	281	4,045.1	340	3.18	200.0	—		35.1	204		—	
1,422.0	342	2,612.8	385	5.48	36.7	34.9	13	30.5	230		12.2	290
1,669.6	311	8,185.0	217	2.46	(0.8)	13.5	90	1.7	384		17.4	187
494.6	457	11,867.3	169	2.82	(6.0)	8.5	155	16.1	317		16.6	208
(421.0)	496	N.A.		N.A.	—	—		—			—	
3,876.8	163	9,778.4	194	2.64	45.1	30.5	16	43.3	159		52.3	1
4,666.2	136	15,142.8	132	6.50	22.4	8.8	149	40.6	176		26.9	48
1,612.5	321	2,024.1	412	(1.19)	—	—		(3.1)	398		0.1	373
1,350.6	351	4,132.9	336	0.17	(83.7)	(12.6)	322	104.9	13		21.2	117
1,502.2	331	2,520.0	389	4.25	(1.4)	20.8	35	14.5	326		12.8	285
1,058.6	380	4,782.9	314	1.63	—	1.9	253	78.0	35		10.8	310
1,060.7	379	2,826.1	376	2.25	—	(0.2)	278	18.6	305		6.0	355
886.2	408	2,780.2	378	1.21	—	27.6	21	40.2	179		30.5	29
3,383.0	181	8,354.2	215	0.94	129.3	3.0	237	14.6	325		15.2	236
4,500.0	144	32,968.7	61	1.00	143.9	23.8	28	41.8	173		39.7	7
2,576.6	229	7,046.7	248	3.26	17.7	6.5	192	19.6	299		9.2	333
5,174.3	122	17,297.8	117	2.94	(19.5)	8.1	165	47.3	134		23.4	86
3,732.0	166	5,782.5	277	0.72	(65.2)	(9.5)	318	13.9	329		13.6	273
3,657.3	167	15,634.5	129	0.79	(42.3)	—		(19.7)	431		—	
760.6	425	2,781.5	377	4.41	(20.4)	0.3	272	(4.0)	400		7.1	349

RANK 1997	COMPANY	REVENUES $ millions	PROFITS $ millions	Rank	ASSETS $ millions	Rank
301	**VF** Wyomissing, Pa.	**5,222.2**	**350.9**	228	**3,322.8**	386
302	**ILLINOIS TOOL WORKS** Glenview, Ill.	**5,220.4**	**587.0**	147	**5,394.8**	301
303	**STAPLES** Westborough, Mass.	**5,181.0**	**130.9**	369	**2,454.5**	426
304	**NORFOLK SOUTHERN** Norfolk, Va.[61]	**5,164.5**[1]	**721.0**	121	**17,350.0**	146
305	**NATIONAL CITY CORP.** Cleveland	**5,152.1**	**807.4**	106	**54,683.5**	58
306	**MELLON BANK CORP.** Pittsburgh	**5,134.0**	**771.0**	115	**44,892.0**	65
307	**IKON OFFICE SOLUTIONS** Valley Forge, Pa.[13,62]	**5,128.4**	**130.4**	372	**5,323.9**	305
308	**AVON PRODUCTS** New York	**5,079.4**	**338.8**	235	**2,272.9**	432
309	**MEAD** Dayton	**5,077.4**	**150.1**	352	**5,229.7**	308
310	**INLAND STEEL INDUSTRIES** Chicago	**5,046.8**	**119.3**	379	**3,646.5**	370
311	**QUAKER OATS** Chicago	**5,015.7**	**(930.9)**	494	**2,697.0**	413
312	**COLUMBIA ENERGY GROUP** Reston, Va.[63]	**4,999.9**E	**273.3**	275	**6,612.3**	263
313	**BLACK & DECKER** Towson, Md.	**4,940.5**	**227.2**	303	**5,360.7**	303
314	**COMCAST** Philadelphia	**4,912.6**	**(238.7)**	482	**12,804.2***	184
315	**SHERWIN-WILLIAMS** Cleveland	**4,881.1**	**260.6**	283	**4,035.8**	359
316	**NORDSTROM** Seattle[1]	**4,851.6**	**186.2**	322	**2,865.2**	404
317	**STONE CONTAINER** Chicago	**4,849.1**	**(417.7)**	488	**5,824.1**	282
318	**MATTEL** El Segundo, Calif.	**4,834.6**	**285.2**	268	**3,803.8**	364
319	**CMS ENERGY** Dearborn, Mich.	**4,787.0**	**268.0**	277	**9,793.0**	212
320	**CHS ELECTRONICS** Miami	**4,756.4**	**48.4**	428	**1,970.1**	449
321	**PRAXAIR** Danbury, Conn.	**4,735.0**	**405.0**	204	**7,810.0**	242
322	**GANNETT** Arlington, Va.	**4,729.5**	**712.7**	126	**6,890.4**	258
323	**SAFECO** Seattle	**4,709.3**	**430.0**	188	**29,467.8**	93
324	**OWENS-ILLINOIS** Toledo	**4,680.1**	**167.9***	337	**6,845.1**	260
325	**EASTMAN CHEMICAL** Kingsport, Tenn.	**4,678.0**	**286.0**	267	**5,742.0**	285

STOCKHOLDERS' EQUITY		MARKET VALUE 3/18/98		EARNINGS PER SHARE					TOTAL RETURN TO INVESTORS			
					% change from 1996	1987–97 annual growth rate			1997		1987–97 annual rate	
$ millions	Rank	$ millions	Rank	1997 $		%	Rank		%	Rank	%	Rank
1,866.8	288	6,046.1	271	2.70	8.9	7.4	181		40.4	177	17.5	183
2,806.5	215	15,403.8	130	2.33	19.5	16.3	67		51.9	110	23.5	81
967.6	392	5,752.8	279	0.51	19.5	—			53.6	104	—	
5,445.0	109	14,685.5	138	1.90	(5.5)	20.1	37		6.6	363	16.9	197
4,281.4	153	15,053.9	134	3.66	11.9	12.1	109		51.2	115	21.6	107
3,845.0	164	16,623.0	120	2.88	11.6	—			75.6	45	26.6	49
1,481.6	334	4,617.9	319	0.83	(43.9)	(0.9)	285		(45.2)	456	15.4	232
285.0	475	10,057.6	191	2.54	7.6	8.4	157		9.7	345	21.6	109
2,288.5	255	3,734.4	349	1.41	(23.4)	(2.0)	291		(1.8)	395	7.7	348
900.1	405	1,378.1	439	2.13	195.8	(6.4)	311		(13.6)	423	(4.3)	375
248.5	481	7,955.7	224	(6.80)	(482.0)	—			42.1	168	13.7	272
1,790.7	295	4,300.9	328	4.90	19.2	—			25.1	268	—	
1,791.4	294	4,860.7	311	2.35	1.3	9.5	140		31.4	224	9.7	325
1,646.5	314	12,700.6	153	(0.75)	—	—			77.9	36	17.9	170
1,592.2	322	5,965.3	273	1.50	12.8	10.8	126		0.5	386	18.5	163
1,475.1	335	4,560.1	321	2.40	31.9	7.8	172		72.1	54	12.9	283
276.9	476	1,278.5	443	(4.29)	—	—			(26.9)	442	(5.8)	378
1,822.1	292	13,102.3	149	0.93	(31.6)	—			35.4	200	35.6	13
1,977.0	279	4,520.9	322	2.61	7.0	2.0	252		35.4	201	15.1	238
670.3	434	899.2	448	1.32	69.2	—			50.0	122	—	
2,122.0	266	7,507.9	238	2.46	39.0	—			(1.6)	394	—	
3,479.7	173	19,427.7	104	2.50	(24.9)	9.7	136		67.8	64	15.1	237
5,461.7	108	7,624.8	232	3.31	(4.6)	5.8	203		27.2	253	17.3	189
1,341.9	353	6,148.0	270	1.24	(20.0)	—			66.8	67	—	
1,753.0	300	5,272.4	295	3.63	(24.2)	—			11.1	341	—	

RANK 1997	COMPANY	REVENUES $ millions	PROFITS $ millions	Rank	ASSETS $ millions	Rank
326	**AIR PRODUCTS & CHEMICALS** Allentown, Pa.[13]	**4,662.0**	**429.3**	189	**7,244.1**	251
327	**BETHLEHEM STEEL** Bethlehem, Pa.	**4,631.2**	**280.7**	270	**4,802.6**	328
328	**PECO ENERGY** Philadelphia	**4,617.9**	**(1,497.1)**	497	**12,356.6**	189
329	**COMPUSA** Dallas[8]	**4,610.5**	**93.9**	397	**1,124.6**	484
330	**PROGRESSIVE** Mayfield Village, Ohio	**4,608.2**	**400.0**	206	**7,559.6**	247
331	**SUNTRUST BANKS** Atlanta	**4,585.0**	**667.3**	132	**57,982.7**	53
332	**DOVER** New York	**4,547.7**	**405.4**	203	**3,277.5**	389
333	**MBNA** Wilmington, Del.	**4,523.9**	**622.5**	140	**21,305.5**	127
334	**UNION CAMP** Wayne, N.J.	**4,476.8**	**81.1**	406	**5,241.7**	307
335	**MICROAGE** Tempe, Ariz.[4]	**4,446.3**	**25.0**	442	**974.1**	488
336	**LTV** Cleveland	**4,446.0**[E]	**30.0**	438	**5,546.0**	293
337	**WILLIAMS** Tulsa	**4,409.6**	**271.4**	276	**13,879.0**	169
338	**NASH FINCH** Edina, Minn.	**4,391.6**	**(1.2)**	456	**906.6**	494
339	**MUTUAL OF OMAHA INSURANCE** Omaha	**4,385.1**	**181.6**	327	**12,692.5**	186
340	**CORESTATES FINANCIAL CORP.** Philadelphia	**4,378.7**	**813.3**	105	**48,461.0**	61
341	**OWENS CORNING** Toledo	**4,373.0**	**47.0**	431	**4,996.0**	315
342	**CINERGY** Cincinnati	**4,352.8**	**253.2***	287	**8,858.2**	222
343	**ALLEGIANCE** McGaw Park, Ill.	**4,350.8**	**90.9**	399	**2,696.6**	414
344	**DOLE FOOD** Westlake Village, Calif.	**4,336.1**	**160.2**	345	**2,463.9**	425
345	**HERSHEY FOODS** Hershey, Pa.	**4,302.2**	**336.3**	236	**3,291.2**	388
346	**CNF TRANSPORTATION** Palo Alto	**4,266.8**	**120.9**	377	**2,421.5**	427
347	**LG&E ENERGY** Louisville	**4,263.8**	**97.8**	391	**3,366.4**	381
348	**OXFORD HEALTH PLANS** Norwalk, Conn.	**4,240.1**	**(291.3)**	484	**1,398.0**	475
349	**NUCOR** Charlotte, N.C.	**4,184.5**	**294.5**	260	**2,984.4**	398
350	**WESTERN DIGITAL** Irvine, Calif.[8]	**4,177.9**	**267.6**	278	**1,307.1**	477

STOCKHOLDERS' EQUITY		MARKET VALUE 3/18/98		EARNINGS PER SHARE				TOTAL RETURN TO INVESTORS			
				1997	% change from 1996	1987–97 annual growth rate %	Rank	1997 %	Rank	1987–97 annual rate %	Rank
$ millions	Rank	$ millions	Rank	$							
2,648.1	222	9,797.3	193	3.90	4.6	10.9	124	20.8	290	17.5	181
1,215.0	366	1,546.6	429	2.03	—	(3.1)	298	(2.1)	396	(5.8)	377
2,864.2	209	4,826.4	313	(6.80)	(403.6)	—		4.1	374	10.4	314
428.0	465	2,651.3	382	0.99	51.1	—		49.4	128	—	
2,135.9	264	8,965.2	203	5.31	28.3	17.3	59	78.3	34	29.0	40
5,199.4	119	15,966.2	125	3.13	13.4	11.2	122	47.1	136	26.2	55
1,703.6	306	8,389.1	214	1.79	5.9	15.8	69	44.7	145	19.0	157
1,970.1	280	18,199.4	111	1.15	29.7	—		50.0	120	—	
2,035.7	272	4,168.8	335	1.16	(5.7)	(8.5)	316	16.3	316	7.7	344
238.0	483	263.4	458	1.40	57.3	8.7	152	(24.7)	437	17.8	173
6,676.0	89	1,329.6	440	0.27	(73.3)	—		(16.0)	428	—	
3,571.7	168	10,546.1	188	0.80	(25.2)	6.4	196	55.5	95	26.5	51
225.6	484	226.5	459	(0.11)	(106.1)	—		(7.3)	411	4.0	363
1,374.8	348	N.A.		N.A.	—	—	—	—		—	
3,237.4	186	17,839.4	116	3.96	34.7	7.3	183	60.7	75	22.0	101
(441.0)	497	1,912.5	415	0.88	—	(15.6)	325	(19.4)	430	7.7	345
2,539.2	231	5,619.7	284	1.59	(24.6)	(0.2)	279	21.0	288	16.7	203
937.2	396	2,301.9	397	1.56	—	—		30.2	236	—	
666.5	435	2,939.4	373	2.65	80.3	4.1	222	36.3	191	11.9	294
852.8	414	10,175.0	190	2.23	27.4	10.5	127	43.7	154	20.4	133
658.1	436	1,753.5	423	2.19	421.4	1.3	262	76.2	43	6.7	351
933.4	397	1,665.9	426	1.47	(6.4)	2.8	243	6.5	364	16.5	209
349.2	470	1,296.4	442	(3.70)	(396.0)	—		(73.4)	461	—	
1,876.4	286	4,927.8	307	3.35	18.4	18.8	46	(4.6)	403	17.9	172
620.0	440	1,447.3	434	2.85	183.6	12.3	103	(43.7)	455	7.0	350

		REVENUES	PROFITS		ASSETS	
RANK 1997	COMPANY	$ millions	$ millions	Rank	$ millions	Rank
351	**LITTON INDUSTRIES** Woodland Hills, Calif.[43]	**4,175.5**	**162.0**	344	**3,519.7**	375
352	**SONAT** Birmingham, Ala.	**4,174.6**	**175.9**	331	**4,431.5**	340
353	**FOSTER WHEELER** Clinton, N.J.	**4,172.0**	**(10.5)**	458	**3,366.4**	382
354	**GPU** Morristown, N.J.	**4,143.4**	**335.1**	237	**12,924.7**	183
355	**W.W. GRAINGER** Lincolnshire, Ill.	**4,136.6**	**231.8**	299	**1,997.8**	445
356	**CORNING** Corning, N.Y.	**4,129.1**	**439.8**	184	**4,811.4**	326
357	**OLSTEN** Melville, N.Y.	**4,113.0**	**93.0**	398	**1,750.2**	461
358	**UNIVERSAL** Richmond[8]	**4,112.7**	**100.9**	389	**1,982.0**	448
359	**AUTOMATIC DATA PROCESSING** Roseland, N.J.[8]	**4,112.2**	**513.5**	168	**4,382.8**	343
360	**BARNETT BANKS** Jacksonville[64]	**4,101.6**	**255.0**	285	**46,534.1**	63
361	**PITNEY BOWES** Stamford, Conn.	**4,100.5**	**526.0**	165	**7,893.4**	240
362	**PARKER HANNIFIN** Cleveland[8]	**4,091.1**	**274.0**	274	**2,998.9**	397
363	**UNUM** Portland, Me.	**4,076.7**	**370.3**	219	**13,200.3**	177
364	**APPLIED MATERIALS** Santa Clara, Calif.[4]	**4,074.3**	**498.5**	172	**5,070.8**	314
365	**PACIFIC LIFE INSURANCE** Newport Beach, Calif.	**4,065.4**	**121.5**	376	**33,911.1**	85
366	**GENERAL DYNAMICS** Falls Church, Va.	**4,062.0**	**316.0**	245	**4,091.0**	357
367	**CONSOLIDATED STORES** Columbus, Ohio[1]	**4,055.3**	**85.9**	403	**1,746.4**	462
368	**MERISEL** El Segundo, Calif.	**4,049.0**	**(15.8)***	461	**747.1**	497
369	**COMPUTER ASSOCIATES INTL.** Islandia, N.Y.[27]	**4,040.0**	**366.0**	221	**6,084.0**	276
370	**AMERICAN FINANCIAL GROUP** Cincinnati	**4,020.7**	**192.3**	319	**15,755.3**	157
371	**ROHM & HAAS** Philadelphia	**3,999.0**	**410.0**	200	**3,900.0**	363
372	**NIAGARA MOHAWK POWER** Syracuse, N.Y.	**3,966.4**	**59.8**	416	**9,584.1**	215
373	**SERVICEMASTER** Downers Grove, Ill.	**3,961.5**	**163.5[65]**	341	**2,475.2**	424
374	**CLARK USA** St. Louis	**3,925.3[E]**	**(109.9)**	473	**1,275.6**	478
375	**PHELPS DODGE** Phoenix	**3,914.3**	**408.5**	201	**4,965.2**	319

STOCKHOLDERS' EQUITY		MARKET VALUE 3/18/98		EARNINGS PER SHARE				TOTAL RETURN TO INVESTORS			
				1997 $	% change from 1996	1987–97 annual growth rate %	Rank	1997 %	Rank	1987–97 annual rate %	Rank
$ millions	Rank	$ millions	Rank								
1,039.0	382	2,716.4	381	3.40	7.9	2.8	244	20.7	291	13.9	267
1,635.4	315	3,629.9	352	2.01	(12.6)	4.5	219	(9.3)	415	19.7	142
619.4	441	1,227.1	445	(0.26)	(112.9)	—		(25.5)	439	9.3	330
3,166.4	192	5,203.6	298	2.77	12.1	3.0	238	32.5	220	17.9	171
1,294.7	359	4,983.8	304	4.54	12.4	11.2	121	22.6	276	14.3	254
1,246.5	363	9,537.4	198	1.85	137.2	5.1	211	(3.6)	399	16.7	202
841.8	417	1,392.4	438	1.15	(11.5)	11.8	113	2.4	377	8.2	341
469.6	459	1,606.9	428	2.88	39.8	5.9	201	32.1	221	15.1	239
2,660.6	221	20,119.5	101	1.76	12.1	14.9	76	44.6	147	19.8	141
3,409.5	178	N.A.		N.A.	—	—		78.8	33	21.9	104
1,872.6	287	14,036.1	142	1.80	15.4	11.0	123	67.8	63	19.6	144
1,547.3	327	5,357.1	291	2.46	14.2	11.4	118	80.2	31	13.9	263
2,434.8	239	7,535.8	237	2.59	60.9	18.2	51	52.6	108	30.2	30
2,942.2	205	12,126.2	163	1.32	(19.3)	100.6	1	67.7	65	37.8	10
944.8	395	N.A.		N.A.	—	—		—		—	
1,915.0	285	5,628.9	283	2.50	17.4	(0.3)	281	25.3	264	22.2	100
1,034.5	384	4,891.2	309	0.77	(23.0)	15.3	72	70.3	58	29.9	32
137.5	486	117.6	463	(0.48)	—	—		164.1	6	—	
1,503.0	330	28,531.1	74	0.97	—	19.5	41	60.1	76	27.8	43
1,662.7	312	2,583.1	387	0.64	(83.1)	3.4	230	9.7	346	10.4	313
1,797.0	293	6,480.2	264	6.39	19.0	8.4	158	19.7	298	14.8	244
3,044.0	199	1,895.5	417	0.16	(68.0)	—		6.3	365	2.7	367
524.4	455	5,015.7	303	0.82	19.4	14.0	87	71.7	55	32.8	18
38.4	490	N.A.		(4.06)	—	—		—		—	
2,510.4	233	3,888.2	343	6.63	(5.0)	7.4	180	(5.3)	404	15.6	230

RANK 1997	COMPANY	REVENUES $ millions	PROFITS $ millions	Rank	ASSETS $ millions	Rank
376	**PROSOURCE** Coral Cables, Fla.	3,901.2	(13.7)*	459	548.1	500
377	**INACOM** Omaha	3,896.3	29.5	439	960.5	491
378	**GIANT FOOD** Landover, Md.[23]	3,881.0	85.5	404	1,503.5	471
379	**SMITHFIELD FOODS** Norfolk, Va.[38]	3,870.6	44.9	434	995.3	486
380	**KELLY SERVICES** Troy, Mich.	3,852.9	80.8	407	967.2	490
381	**NORTHEAST UTILITIES** Berlin, Conn.	3,834.8	(135.7)	476	10,414.4	208
382	**HARRIS** Melbourne, Fla.[8]	3,834.6	207.5	311	3,637.9	372
383	**SOUTHWEST AIRLINES** Dallas	3,816.8	317.8	244	4,246.2	350
384	**CENTEX** Dallas[27]	3,785.0	106.6	387	2,678.8	415
385	**SLM HOLDING** Reston, Va.[66]	3,784.7	507.9	170	39,908.8	72
386	**OFFICEMAX** Shaker Heights., Ohio[1]	3,765.4	89.6	400	1,916.2	454
387	**DTE ENERGY** Detroit	3,764.5	417.3	193	11,222.9	201
388	**MASCO** Taylor, Mich.	3,760.0	382.4	213	4,333.8	345
389	**ALLEGHENY TELEDYNE** Pittsburgh	3,745.1	297.6	258	2,604.5	419
390	**REPUBLIC NEW YORK CORP.** New York	3,738.2	449.1	181	55,638.4	57
391	**H.F. AHMANSON** Irwindale, Calif.	3,732.9	413.8	196	46,678.8	62
392	**SUPERMARKETS GENL. HOLDINGS** Woodbridge, N.J.[56]	3,710.7	(43.8)	465	957.0	492
393	**SOLECTRON** Milpitas, Calif.[18]	3,694.4	158.1	347	1,852.4	457
394	**HARCOURT GENERAL** Chestnut Hill, Mass.[4]	3,691.6	(115.1)	475	3,781.8	365
395	**MAPCO** Tulsa	3,689.7	96.9	394	2,407.7	428
396	**AMERICAN FAMILY INS. GROUP** Madison, Wis.[6]	3,689.4	251.6	288	8,348.3	231
397	**BAKER HUGHES** Houston[13]	3,685.4	97.0	393	4,756.3	330
398	**SERVICE MERCHANDISE** Brentwood, Tenn.	3,662.8	(91.6)	471	1,951.5	452
399	**SILICON GRAPHICS** Mountain View, Calif.[8]	3,662.6	78.6	408	3,344.6	383
400	**BRUNSWICK** Lake Forest, Ill.	3,657.4	150.5	351	3,241.4	390

STOCKHOLDERS' EQUITY		MARKET VALUE 3/18/98		EARNINGS PER SHARE		1987–97 annual growth rate		TOTAL RETURN TO INVESTORS 1997		1987–97 annual rate	
$ millions	Rank	$ millions	Rank	1997 $	% change from 1996	%	Rank	%	Rank	%	Rank
64.4	489	135.6	462	(1.47)	—	—		(36.8)	450	—	
325.2	473	435.1	457	2.17	30.7	9.0	147	(29.8)	445	14.7	246
873.7	410	2,309.5	396	1.43	(16.9)	6.3	197	—	390	9.4	329
307.5	474	1,154.3	446	2.34	178.6	20.3	36	73.7	51	27.5	44
559.8	450	1,323.8	441	2.12	11.0	4.7	215	14.4	327	4.2	362
2,127.2	265	1,741.2	424	(1.05)	(10,600.0)	—		(7.1)	409	2.7	366
1,578.2	325	4,124.6	337	5.27	15.1	9.9	133	36.2	192	16.9	198
2,009.0	275	6,871.2	254	1.40	53.3	31.1	15	68.2	60	29.1	39
835.8	419	2,375.2	394	3.62	97.8	11.4	119	68.1	61	23.0	90
674.6	431	7,846.8	229	2.78	32.9	19.4	42	51.4	113	19.6	146
1,160.6	374	2,116.8	404	0.72	30.9	—		32.6	219	—	
3,561.6	169	5,504.8	287	2.88	35.2	(1.2)	287	14.8	323	18.3	165
2,229.0	259	9,737.6	195	2.30	26.4	3.4	229	44.1	151	11.6	301
999.7	388	4,883.8	310	1.67	40.3	8.2	161	15.2	322	16.5	210
3,438.0	176	7,083.0	246	7.88	11.5	59.6	3	42.5	164	17.3	191
2,395.4	241	7,266.2	243	3.59	290.2	5.9	202	109.8	11	20.2	135
(1,308.0)	500	N.A.		N.A.		—	—	—		—	
919.1	400	4,493.7	324	1.37	25.1	—		55.7	94	—	
845.5	416	3,986.2	341	(1.64)	(162.6)	—		20.5	294	14.0	260
670.7	433	3,024.8	367	1.74	3.0	3.0	239	38.5	183	16.6	206
3,023.0	200	N.A.		N.A.		—	—	—		—	
2,604.6	226	7,004.8	250	0.63	(48.8)	—		27.9	248	14.7	247
336.5	472	207.1	460	(0.92)	(335.9)	—		(48.5)	457	9.7	326
1,839.2	290	2,635.9	384	0.43	(33.8)	7.7	175	(51.7)	459	11.7	298
1,315.0	357	3,345.7	360	1.50	(20.2)	(2.3)	295	28.5	244	10.3	316

RANK 1997	COMPANY	REVENUES $ millions	PROFITS $ millions	Rank	ASSETS $ millions	Rank
401	**TURNER CORP.** New York	**3,639.8**	**5.9***	449	**972.7**	489
402	**REEBOK INTERNATIONAL** Stoughton, Mass.	**3,637.4**	**135.1**	364	**1,756.1**	460
403	**MORTON INTERNATIONAL** Chicago[8]	**3,636.5¶**	**343.0**	232	**2,804.9**	406
404	**ENGELHARD** Iselin, N.J.	**3,630.7**	**47.8**	429	**2,586.5**	421
405	**TEMPLE-INLAND** Diboll, Texas	**3,625.4**	**50.8**	427	**14,364.0**	166
406	**AIRTOUCH COMMUNICATIONS** San Francisco	**3,594.0**	**448.0**	182	**8,970.0**	221
407	**SHAW INDUSTRIES** Dalton, Ga.	**3,575.8**	**29.0**	440	**1,967.6**	450
408	**ECHLIN** Branford, Conn.[18]	**3,568.6**	**(46.9)**	466	**2,374.2**	429
409	**THERMO ELECTRON** Waltham, Mass.	**3,558.3**	**239.3**	296	**5,795.9**	283
410	**PROVIDENT COS.** Chattanooga	**3,553.1**	**247.3**	294	**23,177.6**	118
411	**PROFFITT'S** Birmingham, Ala.[1,67]	**3,544.7**	**62.7**	415	**2,224.9**	434
412	**MCGRAW-HILL** New York	**3,534.1**	**290.7**	263	**3,724.5**	368
413	**MICRON TECHNOLOGY** Boise[18]	**3,515.5**	**332.2**	240	**4,851.3**	324
414	**BORDEN** Columbus, Ohio	**3,481.6**	**278.0**	273	**3,049.7**	396
415	**RYKOFF-SEXTON** Wilkes-Barre, Pa.[8,68]	**3,477.5**	**16.0**	445	**1,219.0**	482
416	**B.F. GOODRICH** Richfield, Ohio	**3,471.0**	**178.2**	330	**3,493.9**	376
417	**RELIANCE GROUP HOLDINGS** New York	**3,442.6**	**229.4**	301	**11,332.5**	198
418	**WILLAMETTE INDUSTRIES** Portland, Ore.	**3,438.7**	**73.0**	409	**4,811.1**	327
419	**STATE STREET CORP.** Boston	**3,428.0**	**380.0**	216	**37,975.0**	77
420	**RICHFOOD HOLDINGS** Mechanicsville, Va.[38]	**3,411.6**	**59.5**	418	**581.5**	499
421	**MAYTAG** Newton, Iowa	**3,407.9**	**180.3**	329	**2,514.2**	423
422	**USF&G** Baltimore	**3,403.9**	**193.9**	316	**15,818.5**	155
423	**ALLMERICA FINANCIAL** Worcester, Mass.	**3,395.6**	**209.2**	309	**22,549.0**	120
424	**PITTSTON** Glen Allen, Va.	**3,394.4**	**110.2**	383	**1,995.9**	447
425	**ESTÉE LAUDER** New York[8]	**3,381.6**	**197.6**	315	**1,873.1**	455

STOCKHOLDERS' EQUITY		MARKET VALUE 3/18/98		EARNINGS PER SHARE				TOTAL RETURN TO INVESTORS			
				1997 $	% change from 1996	1987–97 annual growth rate %	Rank	1997 %	Rank	1987–97 annual rate %	Rank
$ millions	Rank	$ millions	Rank								
76.1	488	144.5	461	0.59	—	—		157.3	7	7.8	343
507.2	456	1,730.0	425	2.32	14.3	4.5	218	(31.4)	446	11.9	295
1,734.3	302	4,107.6	338	2.38	6.3	—		(14.4)	426	—	
785.3	423	2,745.5	380	0.33	(68.0)	(3.6)	301	(7.9)	413	13.8	268
2,045.0	270	3,629.1	353	0.90	(62.3)	(9.1)	317	(1.2)	392	10.4	315
5,529.0	106	23,651.0	85	0.78	116.7	—		64.6	70	—	
637.5	439	1,771.1	422	0.22	(12.0)	0.3	271	0.4	387	21.4	112
913.7	403	3,016.3	368	(0.75)	(132.6)	—		17.0	313	13.9	264
1,997.9	276	5,939.2	275	1.41	20.5	16.9	63	6.7	361	27.0	47
3,279.3	184	4,847.4	312	1.84	27.8	3.9	224	61.6	74	23.5	83
1,094.6	376	2,399.7	393	0.71	8.4	—		54.2	101	27.2	46
1,434.7	340	7,562.6	236	2.91	(41.3)	5.9	200	64.3	71	15.6	228
2,883.1	206	6,705.3	260	1.54	(44.2)	—		(10.9)	419	24.5	72
754.0	426	N.A.		N.A.	—	—		—		—	
354.2	469	N.A.		0.56	—	(2.6)	296	—		—	
1,422.6	341	3,722.7	350	2.41	(2.8)	1.7	255	5.1	371	11.9	293
962.5	393	2,074.6	410	1.94	373.2	1.4	257	59.3	81	14.9	243
1,994.5	278	4,217.6	334	0.65	(62.4)	(5.9)	308	(5.8)	405	14.2	256
1,995.0	277	10,685.5	185	2.32	30.3	15.3	71	81.8	28	29.9	33
258.7	479	1,394.8	437	1.26	58.8	—		17.6	309	—	
615.8	444	4,610.0	320	1.84	38.3	(0.4)	282	93.3	18	9.1	334
2,076.8	267	3,004.6	369	1.63	(16.4)	(7.7)	314	6.9	358	1.9	369
2,381.0	243	3,894.2	342	3.82	5.2	—		49.8	126	—	
685.6	430	2,039.0	411	N.A.	—	—		—		—	
547.7	451	7,747.2	230	1.46	—	—		1.8	383	—	

RANK 1997	COMPANY	REVENUES $ millions	PROFITS $ millions	Rank	ASSETS $ millions	Rank
426	**W.R. GRACE** Boca Raton, Fla.	3,358.0[1]	261.0	282	3,773.0	366
427	**YELLOW** Overland Park, Kan.	3,348.9	52.4	426	1,270.8	480
428	**CYPRUS AMAX MINERALS** Englewood, Colo.	3,346.0	69.0	410	6,459.0	265
429	**AVERY DENNISON** Pasadena	3,345.7	204.8	313	2,046.5	442
430	**NEW CENTURY ENERGIES** Denver[69]	3,342.5	150.9*	350	7,310.3	250
431	**GRAYBAR ELECTRIC** St. Louis	3,338.0	53.0	425	1,051.8	485
432	**TRUSERV** Chicago[39,70]	3,332.0	N.A.		1,436.6	474
433	**TRANS WORLD AIRLINES** St. Louis	3,328.0	(110.8)*	474	2,773.8	408
434	**TIMES MIRROR** Los Angeles	3,318.5	250.3	289	3,415.6	380
435	**FLORIDA PROGRESS** St. Petersburg	3,315.6	54.3	423	5,760.0	284
436	**BALTIMORE GAS & ELECTRIC** Baltimore	3,307.6	282.8	269	8,773.4	224
437	**ALLTEL** Little Rock	3,263.6	507.9	171	5,633.4	287
438	**HORMEL FOODS** Austin, Minn.[4]	3,256.6	109.5	385	1,528.5	470
439	**WHITMAN** Rolling Meadows, Ill.	3,250.1[1]	4.1	451	2,029.7	444
440	**JEFFERSON SMURFIT** St. Louis	3,238.0	1.0	455	2,771.0	409
441	**NEWELL** Freeport, Ill.	3,234.3	290.4	264	3,943.8	360
442	**BEVERLY ENTERPRISES** Fort Smith, Ark.	3,230.3	58.6	420	2,071.1	440
443	**BJ'S WHOLESALE CLUB** Natick, Mass.[1,71]	3,226.5	68.3	412	811.6	496
444	**HANNAFORD BROS.** Scarborough, Me.	3,226.4	59.6	417	1,227.2	481
445	**AGCO** Duluth, Ga.	3,224.4	168.7	336	2,620.9	417
446	**INTERSTATE BAKERIES** Kansas City, Mo.[16]	3,212.4	97.2	392	1,493.1	472
447	**CORPORATE EXPRESS** Broomfield, Colo.[23]	3,196.1	42.0	435	1,844.0	458
448	**AMEREN** St. Louis[72]	3,195.3E	347.2	229	8,827.5	223
449	**YORK INTERNATIONAL** York, Pa.	3,193.7	47.4	430	1,996.3	446
450	**HASBRO** Pawtucket, R.I.	3,188.6	135.0	365	2,899.7	403

STOCKHOLDERS' EQUITY		MARKET VALUE 3/18/98		EARNINGS PER SHARE				TOTAL RETURN TO INVESTORS			
				1997 $	% change from 1996	1987–97 annual growth rate %	Rank	1997 %	Rank	1987–97 annual rate %	Rank
$ millions	Rank	$ millions	Rank								
467.9	460	6,261.4	268	3.45	(88.7)	5.4	207	56.8	89	21.4	114
445.9	462	569.4	454	1.83	—	2.4	248	74.8	48	1.5	370
2,330.0	252	1,542.4	430	0.54	(12.9)	(2.3)	294	(32.2)	447	2.5	368
837.2	418	5,337.6	292	1.93	7.8	16.9	62	28.7	243	18.5	160
2,353.2	248	5,447.5	289	1.44	(48.2)	(7.2)	312	31.9	222	17.5	182
253.1	480	N.A.		10.02	22.5	12.3	106	—		—	
405.8	466	N.A.		N.A.	—	—		—		—	
268.3	477	704.7	452	(2.37)	—	—		53.3	107	—	
876.0	409	5,658.8	282	2.29	49.7	—		24.8	271	—	
1,776.0	297	3,876.5	344	0.56	(75.9)	(13.8)	324	29.7	239	13.5	274
3,080.4	197	4,670.0	316	1.72	(7.0)	(2.9)	297	35.4	202	12.6	287
2,208.5	260	8,093.1	220	2.70	77.6	10.2	128	35.3	203	19.9	138
802.2	422	2,889.0	375	1.43	37.5	9.1	146	24.7	272	14.1	258
539.7	452	2,081.6	409	0.04	(97.0)	(33.1)	333	15.9	320	9.3	331
(374.0)	495	1,796.8	421	0.01	(99.0)	—		(12.1)	421	—	
1,714.3	305	7,971.8	223	1.82	13.0	18.1	53	37.2	190	30.7	28
861.2	413	1,524.5	431	0.57	16.3	—		55.2	98	11.0	307
446.3	461	1,453.3	433	1.81	—	—		—		—	
601.0	445	1,889.4	418	1.40	(20.5)	8.0	169	29.7	238	19.0	155
991.6	390	1,841.9	419	2.71	23.2	—		2.3	380	—	
538.7	453	2,330.9	395	2.55	264.3	—		53.7	103	—	
693.6	429	1,423.1	435	0.31	1,062.5	—		(34.4)	448	—	
3,019.0	201	5,608.7	285	2.44	(10.0)	(1.7)	290	19.8	297	14.3	253
646.3	437	1,813.6	420	1.10	(67.4)	—		(28.4)	444	—	
1,838.1	291	4,954.0	305	1.02	(30.6)	10.8	125	22.9	275	19.3	151

RANK 1997	COMPANY	REVENUES $ millions	PROFITS $ millions	Rank	ASSETS $ millions	Rank
451	**COMERICA** Detroit	3,175.4	530.5	163	36,292.4	80
452	**DARDEN RESTAURANTS** Orlando[16]	3,171.8	(91.0)	470	1,963.7	451
453	**GENAMERICA** St. Louis[6,73]	3,154.0	96.2	396	24,010.1	114
454	**LONG ISLAND LIGHTING** Hicksville, N.Y.[74]	3,147.7	334.0	239	11,907.7	192
455	**3COM** Santa Clara, Calif.[16,75]	3,147.1	374.0	218	2,266.3	433
456	**MERCANTILE STORES** Fairfield, Ohio[1]	3,143.8	129.7	373	2,177.8	436
457	**KNIGHT-RIDDER** Miami	3,139.1	413.0	197	4,355.1	344
458	**AID ASSOCIATION FOR LUTHERANS** Appleton, Wis.	3,129.9	209.8	308	17,974.8	142
459	**INTERPUBLIC GROUP** New York	3,125.8	239.1	297	5,702.5	286
460	**OMNICOM GROUP** New York	3,124.8	222.4	304	4,965.7	318
461	**HARNISCHFEGER INDUSTRIES** St. Francis, Wis.[4]	3,118.2	139.8	361	2,924.5	400
462	**OWENS & MINOR** Glen Allen, Va.	3,116.8	24.3	443	712.6	498
463	**VENCOR** Louisville	3,116.0	130.9	370	3,334.7	385
464	**PETER KIEWIT SONS'** Omaha	3,096.0	248.0	292	2,779.0	407
465	**PENN TRAFFIC** Syracuse, N.Y.[56]	3,074.4	(54.6)	468	1,644.7	465
466	**KOHL'S** Menomonee Falls, Wis.[1]	3,060.1	141.3	359	1,619.7	467
467	**PP&L RESOURCES** Allentown, Pa.	3,048.7	296.2	259	9,485.0	217
468	**MILLENNIUM CHEMICALS** Red Bank, N.J.	3,048.0	185.0	324	4,256.0	349
469	**CAROLINA POWER & LIGHT** Raleigh	3,024.1	388.3	210	8,220.7	234
470	**DEAN FOODS** Franklin Park, Ill.[16]	3,018.4	86.7	402	1,217.4	483
471	**HEALTHSOUTH** Birmingham, Ala.[76]	3,017.3	330.6	241	5,401.1	300
472	**WESTVACO** New York[4]	3,011.0	162.7	342	4,898.8	321
473	**IMC GLOBAL** Northbrook, Ill.	2,988.6	62.9*	414	4,673.9	334
474	**PHOENIX HOME LIFE MUTUAL INS.** Hartford[6]	2,988.3	164.6	338	18,518.7	137
475	**BENEFICIAL** Wilmington, Del.	2,955.7	253.7	286	17,645.1	144

STOCKHOLDERS' EQUITY		MARKET VALUE 3/18/98		EARNINGS PER SHARE				TOTAL RETURN TO INVESTORS			
				1997 $	% change from 1996	1987–97 annual growth rate %	Rank	1997 %	Rank	1987–97 annual rate %	Rank
$ millions	Rank	$ millions	Rank								
2,761.8	216	11,018.4	180	3.19	34.0	13.3	92	77.0	41	26.5	50
1,081.2	378	2,113.6	405	(0.59)	(225.5)	—		44.1	153	—	
1,173.3	371	N.A.		N.A.	—	—		—		—	
2,608.5	225	3,700.2	351	2.23	1.4	2.6	246	46.6	137	23.3	87
1,517.5	329	11,877.8	168	2.02	100.0	26.7	23	(52.4)	460	21.5	111
1,646.8	313	2,480.5	390	3.53	7.0	0.0	276	25.9	261	7.7	347
1,551.7	326	4,493.0	326	4.08	48.4	11.9	110	38.4	184	12.8	286
1,380.5	347	N.A.		N.A.	—	—		—		—	
1,107.2	375	7,996.3	221	1.90	12.2	14.3	84	59.2	82	23.7	77
866.7	411	7,052.0	247	1.37	22.3	14.5	81	88.1	22	28.2	42
764.2	424	1,521.3	432	2.93	21.1	11.8	112	(26.0)	440	7.7	346
259.3	478	593.9	453	0.60	140.0	7.9	170	42.9	161	20.4	130
905.4	404	1,901.5	416	1.92	6.1	—		(22.7)	434	—	
2,230.0	258	N.A.		N.A.	—	—		—		—	
(145.1)	493	56.8	464	(5.02)	—	—		127.6	9	—	
954.8	394	6,583.6	262	1.81	32.1	—		73.6	52	—	
2,859.0	210	3,740.6	348	1.80	(12.2)	0.8	265	12.5	335	11.4	304
1,464.0	337	2,207.2	402	2.47	—	—		36.1	195	—	
2,878.2	207	6,621.8	261	2.66	0.0	3.3	231	22.3	279	16.8	200
567.7	449	2,082.8	408	2.16	—	7.7	174	88.8	21	16.3	215
3,157.4	195	11,437.1	175	0.91	33.8	28.1	19	43.7	155	29.6	37
2,278.6	256	3,154.0	363	1.60	(23.4)	0.6	266	12.6	334	8.8	336
1,935.7	283	4,219.8	333	0.67	(57.1)	—		(15.7)	427	—	
1,628.1	316	N.A.		N.A.	—	—		—		—	
1,772.3	298	6,824.5	256	4.54	(10.1)	2.5	247	34.2	212	21.7	106

RANK 1997	COMPANY	REVENUES $ millions	PROFITS $ millions	Rank	ASSETS $ millions	Rank
476	LONGS DRUG STORES Walnut Creek, Calif.[1]	2,952.9	57.7	421	946.3	493
477	EMC Hopkinton, Mass.	2,937.9	538.5	160	3,490.1	377
478	ALUMAX Atlanta	2,930.9	33.7	437	3,453.0	378
479	GOLDEN WEST FINANCIAL CORP. Oakland	2,913.8	354.1	226	39,590.3	74
480	AIRBORNE FREIGHT Seattle	2,912.4	120.1	378	1,366.0	476
481	LEGGETT & PLATT Carthage, Mo.	2,909.2	208.3	310	2,106.3	439
482	ACE HARDWARE Oak Brook, Ill.[39]	2,907.3	N.A.		976.6	487
483	LUTHERAN BROTHERHOOD Minneapolis	2,900.3	231.6	300	16,441.7	152
484	LYONDELL PETROCHEMICAL Houston	2,878.0	286.0	266	1,559.0	469
485	FLEETWOOD ENTERPRISES Riverside, Calif.[38]	2,874.4	124.8	374	871.5	495
486	USG Chicago	2,874.0	148.0	355	1,926.0	453
487	NEW YORK TIMES New York	2,866.4	262.3	281	3,639.0	371
488	WESTERN ATLAS Houston	2,859.3[1]	(63.1)	469	2,330.7	430
489	SONOCO PRODUCTS Hartsville, S.C.	2,847.8	2.6	452	2,176.9	437
490	READER'S DIGEST ASSOCIATION Pleasantville, N.Y.[8]	2,839.0	133.5	367	1,643.8	466
491	U.S. OFFICE PRODUCTS Washington, D.C.[38]	2,835.9	57.3	422	1,810.4	459
492	FIRSTENERGY Akron[78]	2,821.4	305.8	248	18,080.8	141
493	COMDISCO Rosemont, Ill.[13]	2,819.0	131.0	368	6,350.0	270
494	BECTON DICKINSON Franklin Lakes, N.J.[13]	2,810.5	300.1	254	3,080.3	394
495	ANIXTER INTERNATIONAL Skokie, Ill.	2,805.2	45.3	433	1,440.7	473
496	BARNES & NOBLE New York[1]	2,796.9	53.2	424	1,591.2	468
497	PACIFIC ENTERPRISES Los Angeles	2,777.0	184.0	325	4,977.0	316
498	NORTHERN STATES POWER Minneapolis	2,733.7	237.3	298	7,144.1	253
499	MAXXAM Houston	2,729.1	65.2	413	4,114.2	354
500	ASARCO New York	2,721.0	143.4	358	4,110.4	356
	TOTALS	5,518,510.4	324,229.9		12,881,427.7	

STOCKHOLDERS' EQUITY		MARKET VALUE 3/18/98		EARNINGS PER SHARE				TOTAL RETURN TO INVESTORS			
				1997	% change from	1987–97 annual growth rate		1997		1987–97 annual rate	
$ millions	Rank	$ millions	Rank	$	1996	%	Rank	%	Rank	%	Rank
584.1	448	1,232.9	444	1.47	(0.7)	2.4	250	33.7	215	10.8	309
2,376.3	244	18,909.2	105	1.04	31.6	26.5	24	65.7	69	35.5	14
1,621.7	318	2,476.0	392	0.60	(86.8)	—		2.2	381	—	
2,698.0	219	5,535.6	286	6.13	118.9	10.1	130	55.8	93	23.7	78
670.9	432	2,096.1	407	2.44	281.3	26.9	22	167.7	4	25.6	58
1,174.0	370	5,252.6	297	2.16	41.2	14.3	85	22.6	277	25.0	69
245.8	482	N.A.		N.A.	—	—		—		—	
1,020.6	385	N.A.		N.A.	—	—		—		—	
619.0	442	2,176.4	403	3.58	126.6	—		24.3	273	—	
443.1	463	1,633.8	427	3.19	86.5	14.1	86	57.9	86	20.3	134
147.0	485	2,584.6	386	3.03	877.4	—		44.6	146	—	
1,728.1	304	6,365.4	267	2.66	209.3	3.1	236	76.1	44	10.1	318
886.9	407	4,102.0	339	(1.13)	(148.7)	—		32.6	218	—	
848.8	415	3,755.5	347	N.A.	(100.3)	—		37.2	189	15.9	224
346.0	471	2,768.4	379	1.24	69.9	—		(38.3)	453	—	
921.1	399	2,521.7	388	0.94	154.1	—		(13.7)	425	—	
4,159.6	155	7,006.9	249	1.94	(7.6)	(2.1)	292	27.5	251	11.4	305
865.0	412	3,128.8	364	1.56	17.0	5.0	212	59.2	83	17.1	194
1,385.4	346	8,543.3	210	2.30	9.0	9.9	132	16.6	315	16.4	211
477.0	458	855.6	450	0.95	31.9	—		2.3	379	6.5	352
531.8	454	2,644.3	383	0.76	1.3	—		147.2	8	—	
1,469.0	336	3,213.7	362	2.21	(6.4)	(6.1)	310	29.8	237	3.0	365
2,572.1	230	4,290.6	329	3.21	(16.0)	0.6	267	34.5	209	13.7	271
(2.9)	492	533.4	456	7.14	195.0	43.0	8	(8.4)	414	18.5	162
1,693.9	308	979.2	447	3.42	5.9	(7.4)	313	(7.3)	410	1.1	371
76,233.4		8,110,665.7									

FOOTNOTES TO THE 1998 FORTUNE 500

▲▼▲

N.A. Not available.

ᴱ Excise taxes have been deducted.

* Reflects extraordinary charge of at least 10%.

¶ Includes revenues of discontinued operations of at least 10%.

▶ **1–9**

[1] Figures are for fiscal year ended Jan. 31, 1998.

[2] Revenues for 1996 included the discontinued operations of Lucent Technologies (1997 rank: 37) and NCR (1997 rank: 247).

[3] Acquired McDonnell Douglas (1996 rank: 87), Aug. 1, 1997.

[4] Figures are for fiscal year ended Oct. 31, 1997.

[5] Acquired Salomon (1996 rank:163), Nov. 26, 1997.

[6] A mutual company; the figures here, however, follow Generally Accepted Accounting Principles.

[7] 1997 figure is not comparable with 1996, because the company changed from statutory reporting to GAAP reporting.

[8] Figures are for fiscal year ended June 30, 1997.

[9] Acquired Nynex (1996 rank: 91), Aug. 14, 1997.

▶ **10–19**

[10] Data are combined statutory financials for Teachers Insurance & Anuity Association and College Retirement Equities Fund. Prior to this year, these affiliated companies reported separately.

[11] Figures are for fiscal year ended Nov. 30, 1997.

[12] Name changed from Dean Witter Discover & Co., after acquiring Morgan Stanley Group (1996 rank: 96), May 31, 1997.

[13] Figures are for fiscal year ended Sept. 30, 1997.

[14] Acquired Pacific Telesis Group (1996 rank: 154), April 1, 1997.

[15] Acquired Tandem Computers (1996 rank: 552), Aug. 29, 1997.

[16] Figures are for fiscal year ended May 31, 1997.

[17] Acquired Vons (1996 rank: 266), April 8, 1997.

[18] Figures are for fiscal year ended Aug. 31, 1997.

[19] Figures do not include Barnett Banks (1997 rank: 360), acquired Jan. 9, 1998.

▶ **20–29**

[20] Acquired Portland General (1996 rank: 911), July 1, 1997.

[21] Acquired Healthsource (1996 rank: 700), July 31, 1997.

[22] Acquired Value Health (1996 rank: 615), Aug. 6, 1997.

[23] Figures are for fiscal year ended Feb. 28, 1997.

[24] Name changed from Duke Power after acquiring PanEnergy (1996 rank: 192), June 18, 1997.

[25] Acquired Valero Energy (1996 rank: 287), July 31, 1997.

[26] Acquired Signet Banking Corp. (1996 rank: 913), Nov. 30, 1997.

[27] Figures are for fiscal year ended March 31, 1997.

[28] Name changed from ITT Hartford Group, May 2, 1997.

[29] Acquired First USA (1996 rank: 734), June 27, 1997.

▶ **30–39**

[30] Acquired Revco D.S. (1996 rank: 280), May 30, 1997.

[31] Figure is for Sept. 30, 1997.

[32] Acquired Alex. Brown (1996 rank: 948), Aug. 29, 1997.

[33] Name changed from Federal Express after acquiring Caliber System, Jan. 27, 1998. Figures do not include Caliber System (1996 rank: 482).

[34] Acquired BDM International (1996 rank: 985), Dec. 26, 1997.

[35] The company and Norfolk Southern (1997

rank: 304) acquired Conrail (1996 rank: 366), May 23, 1997.

[36] Name changed from CPC International, Jan. 1, 1998.

[37] Name changed from Westinghouse Electric, Dec. 1, 1997.

[38] Figures are for fiscal year ended April 30, 1997.

[39] Cooperatives provide only net margin figures, which are not comparable with the profit figures on the list.

▶ **40–49**

[40] Acquired FHP International (1996 rank: 325), Feb. 14, 1997.

[41] Acquired USLife Corp. (1996 rank: 654), June 17, 1997.

[42] Acquired OrNda HealthCorp (1996 rank: 580), Jan. 30, 1997.

[43] Figures are for fiscal year ended July 31, 1997.

[44] Acquired Enserch Corp (1996 rank: 583), Aug. 5, 1997.

[45] Acquired Physician Corp. of America (1996 rank: 767), Sept. 8, 1997.

[46] Acquired Great Western Financial (1996 rank: 381), July 1, 1997.

[47] Name changed from James River Corp. of Virginia after acquiring Fort Howard (1996 rank: 718), Aug. 13, 1997.

[48] Name changed from Health Systems International after acquiring Foundation Health (1996 rank: 382), April 1, 1997.

[49] Name changed from Consolidated Edison of New York, Jan. 1, 1998.

▶ **50–59**

[50] Name changed from American Brands, May 30, 1997.

[51] Acquired Thrifty Payless (1996 rank: 295), Dec. 12, 1996.

[52] Name changed from First Bank System Inc., after acquiring U.S. Bancorp (1996 rank: 445), Aug. 1, 1997.

[53] Diluted EPS for 1996—not adjusted for mergers—was not available. Therefore, primary EPS for 1996 was used in the percent change calculation.

[54] Acquired NorAm Energy (1996 rank: 296), Aug. 6, 1997.

[55] Figures do not include Hudson Foods (1997 rank: 724), acquired Jan. 9, 1998.

[56] Figures are for the four quarters ended Oct. 31, 1997.

[57] Acquired Smith's Food & Drug Centers (1996 rank: 461), Sept. 9, 1997.

[58] Figures do not include Quality Food Centers (1997 rank: 649), acquired March 9, 1998.

[59] Fiscal year-end changed from Jan. 31.

▶ **60–69**

[60] Name changed from CUC International, Dec. 18, 1997.

[61] The company and CSX (1997 rank: 147) acquired Conrail (1996 rank: 366), May 23, 1997.

[62] Excludes discontinued operations of Unisource Worldwide (1997 rank: 220).

[63] Name changed from Columbia Gas System, Jan. 20, 1998.

[64] Acquired by NationsBank (1997 rank: 54), Jan. 9, 1998.

[65] Limited partnership; after tax estimated at corporate rate.

[66] Name changed from Student Loan Marketing Association, Aug. 7, 1997.

[67] Acquired Carson Pirie Scott (1996 rank: 919), Jan. 31, 1998.

[68] Acquired by U.S. Foodservice (1997 rank: 713), Dec. 23, 1997.

[69] Name changed from Public Service Co. of Colorado, Aug. 1, 1997.

▶ **70–78**

[70] Name changed from Cotter & Co., July 1, 1997.

[71] Spun off from Waban, now known as HomeBase (1997 rank: 783), July 28, 1997.

[72] Name changed from Union Electric, Dec. 31, 1997.

[73] Name changed from General American Life Insurance, April 24, 1997

[74] Figures are for the 12 months ended Dec. 31 and are unaudited. Company changed fiscal year-end from Dec. 31 to March 31.

[75] Figures do not include U.S. Robotics (1996 rank: 614), acquired June 12, 1997.

[76] Acquired Horizon/CMS Healthcare (1996 rank: 668), Oct. 29, 1997.

[77] Due to change in fiscal year-end, percent change is not calculated.

[78] Name changed from Ohio Edison after merger with Centerior Energy (1996 rank: 503), Nov. 7, 1997.

THE 1998
FORTUNE 500 INDEX

▲▼▲

AMERICA'S MOST ADMIRED COMPANIES, 1998

▲▼▲

Intensity of interest in FORTUNE's Most Admired Companies list increases every year, so plenty of executives, directors, investors, shareholder activists, and researchers are sure to focus on a change we've made: Our ranking of the top ten most admired was determined in a new way for the 1998 ranking. For the first time, we asked all 12,600 ballot recipients simply to tell us which companies, regardless of industry, they admire most. Since those ballot recipients are the most knowledgeable people in U.S. business, their verdict yields the true A list.

Traditionalists will be relieved to know we perform the same underlying research we've done the past 16 years—every bit of it. We ask top executives, outside directors, and securities analysts to evaluate the companies in their industry on each of eight criteria: quality of management, quality of products or services, ability to attract, develop and keep talented people, value as a long-term investment, use of corporate assets, financial soundness, innovativeness, and community and environmental responsibility. In past years we picked out the top scores to create our top-ten ranking. But some industries could have been generally more lavish or stinting with praise than others, so the scores might not have been directly comparable. Now that potential problem doesn't arise.

The value of corporate reputation turns out to be a deep topic. Our survey has been the subject of countless research papers, dozens of corporate tracking studies, and at least one major university symposium. Apparently, being admired has never been more valuable.

MONEY CENTER BANKS

Rank	Last Year	Company	Score
1	1	J.P. Morgan	8.16
2	2	Citicorp	7.55
3	6	Chase Manhattan	7.22
4	9	Bankers Trust New York	6.62
5	8	First Chicago NBD	6.61
6	•	Bank of New York	6.60
7	•	Republic New York	6.40

SAVINGS INSTITUTIONS

Rank	Last Year	Company	Score
1	2	Golden West Financial	7.04
2	4	Charter One Financial	6.69
3	1	Washington Mutual	6.55
4	5	H.F. Ahmanson	6.05
5	3	Standard Federal Bancorp.	5.54
6	•	Dime Bancorp	5.36
7	7	Glendale Federal Bank	5.21
8	•	California Federal Bank	4.99
9	•	Greenpoint Financial	4.91
10	6	Great Western Financial	4.34

SECURITIES

Rank	Last Year	Company	Score
1	1	Merrill Lynch	8.13
2	2	Morgan Stanley Group	7.59
3	3	Charles Schwab	7.07
4	5	A.G. Edwards	6.48
5	•	Alex. Brown	6.38
6	•	Franklin Resources	6.36
7	4	Bear Stearns	6.34
8	6	Salomon	5.71
9	8	Lehman Brothers Holdings	5.68
10	7	Paine Webber Group	5.09

INSURANCE: LIFE AND HEALTH

Rank	Last Year	Company	Score
1	1	Northwestern Mutual Life Insurance	7.49
2	3	Principal Financial Group	6.77
3	2	New York Life Insurance	6.62
4	4	TIAA	6.46
5	•	Massachusetts Mutual Life Insurance	6.45
6	6	Metropolitan Life Insurance	6.16
7	•	John Hancock Mutual Life Insurance	6.10
8	8	Cigna	6.00
9	9	Aetna	5.61
10	10	Prudential Insurance of America	4.91

INSURANCE: PROPERTY AND CASUALTY

Rank	Last Year	Company	Score
1	1	Berkshire Hathaway	7.78
2	1	USAA	7.31
3	2	American International Group	7.30
4	3	General Re	7.08
5	5	State Farm Insurance	7.03
6	6	Allstate	6.99
7	7	Travelers Group	6.78
8	8	Hartford Financial Services Group	6.54
9	7	Nationwide Insurance Enterprise	6.37
10	10	Liberty Mutual Insurance Group	5.95

SUPERREGIONAL BANKS

Rank	Last Year	Company	Score
1	•	Norwest	7.52
2	7	First Union	7.19
3	3	BankAmerica	7.10
4	4	NationsBank	7.08
5	5	Banc One	7.07
6	•	BankBoston	6.55
7	10	Fleet Financial Group	6.54
8	•	Wells Fargo	6.35
9	•	PNC Bank	6.23
10	•	KeyCorp	6.21

CONSUMER CREDIT

Rank	Last Year	Company	Score
1	6	American Express	7.56
2	•	MBNA	7.42
3	•	First USA	6.66
4	•	Capital One Financial	6.26
5	4	Household International	6.20
6	7	Dean Witter Discover	6.01
7	•	Beneficial	5.41
8	•	Advanta	4.04

AEROSPACE

Rank	Last Year	Company	Score
1	1	Boeing	7.83
2	3	AlliedSignal	7.38
3	2	Lockheed Martin	7.29
4	4	United Technologies	7.02
5	5	Textron	6.81
6	7	General Dynamics	6.60
7	9	Sundstrand	6.38
8	8	B.F. Goodrich	6.36
9	10	Northrop Grumman	6.32
10	6	McDonnell Douglas	6.04

AIRLINES

Rank	Last Year	Company	Score
1	1	Southwest Airlines	7.14
2	2	AMR	7.07
3	6	Continental Airlines	6.41
4	3	UAL	6.26
5	4	Northwest Airlines	6.11
6	7	Alaska Air Group	5.86
7	5	Delta Air Lines	5.64
8	9	US Airways Group	5.21
9	8	America West Holdings	4.64
10	10	TWA	3.54

MAIL, PACKAGE, AND FREIGHT DELIVERY

Rank	Last Year	Company	Score
1	1	United Parcel Service	8.00
2	2	Federal Express	7.33
3	4	Airborne Freight	6.08
4	3	Air Express International	6.07
5	5	Pittston	5.55

INDUSTRIAL AND FARM EQUIPMENT

Rank	Last Year	Company	Score
1	1	Caterpillar	7.65
2	2	Deere	7.34
3	7	Cummins Engine	6.52
4	4	Ingersoll-Rand	6.43
5	5	Dover	6.34
6	3	Parker Hannifin	6.28
7	6	Black & Decker	6.20
8	9	Case	6.01
9	10	Dresser Industries	5.95
10	8	American Standard	5.93

TRUCKING

Rank	Last Year	Company	Score
1	1	Ryder System	6.53
2	6	CNF Transportation	6.20
3	8	Yellow	6.03
4	2	Roadway Express	5.55
5	5	J.B. Hunt Transport Services	5.39
6	7	Caliber System	5.37
7	3	USFreightways	5.34
8	•	Consolidated Freightways	5.04
9	9	Arkansas Best	4.61
10	10	Amerco	4.30

MOTOR VEHICLES AND PARTS

Rank	Last Year	Company	Score
1	•	Toyota Motor Sales U.S.A.	7.56
2	7	Daimler-Benz N.A.	7.24
3	1	Chrysler	7.18
4	2	American Honda Motor	6.98
5	4	Ford Motor	6.85
6	3	Johnson Controls	6.72
7	5	TRW	6.63
8	8	Tenneco	6.29
9	10	General Motors	6.28
10	9	ITT Industries	6.07

RAILROADS

Rank	Last Year	Company	Score
1	1	Norfolk Southern	7.88
2	4	Burlington Northern Santa Fe	6.98
3	3	CSX	6.92
4	2	Union Pacific	6.47
5	5	Conrail	5.87

APPAREL

Rank	Last Year	Company	Score
1	•	Nike	7.59
2	2	Liz Claiborne	7.09
3	3	VF	6.85
4	•	Jones Apparel Group	6.58
5	•	Reebok International	6.42
6	4	Russell	6.16
7	6	Kellwood	5.89
8	5	Warnaco Group	5.87
9	7	Fruit of the Loom	4.85

WHOLESALERS

Rank	Last Year	Company	Score
1	1	Cardinal Health	7.68
2	•	Ingram Micro	7.08
3	2	Sysco	6.99
4	4	McKesson	6.93
5	6	Arrow Electronics	6.56
6	5	Genuine Parts	6.55
7	7	Bergen Brunswig	6.33
8	8	Supervalu	6.28
9	3	Ikon Office Solutions	6.00
10	9	Fleming	5.48

FURNITURE

Rank	Last Year	Company	Score
1	1	Herman Miller	8.14
2	2	Leggett & Platt	7.67
3	3	Hon Industries	7.55
4	5	Furniture Brands International	6.37

SPECIALTY RETAILERS

Rank	Last Year	Company	Score
1	1	Home Depot	8.07
2	4	Toys "R" Us	6.47
3	7	Costco	6.43
4	2	Circuit City Group	6.28
5	5	Lowe's	6.10
6	•	TJX	6.04
7	6	Limited	5.93
8	9	CVS	5.93
9	•	Best Buy	4.94
10	10	Woolworth	3.99

FOOD

Rank	Last Year	Company	Score
1	5	Nestlé USA	7.42
2	3	Sara Lee	7.21
3	1	Campbell Soup	7.20
4	4	ConAgra	7.03
5	6	CPC International	6.67
6	7	H.J. Heinz	6.62
7	8	RJR Nabisco Holdings	6.28
8	9	IBP	5.99
9	•	Farmland Industries	5.75
10	10	Archer Daniels Midland	5.18

FOOD AND DRUG STORES

Rank	Last Year	Company	Score
1	2	Walgreen	7.34
2	3	Publix Super Markets	7.20
3	4	Safeway	7.09
4	1	Albertson's	6.96
5	5	Kroger	6.82
6	6	American Stores	6.36
7	•	Rite Aid	6.04
8	7	Winn-Dixie Stores	5.77
9	8	Food Lion	5.59
10	10	A&P	4.70

FOOD SERVICES

Rank	Last Year	Company	Score
1	1	McDonald's	7.15
2	2	PepsiCo	7.04
3	4	Wendy's International	6.89
4	•	Host Marriott Services	6.50
5	3	Brinker International	6.00
6	5	Aramark	5.71
7	10	Viad	5.17
8	•	Darden Restaurants	4.96
9	7	Shoney's	4.50
10	10	Flagstar	3.37

GENERAL MERCHANDISERS

Rank	Last Year	Company	Score
1	1	Wal-Mart Stores	7.23
2	2	Nordstrom	7.11
3	6	Dayton Hudson	6.87
4	3	Sears Roebuck	6.72
5	4	May Department Stores	6.69
6	7	Federated Department Stores	6.27
7	5	J.C. Penney	6.14
8	8	Dillard's	6.05
9	9	Fred Meyer	5.69
10	10	Kmart	4.51

SOAPS, COSMETICS

Rank	Last Year	Company	Score
1	1	Gillette	8.29
2	1	Procter & Gamble	8.19
3	4	Colgate-Palmolive	7.27
4	2	Estée Lauder	7.19
5	5	Unilever U.S.	6.91
6	3	Clorox	6.86
7	6	International Flavors & Fragrances	6.72
8	7	Avon Products	6.67
9	•	Revlon	6.33
10	9	Alberto-Culver	5.85

HEALTH CARE

Rank	Last Year	Company	Score
1	2	United HealthCare	6.98
2	5	Tenet Healthcare	6.77
3	6	WellPoint Health Networks	6.59
4	3	PacifiCare Health Systems	6.40
5	•	MedPartners	6.08
6	•	Allegiance	6.02
7	8	Humana	5.79
8	•	Foundation Health	5.43
9	9	FHP International	5.25
10	1	Columbia/HCA Healthcare	4.75

TEMPORARY HELP

Rank	Last Year	Company	Score
1	1	Manpower	6.71
2	•	Norrell	6.66
3	•	Interim Services	6.45
4	3	Kelly Services	6.06
5	5	Volt Information Sciences	5.93
6	2	Olsten	5.86
7	4	CDI	5.79
8	•	Accustaff	5.75

BEVERAGES

Rank	Last Year	Company	Score
1	1	Coca-Cola	8.68
2	2	Coca-Cola Enterprises	7.41
3	3	Anheuser-Busch	7.13
4	4	Adolph Coors	6.24
5	5	Brown-Forman	5.89
6	6	Joseph E. Seagram & Sons	5.72
7	7	Whitman	5.16
8	8	Canandaigua Wine	4.83

TOBACCO

Rank	Last Year	Company	Score
1	1	Fortune Brands	8.01
2	2	Philip Morris	5.51
3	3	UST	4.67
4	4	Universal	4.66
5	5	DIMON	4.43
6	6	Standard Commercial	3.97

ELECTRIC AND GAS UTILITIES

Rank	Last Year	Company	Score
1	2	FPL Group	6.84
2	1	Southern	6.84
3	5	Edison International	6.66
4	4	PG&E	6.29
5	3	American Electric Power	6.27
6	6	Texas Utilities	5.99
7	7	Entergy	5.86
8	8	Public Service Enterprise Group	5.61
9	9	Consolidated Edison of New York	5.52
10	10	Unicom	5.20

MINING, CRUDE OIL

Rank	Last Year	Company	Score
1	•	Burlington Resources	6.65
2	•	Union Texas Petroleum Holdings	6.57
3	4	Vulcan Materials	6.50
4	3	Cyprus Amax Minerals	6.42
5	5	Mitchell Energy & Development	6.31
6	2	Freeport-McMoRan Copper & Gold	6.24
7	7	Asarco	6.05
8	6	Oryx Energy	5.90

PETROLEUM REFINING

Rank	Last Year	Company	Score
1	1	Shell Oil	7.44
2	3	Exxon	7.35
3	2	Mobil	7.30
4	5	Chevron	6.84
5	4	Amoco	6.84
6	6	BP America	6.70
7	7	Texaco	6.50
8	8	Atlantic Richfield	6.19
9	9	Phillips Petroleum	6.13
10	10	USX	5.63

PIPELINES

Rank	Last Year	Company	Score
1	1	Enron	7.79
2	2	Williams	7.54
3	3	PanEnergy	7.11
4	4	Sonat	6.83
5	5	NGC	6.66
6	7	Tejas Gas	6.49
7	•	El Paso Natural Gas	6.36
8	•	Western Gas Resources	5.86
9	9	NorAm Energy	5.64
10	10	Enserch	5.41

WASTE MANAGEMENT

Rank	Last Year	Company	Score
1	•	USA Waste Services	6.95
2	•	Browning-Ferris Industries	5.60
3	•	Waste Management	5.43
4	•	Ogden	5.16

ENGINEERING, CONSTRUCTION

Rank	Last Year	Company	Score
1	1	Fluor	6.62
2	3	Jacobs Engineering Group	6.58
3	2	Halliburton	6.56
4	5	Centex	6.46
5	7	Peter Kiewit Sons'	6.36
6	4	Foster Wheeler	6.34
7	6	Pulte	6.34
8	8	Fleetwood Enterprises	6.13
9	9	Turner	5.82
10	•	Kaufman & Broad Home	5.79

METAL PRODUCTS

Rank	Last Year	Company	Score
1	2	Tyco International	7.45
2	3	Illinois Tool Works	7.36
3	5	Newell	6.72
4	•	Danaher	6.60
5	7	Masco	6.58
6	•	Hillenbrand Industries	6.40
7	4	Stanley Works	6.36
8	6	Crown Cork & Seal	6.36
9	10	Ball	5.75
10	8	U.S. Industries	5.73

METALS

Rank	Last Year	Company	Score
1	1	Alcoa	7.14
2	2	Nucor	7.10
3	•	Allegheny Teledyne	6.77
4	3	Phelps Dodge	6.40
5	5	Reynolds Metals	6.10
6	6	Alumax	5.83
7	7	LTV	5.49
8	8	Inland Steel Industries	5.18
9	9	Maxxam	4.89
10	10	Bethlehem Steel	4.86

BUILDING MATERIALS, GLASS

Rank	Last Year	Company	Score
1	1	Corning	7.40
2	2	Armstrong World Industries	7.13
3	3	Owens-Corning	6.14
4	5	USG	6.05
5	4	Owens-Illinois	6.01
6	6	Johns Manville	5.51

PHARMACEUTICALS

Rank	Last Year	Company	Score
1	1	Merck	7.99
2	3	Pfizer	7.95
3	2	Johnson & Johnson	7.79
4	8	Bristol-Myers Squibb	7.36
5	5	Eli Lilly	7.20
6	4	Abbott Laboratories	6.73
7	9	Warner-Lambert	6.61
8	6	Schering-Plough	6.60
9	7	American Home Products	6.27
10	10	Pharmacia & Upjohn	4.84

TEXTILES

Rank	Last Year	Company	Score
1	1	Unifi	7.29
2	2	Springs Industries	6.81
3	4	WestPoint Stevens	6.75
4	•	Interface	6.69
5	3	Shaw Industries	6.63
6	7	Mohawk Industries	6.36
7	6	Burlington Industries	5.95
8	9	Triarc	5.29
9	10	Fieldcrest Cannon	5.25

RUBBER AND PLASTIC PRODUCTS

Rank	Last Year	Company	Score
1	2	Goodyear Tire & Rubber	7.58
2	1	Rubbermaid	7.29
3	3	M.A. Hanna	7.16
4	6	Cooper Tire & Rubber	6.64
5	•	Tupperware	6.60
6	•	Standard Products	6.32
7	4	Premark International	6.29
8	8	Mark IV Industries	6.09
9	7	Bridgestone/Firestone	6.08
10	•	GenCorp	6.06

CHEMICALS

Rank	Last Year	Company	Score
1	1	Du Pont	7.89
2	3	Monsanto	7.29
3	2	Dow Chemical	7.13
4	4	PPG Industries	6.93
5	5	Bayer	6.63
6	6	Union Carbide	6.39
7	8	BASF	6.33
8	7	Celanese	6.18
9	9	W.R. Grace	5.37
10	10	Occidental Petroleum	5.29

FOREST AND PAPER PRODUCTS

Rank	Last Year	Company	Score
1	1	Kimberly-Clark	7.35
2	3	Mead	6.52
3	2	Weyerhaeuser	6.51
4	4	International Paper	6.18
5	5	Union Camp	6.16
6	6	Georgia-Pacific	5.67
7	7	Champion International	5.44
8	8	Fort James	5.34
9	9	Boise Cascade	4.93
10	10	Stone Container	4.47

ADVERTISING, MARKETING

Rank	Last Year	Company	Score
1	1	Omnicom Group	7.59
2	2	Interpublic Group	7.23
3	3	CUC International	7.06
4	4	ADVO	6.69

PUBLISHING, PRINTING

Rank	Last Year	Company	Score
1	3	Tribune	7.20
2	2	Gannett	7.07
3	5	New York Times	6.96
4	4	Knight-Ridder	6.55
5	10	Times Mirror	6.31
6	8	R.R. Donnelley & Sons	6.29
7	9	McGraw-Hill	6.18
8	1	Dow Jones	6.05
9	6	American Greetings	6.00
10	7	Reader's Digest Association	5.11

ENTERTAINMENT

Rank	Last Year	Company	Score
1	1	Walt Disney	7.61
2	4	Time Warner	6.74
3	10	Westinghouse Electric	6.22
4	3	Viacom	5.64
5	•	News America Publishing	5.56

HOTELS, CASINOS, RESORTS

Rank	Last Year	Company	Score
1	1	Mirage Resorts	7.98
2	2	Marriott International	6.98
3	3	Hilton Hotels	6.59
4	6	Harrah's Entertainment	6.14
5	4	Circus Circus Enterprises	5.76
6	7	ITT	4.81

RECREATIONAL EQUIPMENT

Rank	Last Year	Company	Score
1	1	Brunswick	7.70
2	2	Polaris Industries	6.26
3	3	Coleman Holdings	5.26
4	4	Outboard Marine	4.12

COMPUTER AND DATA SERVICES

Rank	Last Year	Company	Score
1	3	First Data	6.69
2	5	Automatic Data Processing	6.67
3	•	Equifax	6.44
4	•	A.C. Nielsen	6.07
5	7	Comdisco	6.05
6	•	America Online	6.01
7	8	Dun & Bradstreet	6.01
8	•	Ceridian	5.86
9	•	Micro Warehouse	5.75
10	10	Unisys	5.19

COMPUTERS, OFFICE EQUIPMENT

Rank	Last Year	Company	Score
1	1	Hewlett-Packard	7.90
2	3	Compaq Computer	7.50
3	4	International Business Machines	7.26
4	5	Dell Computer	7.18
5	2	Sun Microsystems	7.09
6	2	Xerox	7.00
7	8	Canon U.S.A.	5.98
8	•	Gateway 2000	5.85
9	9	Digital Equipment	4.93
10	10	Apple Computer	3.73

SCIENTIFIC, PHOTOGRAPHIC, AND CONTROL EQUIPMENT

Rank	Last Year	Company	Score
1	1	Minnesota Mining & Manufacturing	7.93
2	•	Medtronic	7.57
3	5	Thermo Electron	6.76
4	4	Honeywell	6.71
5	•	Tektronix	6.48
6	6	Becton Dickinson	6.34
7	3	Eastman Kodak	6.32
8	7	Baxter International	6.31
9	10	Polaroid	5.93
10	9	Bausch & Lomb	5.88

TELECOMMUNICATIONS

Rank	Last Year	Company	Score
1	1	SBC Communications	7.23
2	2	BellSouth	6.74
3	4	Ameritech	6.40
4	6	Bell Atlantic	6.39
5	3	Sprint	6.32
6	7	GTE	5.66
7	5	MCI Communications	5.52
8	8	AT&T	5.44
9	9	US West	5.39
10	10	Nynex	5.02

ELECTRONICS, ELECTRICAL EQUIPMENT

Rank	Last Year	Company	Score
1	2	General Electric	8.18
2	3	Motorola	7.66
3	4	Emerson Electric	7.50
4	7	Siemens	6.51
5	6	Rockwell International	6.49
6	•	Toshiba America	6.45
7	8	Raytheon	6.27
8	•	Eaton	6.21
9	9	Whirlpool	6.16
10	•	Philips Electronics N.A.	6.16

COMPUTER PERIPHERALS

Rank	Last Year	Company	Score
1	•	EMC	7.30
2	•	Western Digital	6.94
3	6	Seagate Technology	6.82
4	•	Iomega	6.52
5	•	Lexmark International Group	6.37
6	•	Quantum	6.33
7	•	Storage Technology	5.95
8	•	Maxtor	5.09

COMPUTER SOFTWARE

Rank	Last Year	Company	Score
1	1	Microsoft	8.28
2	2	Oracle	7.26
3	4	Computer Associates International	7.08
4	6	Computer Sciences	6.97
5	9	Novell	5.67
6	•	Sybase	5.63
7	•	Cognizant	5.60

ELECTRONICS, NETWORKS

Rank	Last Year	Company	Score
1	•	Cisco Systems	8.17
2	•	3Com	7.18
3	•	U.S. Robotics	6.40
4	•	Cabletron Systems	5.90
5	•	Bay Networks	5.80

ELECTRONICS, SEMICONDUCTORS

Rank	Last Year	Company	Score
1	1	Intel	8.75
2	•	Applied Materials	7.59
3	5	Texas Instruments	7.51
4	•	Analog Devices	6.74
5	•	Atmel	6.29
6	•	LSI Logic	6.27
7	•	National Semiconductor	5.97
8	•	Advanced Micro Devices	5.09
9	•	Cirrus Logic	4.88